INTENSIVE SHORT-TERM
DYNAMIC PSYCHOTHERAPY

INTENSIVE SHORT-TERM DYNAMIC PSYCHOTHERAPY

THEORY AND TECHNIQUE

Patricia Coughlin Della Selva

Foreword by David Malan

Routledge
Taylor & Francis Group

LONDON AND NEW YORK

Errata
Page 2: "Tenants" should be printed "Tenets"
Throughout the book: the name "Ferenzi" should be printed as "Ferenczi"
Throughout References: "International University Press" should be printed
"International Universities Press"

First published 1996 by John Wiley & Sons, Inc.

Published 2004 by Karnac Books Ltd.

Published 2018 by Routledge
2 Park Square, Milton Park, Abingdon, Oxon OX14 4RN
711 Third Avenue, New York, NY 10017, USA

Routledge is an imprint of the Taylor & Francis Group, an informa business

British Library Cataloguing in Publication Data
A C.I.P. for this book is available from the British Library

ISBN: 9781855753020 (pbk)

For those who matter most
Jeremy, Megan, Katie, and Anthony

Preface

My experiences as a psychodynamic psychotherapist are not unique. Like many before me, I came to believe in the power of unconscious forces in the creation and maintenance of neurotic suffering. I dedicated myself to the study and practice of psychoanalytic theory in an attempt to free patients of this suffering. Although occasionally meeting with success, nagging questions persisted. Why did treatment take so long and why were the results so sporadic and unpredictable? Was it my lack of formal analytic training, countertransference, the patient's fragility—or was I just expecting too much?

In 1987, my family and I moved to Toronto. There, in Canada, I had a chance to enroll in a psychoanalytic institute that was opened to clinical psychologists. Perhaps more study and supervision would increase my effectiveness. Several months before my analytic training was to begin, I received a notice announcing a weekend seminar in Intensive Short-Term Dynamic Psychotherapy to be given by Dr. Habib Davanloo. A vague recollection of a videotaped segment of his work, viewed in a psychotherapy course during graduate school, emerged in my mind and motivated me to attend.

That weekend was a revelation. During those 16 hours, most of them spent in a dark auditorium viewing actual therapy sessions on videotape, I witnessed something truly revolutionary.

In the past, increasing the *quantity* of therapeutic contact was the only way I had learned to intensify patient's conflicts and deepen their access to unconscious thoughts and feelings. Patients were generally seen from two to five times a week for a period of years. Dr. Davanloo presented us with unequivocal evidence that it was possible to accelerate and condense the analytic process by increasing the *quality* of therapeutic interventions. The videotaped material demonstrated a treatment protocol of unparalleled effectiveness as well as efficiency. My decision was clear. I would pursue training and supervision with Dr. Davanloo.

This book will outline what I have learned from this training. Obviously, this book reflects my understanding of Davanloo's theory and techniques. Over time I have added and integrated elements of style and substance which depart from Davanloo and these deviations are noted. Dr. Davanloo's approach remains faithful to psychoanalytic theory while radically altering standard analytic techniques. The techniques he has developed to dismantle defenses, intensify the patient's affective involvement in treatment, and identify the transference pattern of behavior result in a rapid "unlocking of the unconscious." Because these powerful techniques must be used with prudence and skill, they require a thorough understanding of the metapsychology of the unconscious in addition to careful supervision.

The book will begin from this premise, reviewing the basic concepts involved in the psychoanalytic theory of neurosis. The first chapter will outline operational definitions of dynamic concepts and strategies for developing a series of systematic interventions based on an understanding of unconscious processes.

The main body of the book will proceed in a fashion roughly parallel with the process of psychotherapy. Chapter 2 details the requirements of the initial evaluation, so crucial in determining suitability for treatment. Chapters 3 and 4 focus on techniques for working with defenses, a critical step in eliminating the resistances that prolong or disrupt treatment. Chapters 5 and 6 describe the role of affect in the creation and remediation of psychopathology, as well as techniques to intensify affective experience and facilitate its expression. Chapter 7 enumerates the various elements required to enhance and complete the process of working through. Finally, Chapter 8 discusses the process of termination and the role of follow-up in Intensive Short-Term Dynamic Psychotherapy (ISTDP).

My hope is that this introduction to the theory and technique of ISTDP will whet your appetite, increase your interest in doing effective and efficient treatment of real depth and intensity and, in so doing, revive hope and optimism about the unique effects of dynamic psychotherapy.

PATRICIA COUGHLIN DELLA SELVA, PhD

Albany, New York

Acknowledgments

I feel blessed to have had the guidance and support of so many friends and colleagues through the years. I must start with my first mentor, Dr. Hal Arkes who displayed great faith in me and helped me to believe I might have something special to offer the field of clinical psychology. During my years of graduate study at Syracuse University, Drs. Jay Land and Ruth Burton stood out as models of integrity and had a profound and lasting influence on my personal and professional life.

During my years in Chicago, as a resident and a member of the faculty at Northwestern University Medical School, I was surrounded by bright, dedicated, and compassionate professionals. Drs. Edward Sheridan and Mary Dohney were most influential during my residency. Alma Rolfs, MSW, and Barbara Muday, CSW, became close personal friends as well as stimulating colleagues and models of dedicated service. Drs. Merton Gill and Ruth Westheimers were superb clinicians whose supervision proved to be an invaluable aid in my development as a therapist.

In 1987, I attended a weekend seminar offered by Dr. Davanloo, and it is no exaggeration to say that the experience changed my professional life (and undoubtedly my personal life as well). All my subsequent clinical work, teaching, and writing, reflect the influence of my exposure to this brilliant man. Others who have helped immeasurably in my understanding and integration of the theories and techniques developed by Dr. Davanloo include Dr. George Glumac and the faculty at the Ontario Institute for STDP, Drs. Jim Schubmehl, Michael Alpert, Diana Fosha, David Malan, and Leigh McCullough Vaillant.

A deep debt of gratitude is extended to Pearl Mindell, a woman of grace and dignity, who helped me travel through the darkest night of my soul. Her influence has been deep and abiding.

My patients have granted me the rare privilege of intimate knowledge of their deepest thoughts and feelings. I have been inspired by their courage and have grown from their journeys. The generosity of spirit evident in those who have allowed their treatment to be videotaped, written about, and even viewed to professional audiences for our learning, is a gift of immeasurable value. I thank each and every one of them. Verbatim transcripts of therapy sessions are used throughout the book. Identifying information has been deleted or altered in order to preserve patient's privacy.

Most of all, I want to thank my family for their love and support over the years, and especially during the writing of this book. I thank my mother for teaching me a love of learning and compassion for the suffering of others. To my father, who died while this manuscript was in progress, I am most grateful for his integrity of being. To my children, Megan, Katherine, and Anthony, thanks for making me happy to wake up each morning.

Finally, I want to thank Steven Sandler, MD, for his careful reading of this manuscript and my editor, Kelly Franklin. Her keen intellect and enthusiastic support were invaluable assets. This book is far better for her involvement.

Contents

Foreword

Of all the factors standing in the way of therapies based on psychody-namics—which of course includes psychoanalysis—*resistance* is the most intractable. In my own practice, I recognized this many years ago, and desperation led me to try many devices for overcoming it. Most of these were derived from "alternative" psychotherapies and included using hypnosis, LSD, and Gestalt techniques, and encouraging my patients to go to encounter groups. None were of the slightest value. The attempts to shorten psychotherapy by the use of active and purely interpretive techniques, though successful, have essentially *avoided* the problem because both Balint's group in London and Sifneos's in Boston have been forced to select patients who are not resistant but highly motivated and responsive. But, in face of the kind of resistance shown by the majority of patients—perhaps 80% or 90% of the psychotherapeutic population—such methods are helpless.

In the 1970s, it became clear that Davanloo had solved the problem of resistance, without any use of alternative techniques, to an extent that would have been unbelievable if it had not been supported by videotape. In 1980, I referred to Davanloo's work as "the most important development in psychotherapy since the discovery of the unconscious"; and earlier, in 1979, I had predicted, "His work is destined to revolutionize both the practice and the scientific status of dynamic psychotherapy within the next 10 years."

I stand by the first statement, but the hope expressed in my prediction was destined to be disappointed; this simply hasn't happened. The reasons seem to include, above all, the extreme difficulty of learning Davanloo's technique, with the result that only a handful of therapists other than Davanloo himself can use it effectively. This partly stems from his use and advocacy of a highly confrontational, almost adversarial, style.

Although such an approach is extremely effective in his hands, many other therapists do not feel comfortable with it. Moreover, there has never been any textbook to facilitate the learning process.

Yet, the importance of his work cannot be overstated: He has demonstrated that a technique exists for completely overcoming the problem of resistance, resulting in a method of short-term psychotherapy with unparalleled effectiveness. The question is then whether this technique can be modified to preserve the essentials and yet permit its use by other therapists. Many professionals are attempting this task, and there are promising developments, but the results have not yet been fully documented.

That is, until the work of Dr. Coughlin Della Selva described here. She has taken hold of Davanloo's technique and passed it through the furnace of her own personality, from which it has emerged softened but otherwise unchanged, and apparently equally effective—as is attested by the numerous verbatim transcripts of her interviews. There is the same persistent concentration on the defenses and the same minute attention to the transference, demonstrating that it is possible to break through lifelong defenses within the span of a single interview and thus to "unlock" the patient's unconscious. The series of observations that follow from this achievement are by now familiar, but when first made, they were equally astonishing and contradicted many pessimistic beliefs based on decades of experience with psychoanalysis: Many patients can bear having the whole of their neurosis exposed within a few hours; patients rapidly reach a stage that allows direct access to the past so transference is no longer an issue; the transference neurosis can be entirely avoided; prolonged working through is not necessary; therapeutic effects can follow within a few weeks and can be *total*. Moreover, the essential therapeutic mechanism that emerges from all these therapies—as in those of Davanloo—is of extraordinary simplicity: It is the derepression and direct experience of infinitely painful feelings and memories concerned with *family relationships* throughout the whole of the patient's upbringing.

Dr. Coughlin Della Selva has mastered completely both the moment-to-moment use of her technique and the theory behind it. Above all, she confronts the transference as soon as it becomes an issue; she also knows when it is necessary to back off to reduce the patient's anxiety, particularly with depressives; she understands how to judge, from physical signs, the degree to which patients are in touch with their feelings; and she is well aware of the possible danger to patients of being exposed to her powerful technique and therefore quickly detects when candidates are unsuitable and should be referred elsewhere.

It is important to say that Dr. Coughlin Della Selva does not follow Davanloo's technique slavishly; she differs from him on a number of issues. She emphasizes even more than he does the importance of defenses against emotional closeness; she explicitly points out to her patients that in childhood their defenses were essential to survival; she openly acknowledges the pathology and destructiveness in other family members; she emphasizes the need to reinforce and develop the vital functions of self-care and self-protection; and she often gives the patient words of sympathy and encouragement. All these are examples of the softening that must make her technique more acceptable to other therapists and easier to use; but it in no way diminishes her toughness and determination not to let go, and therefore the effectiveness of her therapeutic work.

The book is written with exceptional clarity—the reader never has to go back and read a sentence again to understand it, but on the contrary is eager to read on.

To return to the earlier theme: In 1995, I wrote that perhaps Davanloo's most important contribution has simply been the demonstration that widely applicable brief psychotherapy is *possible,* so that other therapists are encouraged to use some of his ideas to find equally effective methods that suit their own personalities. Dr. Coughlin Della Selva has unquestionably done this, and the next step will be much easier; namely, for yet other therapists to adapt her technique to suit *their* personalities—in which process the publication of this book will play an essential part. I hope the result will be a chain reaction by which the whole status of psychotherapy may ultimately be transformed.

DAVID MALAN

Hants, England

CHAPTER 1

The Integration of Theory and Technique in Davanloo's Intensive Short-Term Dynamic Psychotherapy

I hear a distant drum beat
A heart beat pulsing low
Is it coming from within
A heart beat I don't know
A troubled soul knows no peace
A dark and poisoned pool
Of liberty now lost
A pawn, the oppressor's tool.
*Loreena McKennitt**

In many ways, this songwriter has articulated the plight of neurotics, blind to their own inner world and, as such, destined to live the life of a prisoner. The discovery of such a rich and complex inner life began with Breuer and was elaborated on in great detail by Freud (Breuer & Freud, 1895).

*From "Breaking the Silence." Music and lyrics by Loreena McKennitt. "Parallel Dreams" Quinlan Road 1989.

BASIC TENANTS OF PSYCHOANALYTIC THEORY

Breuer's (Breuer & Freud, 1895) pioneering work with Anna O. led to the discovery of the dynamic unconscious and laid the foundation for psychoanalysis. He placed the patient under a hypnotic trance and discovered, quite by chance (Schoenewolf, 1990), that her current physical symptoms were connected to traumatic experiences from the past (caring for her sick and dying father). When he was able to get her to verbalize her feelings about these traumatic experiences, the symptoms vanished. Again and again, he found that the recall of memories and reliving of the emotions associated with the memories led to symptom removal. The original forgetting was labeled "repression," and the remembering, "catharsis" (Fisher & Greenberg, 1977). Although this cathartic treatment led to immediate relief, there were frequent relapses and no lasting cure. An additional problem arose in the treatment relationship when Anna began to have strong loving and sexual feelings toward Breuer. He became frightened and abruptly ended her treatment. In fact, he abandoned this kind of work altogether.

Freud took over where Breuer left off, making changes designed to address the problems encountered with hypnotic treatment. He decided to abandon hypnosis because this technique only provided temporary relief. He felt that the conscious ego must learn to deal directly with the trauma and integrate these memories and feelings into awareness. The task was to develop a treatment that would enable the patient to consciously tolerate what had been previously experienced as unbearable. By encouraging patients to say whatever came to mind and following their associations, Freud found that they would gradually approach previously avoided topics. The technique of free association, designed to enable patients gradually to become aware of unconscious feelings, memories, and fantasies, was the first major change in psychoanalytic technique to follow hypnosis.

As Freud began to encourage patients to say whatever came to mind, he confronted a counterforce working against remembering and reexperiencing painful and anxiety-provoking events. He labeled this force resistance and found it became the greatest obstacle to successful treatment. In many ways, all developers of subsequent technique, including the short-term dynamic psychotherapists such as Malan, Mann, Sifneos, and Davanloo, have tried to find methods for circumventing, reducing, or eliminating resistance so that patients will reach therapeutic goals. The tension between the patient's desire to get well and the desire to avoid that which is painful by resisting therapeutic intervention, is the essence of psychic conflict. How professionals deal with this conflict in the therapeutic setting is of pivotal importance and will be covered extensively in the present volume.

Another essential change in technique that followed the use of hypnosis involved using, rather than avoiding, the feelings evoked within the treatment relationship. Freud came to realize that the patient's feelings toward and perceptions of the therapist were not random, but constituted a projection or transference of feelings and perceptions having to do with significant figures from the patient's past. He called this the phenomenon of transference and used it to bring the patient's inner conflicts to life in the therapeutic setting.

He combined these changes (i.e., free association, a focus on resistance and analysis of the transference) as he developed the technique of psychoanalysis. He would actively interpret the patient's defensiveness and resistance to remembering and experiencing painful experiences from the past. These interpretations were designed to release buried feelings. The process itself tended to elicit feelings toward the doctor, which were then associated to prominent figures from the patient's past. This basic technique of interpreting defense, and releasing buried feelings and memories, enabled patient and therapist to gain insight into links between the forgotten past and current behavior. This remains the essence of psychodynamic psychotherapy.

As Alexander (Alexander & French, 1946) understood it, it was not necessary for patients to remember all the events from their past that caused neurotic reactions. The essential element was the therapist's ability to reestablish the core conflictual situation in the transference relationship so that "the adult ego has the opportunity to grapple with it in a new attempt at mastery" (Alexander & French, 1946, p. 163). Being able to withstand the full impact of the previously repressed intense feelings and reactions from the past in the current relationship with the therapist, without resorting to regressive defenses, was designed to increase the patient's ego-adaptive capacity. Thus, the new experience in the transference would restructure the patient's defensive system. This shift in focus from emotional catharsis to conscious recall was accompanied by a shift in therapeutic goals, from that of mere symptom removal, to a permanent change in the patient's ego functioning. Dynamic psychotherapy, which had been fairly brief during Freud's early days, got increasingly protracted as the goals of treatment expanded. Following each extension of therapy, came clinicians attempting to find ways to shorten the process. Contributions of the major theorists in the short-term dynamic psychotherapy movement will be reviewed in subsequent chapters.

THE IMPORTANCE OF THEORY-GUIDED TECHNIQUE

Freud was a theorist, researcher, and clinician who wrote relatively little on technique. In his paper entitled "On the History of the Psychoanalytic Movement" (Freud, 1914), he remained vague about technique, stating that any psychotherapy which recognized the phenomena of transference and resistance as facts and made them central in the work could be considered psychoanalysis. There was little improvement in this regard over time. Analysts as a group have proven unable to agree on theory or technique. A survey of British analysts (Glover, 1958) revealed that half of the respondents reported approaching their analytic work *without* any theoretical outline in mind. A study conducted in Chicago (Henry, Sims, & Spicey, 1968) revealed that 61% of the analysts there responded in a similar fashion. Given the lack of a cohesive theoretical paradigm for understanding patient material, it should come as no surprise that other surveys were unable to find any agreement on the goals of psychoanalytic treatment (Seward, 1962–1963). In fact, the 65 analysts studied by Seward could only agree on what they *did not* expect to accomplish, including symptom relief, self-acceptance or expression, and an increase in personal responsibility. These findings have been corroborated by others (Sklansky, Isaacs, Levitor, & Haggard, 1966) who have found that analysts were "highly idiosyncratic" in their interventions.

Davanloo (1980, 1990) has attempted to correct many of these inconsistencies by having a clear grasp on the metapsychology of the unconscious, developing a systematic method of intervention based on theory, closely examining patients' responses to intervention (asking questions rather than assuming or making interpretations), and using videotapes to study the process. He has labeled this form of treatment Intensive Short-Term Dynamic Psychotherapy (ISTDP). He has repeatedly emphasized that a thorough understanding of the metapsychology of the unconscious is essential to the proper use of the techniques he has developed. Following his suggestion, this chapter will outline the metapsychological assumptions underlying Davanloo's method and then detail the technical interventions based on this theoretical understanding.

Freud's Second Theory of Anxiety

The theoretical underpinnings of Davanloo's model have been derived from Freud's second theory of anxiety. Originally, Freud viewed anxiety as a reaction to the build-up of instinctual tensions, assuming an "inherent tendency in the nervous system to reduce, or at least keep constant, the amount of excitation present in it" (Freud, 1926, p. 4). This is the essence of drive theory, which hypothesizes a motivation toward the reduction or discharge of instinctual tensions. As early as 1897 (Freud, 1950, Letter 75), Freud expressed doubts about a direct link between accumulated excitation and anxiety. Still, it was not until the publication of *Inhibitions, Symptoms and Anxiety* in 1926 that he explicitly stated his revised view, that anxiety is a danger signal to the ego, warning of the occurrence of trauma. Trauma, as he defined it, "involves separation from, or loss of, a loved object or a loss of its love" (Freud, 1926, p. 151). That such a separation or loss would constitute trauma is readily explained by the infant and child's prolonged state of mental and physical helplessness and utter dependence on caretakers for survival and well-being. As such, anxiety serves an indispensable biological function, alerting the ego to the probability of trauma.

This revision implies the central nature of human attachments and is the beginning of an object relations theory (Della Selva, 1992, 1993; Greenberg & Mitchell, 1983). Because of the child's dependence and the centrality of human attachments, any thought, feeling, or action which has led to unwanted separation from or loss of an attachment figure or their love is experienced as dangerous, evokes anxiety, and is avoided. Symptoms are considered to be compromises between the competing need to express the feeling and to defend against it. Symptoms and defenses keep the anxiety, and the feelings propelling it, out of awareness.

The following example of this theory involves a depressed woman who came for treatment. As she described a recent interaction with her father, she realized that she'd had a stubborn headache ever since the visit with him. After describing the incident, we focused on her feelings toward her father. She began to get in touch with a rage toward him that had mobilized a violent impulse. She imagined smashing his head and poking out his eyes, leaving him dead in a pool of blood. This feeling and the accompanying impulse were experienced as very dangerous and aroused considerable anxiety. There was little love lost with her father, but she imagined her mother would be furious with her. It was her mother's love and attention she felt she couldn't afford to lose. The anxiety served as a signal to repress this feeling from consciousness. Still, the feelings and impulses were very strong and were pushing for expression. The compromise between the impulse (smashing his head and poking his eyes) and the defense against it (displacement) was a headache. Following the experience of anger in the therapy session, the headache disappeared, providing compelling evidence that, once the patient was able to consciously tolerate the direct experience and expression affect, the need to defend against it by becoming symptomatic was no longer necessary.

Two Triangles

Menninger (1958) operationalized the notion of intrapsychic conflict by drawing a "triangle of insight" in which impulses and feelings, defenses, and anxiety each occupy one of the three corners. Malan (1979) went one step further by linking the triangle that depicts intrapsychic conflict with another triangle that represents significant others in the patients's life (called the triangle of conflict and triangle of the person, respectively). The relationship between these two triangles indicates, once again, the central importance of the interpersonal context within which psychic conflict is experienced (Figure 1.1).

Feelings do not exist in a vacuum, but arise both toward and in reaction to others. There is always an interpersonal context to the arousal of emotion, even if only in fantasy. It is hypothesized that those affective states which caretakers did not tolerate will be suffused with anxiety and lead to the operation of a defense. We cannot assume that only certain feelings, such as anger, will be prohibited; for in some families

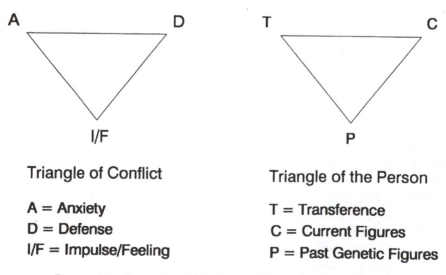

Triangle of Conflict

A = Anxiety
D = Defense
I/F = Impulse/Feeling

Triangle of the Person

T = Transference
C = Current Figures
P = Past Genetic Figures

Figure 1.1   Triangle of Conflict and Triangle of the Person

nothing is experienced as more threatening and, therefore, is more heavily prohibited than the expression of tender feelings (Suttie, 1937, 1988). Careful exploration of anxiety as it arises in the dynamic interaction between patient and therapist is the most accurate way to assess this for a given patient.

OPERATIONAL DEFINITIONS OF DYNAMIC CONCEPTS

Davanloo (1980, 1990) has made extensive use of the two triangles as a means for conceptualizing intrapsychic conflict. As such, the triangles serve as both a diagnostic tool and guide to systematic intervention. Since a full and detailed understanding of the two triangles is of such great importance in Davanloo's system, each element will be specifically and operationally defined.

Feelings and Impulses

Feelings are considered the engine of the intrapsychic system and have been placed at the bottom of the triangle. Primary feelings include joy and happiness, sexual desire and arousal, anger, and sadness or grief. Davanloo has identified three components to feeling that must be present for a patient to be considered "in touch with" the experience of affect (Laikin, Winston, & McCullough, 1991). These three components represent the cognitive, physiological, and motoric elements of emotional experience (Figure 1.2). The cognitive component involves the accurate labeling of the emotion ("I am angry"). The physiological component includes all the physical and visceral sensations that accompany the emotion ("I am feeling hot, like my temperature is up and my blood is pumping. My muscles feel strong"). Finally, the motoric element of the emotion involves mobilization of an impulse ("I feel like punching him in the face").

```
                    ---->  COGNITIVE
                           ("I am angry")

AFFECT/FEELING     ---->  PHYSIOLOGICAL AROUSAL
   (e.g. Anger)            ("I feel hot and reved up")

                    ---->  MOTORIC/IMPULSE
                           ("I feel like punching him in the nose")
```

Figure 1.2 Components of an Affective Experience

The absence of any one of the components of feelings indicates the operation of defense. This detailed conceptualization of feeling allows the clinician to pinpoint the specific aspect of the feeling that is being defended against and can serve as a guide to specific interventions.

For example, histrionic patients tend to experience the physiological and motoric aspects of feeling but defend against knowing *what* it is they are feeling and *toward whom* (the cognitive element of feeling). On the other hand, obsessive patients might be able to label their feeling (cognitive) and even elaborate a fantasy of what they want to do with the feeling (motoric), but they defend against the physiological experience of the feeling, remaining emotionally detached. This brings us to the defense corner of the triangle.

Defenses

Defenses consist of cognitive, emotional, and interpersonal strategies employed by patients to keep anxiety-provoking thoughts and feelings out of awareness (Figure 1.3). Several categories of defense mechanisms will be explored here.

Formal Defenses.   The formal defenses, designed to prevent conscious awareness of thoughts and feelings experienced as dangerous, can be grouped into two general categories, repressive and regressive. The repressive defenses include intellectualization, rationalization, minimization, displacement, and reaction formation. Regressive defenses include denial, projection, and somatization. Identifying the patient's characteristic defenses yields diagnostic information regarding their current level of ego functioning. For example, a reliance on regressive defenses such as denial and projection indicates greater impairment in

FORMAL		TACTICAL	
REPRESSIVE	REGRESSIVE	VERBAL	NON−VERBAL
Intellectualization	Projection	Vague/General	Avoiding Eye Contact
Rationalization	Somatization	Diversification	Smiling/Laughing
Minimization	Denial	Sarcasm	Weepiness
Displacement	Acting Out/	Argumentativeness	Arms/Legs Crossed
Reaction Formation	Discharge of Impulse		

Figure 1.3   Defenses

ego functioning than would the characteristic use of repressive defenses, such as rationalization and displacement.

Tactical Defenses.   In addition to the formal defenses, Davanloo pays strict attention to what he has labeled "tactical defenses." Whereas formal defenses are largely intrapsychic in nature, tactical defenses are employed interpersonally to prevent emotional closeness. Tactical defenses include all the verbal and nonverbal maneuvers patients use interpersonally to deflect or prevent meaningful emotional contact.

Verbal tactical defenses include vagueness and a tendency toward generalities, the use of contradictory statements, sarcasm, a high level of verbal activity making a dialogue impossible, or diversification (jumping from topic to topic). Some examples of nonverbal tactical defenses include avoidance of eye contact, smiling and giggling, weepiness, or an air of detachment. Posture is also included here, with either great stiffness and immobility or limpness indicating the presence of a defensive barrier against meaningful interpersonal contact.

Assessing Whether Defenses Are Syntonic or Dystonic

Patients are sometimes aware that they are avoiding the experience of painful feelings by utilizing formal defenses. Such an awareness indicates that this particular defense is dystonic and suggests a high level of ego-adaptive capacity (specifically a good observing ego). Tactical defenses are almost always automatic and unconscious. Together, the various tactical defenses a patient employs tend to be embedded in the character and are quite syntonic ("That's just the way I am").

So, at the micro-level, the patient employs specific defenses against the experience of painful and anxiety-laden feelings, but on a macro-level, these individual defenses link together to form a barrier or wall against meaningful emotional contact with others, including the therapist (Laikin et al., 1991). To intervene effectively, the therapist must ascertain which level of defensive operation is most prominent, so that therapy can specifically address it. For example, challenging a patient on a specific defense (minimization) against a particular feeling (grief about the loss of loved one), will have very little impact if the patient has erected a massive wall against meaningful involvement with the therapist (made up of minimal eye contact, a monotone voice, and a passive, compliant stance). The therapist must proceed from the outside in, and should begin with any defenses against emotional closeness.

Anxiety

Defenses are employed in an effort to reduce the anxiety that accompanies "forbidden" thoughts and feelings. Understanding the nature of the patient's anxiety, the level of anxiety experienced, and the ways in which the patient typically channels anxiety is of great diagnostic significance and should be monitored throughout treatment. Davanloo has classified three primary channels of anxiety (Figure 1.4).

Striated Muscle.   One very common channel or pathway of anxiety is into the striated or voluntary muscle. Patients who channel their anxiety into striated muscle tend to associate their physical tension with anxiety and to have a fairly accurate idea what they are anxious about, indicating some degree of integration between thoughts and feelings and suggesting a fairly high level of ego functioning. For example, a 40-year-old married man reported feeling "a little nervous" about our first meeting. When I asked how he experienced his anxiety, he said he felt physically tense (voluntary muscle). I then asked when it started and what he thought the anxiety was about. He said that his anxiety had only kicked in once he was actually in the waiting room and that, since most of his problems were of an intimate, sexual nature, he felt uncomfortable discussing them openly with "a young, attractive woman." This interchange provided evidence of a fairly high level of ego-adaptive capacity, as the anxiety was being channeled into the striated muscle and the patient was able to make a connection between his anxiety and an upsurge of feeling in the transference.

Smooth Muscle.   The second channel of anxiety Davanloo has identified is into the smooth, involuntary muscle. These are patients who channel their anxiety into the soma. Frequently, they are unaware of any link between their physical state of distress (e.g., headache, or gas pains and diarrhea) and the emotional state of anxiety and nervousness. Often

```
                  --->   STRIATED MUSCLE

ANXIETY           --->   SMOOTH MUSCLE

                  --->   COGNITIVE DISRUPTION/DISCHARGE
```

Figure 1.4   Channels of Anxiety

they will vehemently deny any such link, insisting, "It's only physical." In such cases, preparatory work is required to increase their capacity to consciously tolerate the experience of anxiety before moving on to more intense, affect-laden work. Failure to do so could lead to an exacerbation of the patient's physical ailment (headaches, irritable bowel, ulcerative colitis, asthma).

An example of a patient in this category was an older man who presented himself as "calm, cool, and collected." He reported being very interested in the process of therapy and said he look forward to our meeting. When I asked him about any physical difficulties, he reported sleep disturbance and diarrhea, both of which had been particularly bad the day or two before our meeting. His detachment from the experience of his anxiety and failure to connect his physical symptoms with the anxiety about meeting with me indicated a lower level of ego functioning than with the man previously mentioned.

Cognitive Disruption.   The third channel of anxiety is that which affects cognitive functioning. When anxious, these patients experience some sort of cognitive disruption; either losing track of their thoughts, getting weak and dizzy, dissociating, or reporting an urge to discharge their anxiety in an impulsive manner. Evidence of the use of this channel of anxiety generally signifies some fragility of the ego and is a contraindication for rapid movement into the unconscious.

For example, a young college student presented herself in a rather bubbly and effervescent manner. When asked how she felt about coming to see me, she said she was really excited about it. She had actually arrived a half hour late for our appointment. As we explored this, she revealed that she had been up all night, unable to sleep, and had lost directions to the office. Her thinking was scattered and she had a great deal of difficulty articulating the nature of her problems. Further inquiry revealed pervasive cognitive disruption in the face of anxiety that had significantly affected her ability to complete schoolwork. In fact, she was on academic probation. All these factors suggested that a very high level of anxiety was seriously interfering with her ability to think clearly and indicated some fragility of the ego.

Obtaining a Baseline of Anxiety.   In addition to identifying the primary channel of anxiety in evidence at the time of the interview (it's not unusual to find a mix), a baseline needs to be obtained. One patient entered the evaluation with a cordless phone in hand saying, "I've brought this in case I need to dial 911. When I get anxious, I pass out." It would be easy to assume that his anxiety was exceptionally high because he was about to begin the process of psychotherapy. When asked, "How does this anxiety compare with what you experience in other situations?", he replied, "Oh, this is fairly mild. I'm least anxious when I'm alone in my apartment, and I'm also pretty good if I'm at a hospital or in a doctor's office. It's being out there with people I can't tolerate." This comparative analysis yielded valuable diagnostic data suggesting a high degree of ego fragility.

Therapeutic Implications of Theory

Psychodynamic theory suggests that all the repressed feelings and reactions to the ruptures in significant relationships lie at the root of neurotic suffering. Davanloo believes, "The vast majority of neurosis stems from the patient's conflicting feelings within family relationships . . ." (1990, p. 190).

How do these mixed and conflictual feelings develop (Figure 1.5)? At the very center of human experience, there is an innate capacity to form close emotional attachments to caretakers (Bowlby, 1973). Davanloo has clearly stated, "Only the capacity to develop warm emotional ties to caretakers is innate" (1987a, 1987b). These attachment strivings are

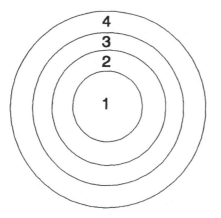

1 = Attachment Strivings
2 = Pain and Grief
3 = Reactive Rage
4 = Defense against Emotional Closeness

Figure 1.5 Genetic System within the Unconscious

inevitably frustrated, which causes internal pain and grief and gives rise to reactive anger toward the frustrating and depriving (if not, at times, abusive) attachment figure. At times, the pain and anger seem so great and so unbearable that the patient unconsciously decides that no one will ever get close enough to cause such harm again. Consequently, the person builds a layer of defense around the entire intrapsychic system. This protective layer serves a dual function by fending off real or anticipated pain from both internal and external sources. Davanloo (1990–1991) refers to this as a defense against emotional closeness (DAEC). Others have called this type of defense "character armor" (Reich, 1933) or "false self" (Winnicott, 1965). What began as a layer of protection for many patients becomes an immovable barrier to satisfying human contact. These patients are often referred to as character disordered.

Traditionally, patients with a significant layer of character pathology have proven resistant to treatments of all sorts, even medication (Reitav, 1991). In all likelihood, this is the result of the therapist's failure to effectively penetrate the defensive armor of the patient.

The resistance employed by the patient has been a long-standing problem for analysts. Malan (Davanloo, 1980) has suggested that Freud took a "wrong turn" when he reacted to increasing resistance with increased passivity. Not only did this passivity on the part of the analyst prolong treatment, it frequently proved ineffective and patients failed to improve despite years of treatment. Reich (1933) expressed the opinion, "If one neglects such character resistances, and instead simply follows the line of the material, such resistances form a ballast which is difficult, if not impossible to remove" (p. 51).

Davanloo (1987a, 1987b) has developed a series of techniques designed to directly address, and then break through, defensive barriers that will otherwise become a resistance in treatment. He has found that clarification of defense and resistance, followed by pressure and challenge to the patient's defensive barrier, must occur from the start of treatment. This technique stirs up strong mixed feelings in the transference, followed by the patient's characteristic defenses against same. This conflict serves as a trigger to similar conflicts from the past. Davanloo has repeatedly demonstrated that, if the defenses can be penetrated, and the feelings in the transference experienced and expressed directly, an opening into the genetic unconscious will be achieved. Theory suggests that, once patients can consciously face that which they had previously avoided, they will no longer need to rely on regressive and self-defeating defenses. The ego regains autonomy, and patients can function at their highest level of ability.

Resistance versus Alliance

The central role of conflictual feelings in the development of neurosis makes it inevitable that patients arrive for treatment in a state of ambivalence. Patients want help from the therapist in getting to the bottom of their difficulties and achieving freedom from suffering. This part of the patient is available for the development of a therapeutic alliance. At the same time, another part of the patient operates in opposition to the therapist. This part wants to run, hide, and avoid the pain and grief the therapeutic process will entail. It is this part of the patient that fuels the resistance. Davanloo (1987a, 1987b) has found that these two variables, the therapeutic alliance and resistance, exist in inverse proportion to one another. Our job involves creating a shift within the patient from resistance to alliance. How this is achieved is a central question for all dynamic psychotherapists.

Therapeutic Stance

Many therapists have experienced occasional success in helping patients to achieve deep and long-lasting change in a brief time. The question has always been how to do so with some consistency. Alexander and French (1946), Malan (1976, 1979; Malan & Osimo, 1992), and Davanloo (1980) have all found that those most likely to make rapid and enduring changes were in some sort of acute crisis. In these cases, some external event had evoked such intense feelings and conflict that the patients' characteristic defenses were not sufficient to contain them. So these patients entered treatment with little defense in operation, and strong feelings close to the surface. In addition, the pain they were already experiencing served as a potent motivator. These factors all contributed to rapid movement. Yet, this group of patients constitutes only about 20% of those seeking outpatient psychotherapy. In most cases, patients are suffering from chronic difficulties with anxiety, depression, and interpersonal relatedness. It has been assumed such patients would not be able to benefit from short-term dynamic psychotherapy. Davanloo has challenged this assumption by developing specific methods for *creating* an intrapsychic crisis in these patients. How is this accomplished?

According to Davanloo (1980, 1990), the therapist must abandon the passive stance and work actively to bring the patient's conflict into focus, intensifying the affective involvement and creating an intrapsychic crisis that makes rapid change possible. The therapist makes a direct appeal to the healthy part of the ego seeking freedom, while exerting pressure on the defenses. In this way, the ISTDP therapist is not neutral but adopts a therapeutic stance that advocates openness and honesty, even when painful. The therapist communicates a serious but dedicated approach to getting at the truth (Malan has referred to this as "the iron hand in the velvet glove"). It is clear to the patient from the outset that the therapist is working diligently and is presenting a challenge to the patient to join in and work at his or her highest level of ability.

Michael Balint (1957) has written about the element of surprise in psychotherapy and advocated presenting the patient with a counter-offer. In Freud's day, it was startling for the therapist to offer an atmosphere in which the patient could say whatever comes to mind. This was in stark contrast to the repressive attitudes of the day. In post-Freudian America, it is assumed that therapy will consist of endless talk, and it is startling for the therapist to suggest that meaningful work can occur rapidly. This counter-offer consists of the therapist's placing pressure on the patient to abandon defenses while simultaneously displaying a keen interest in getting to know the patient deeply enough to be of help. Such a unique and unexpected offer evokes strong mixed feelings in the transference. In part, the patient is alarmed that the therapist wants to enter into his or her inner world, possibly closer than anyone has come before. Resistance against this is mobilized as "an inevitable consequence of the basic mechanism underlying neurosis, namely repression of feelings that are painful, anxiety-laden, and considered dangerous and unacceptable" (Davanloo, 1987).

On the other hand, there is a healthy, maturational force within the patient that yeans for the kind of emotional closeness the therapist is offering. Establishing such a relationship would help the patient openly deal with difficulties and gain freedom from suffering. The mobilization of these strong, conflicting feelings creates an intrapsychic crisis within the patient. It is the direct experience of all these conflicted feelings in the transference that provides the key to unlock the unconscious system (Davanloo, 1990).

All the techniques developed by Davanloo have been aimed at bringing buried feelings to the surface, so they can be faced directly by the patient and resolved in an adaptive manner.

CENTRAL DYNAMIC SEQUENCE

The central dynamic sequence encapsulates the procedure developed by Davanloo (1988) to assess suitability for an unlocking of the unconscious and then guiding the process, should such a procedure be deemed appropriate. Malan (1980) has called Davanloo's development of this elegant and comprehensive system of intervention "the most important development in psychotherapy since the discovery of the unconscious."

The central dynamic sequence involves five phases:

1. Inquiry and survey of patient's difficulties.
2. Defense analysis.
3. Rise and breakthrough of complex transference feelings.
4. De-repression of significant memories and associations allowing for a meaningful exploration of the patient's developmental history.
5. Interpretation and consolidation of insights obtained in the process.

Phase 1. Inquiry

Davanloo advocates a descriptive, phenomenological approach to inquiry. This includes taking a survey of the patient's symptomatic and characterological difficulties, with an emphasis on specificity and a focus on feeling. Recent examples of the problems being reported are requested to aid in this process.

Specificity.   To obtain an accurate assessment of the patient's difficulties, the therapist must make specific inquiries. For example, a patient comes in complaining of depression and inhibition at work. The therapist inquires, "What do you mean by depression? Could we look at a recent example of a time when you felt depressed? What is it that you actually experienced inside, on an emotional level, that you refer to as being depressed?"

If the patient is able to provide detailed information regarding such an experience, then a baseline and brief history of the presenting problem should be obtained before moving on to other areas of disturbance. To continue with our example, the therapist would ask, "So how long have you been depressed? Have you had other periods of depression in your life? What is the worst it has ever gotten?"

The answers to these questions suggest the nature of the underlying difficulty, as well as providing some information on the patient's ego adaptive capacity. For example, if the patient has recently become depressed in reaction to the death of a friend and reports a history of depression following previous losses, it suggests the presence of pathological mourning. If the depression is experienced as sadness, lethargy, and pessimism about the future, but does not involve vegetative symptoms or an inability to function, the patient is likely to have fairly good ego-adaptive capacity that has been temporarily depleted and can be rapidly mobilized to deal actively with an acute grieving process.

If, on the other hand, the patient can't sleep, has lost 15 pounds in the past month, and has been calling in sick at work, the ego is so depleted there will be little energy in the system to mobilize for the work of an uncovering psychotherapy. Either medication or supportive and restructuring work would be necessary to build the ego to the point where the patient could tolerate the repressed feelings that need to be uncovered.

Obtaining a Survey of Difficulties.   Once the presenting complaints have been explored, the therapist should ask about other areas of difficulty. At times, patients will report needing help with only one circumscribed problem. The therapist might say, "So, other than this conflict with your boss, you have no other problem in your life? You are 100% satisfied in other areas?" If the patient says, "Yes, that's it," then you are sitting with one of those rare patients (5%–10% of those seeking outpatient psychotherapy) who has one circumscribed area of conflict that should be worked through in a number of hours. More often, however, patients will then volunteer several other problems.

Challenge to Lack of Clarity.   The only challenge to the patient at this point in the sequence is to provide specific data necessary to delineate the areas of difficulty. In response to vagueness, the therapist might say, "It is important that you be specific so I can understand the nature of your difficulties. Could you give me an example?"

It is not uncommon for patients to externalize and either talk about problems that other people have or to say they have come at the insistence of someone else. When I asked a college student why she had come to see me, she said that her roommates were a pain in the neck, and went on to detail *their* problems. Sometimes a simple redirection will suffice to get inquiry on track. I replied, "You're telling me about some problems your roommates are having. What difficulties are you having that I could help you with?"

Securing the Patient's Will to Work.   The therapist should explore immediately a patient's report that he is seeking psychotherapy at someone else's behest. It must be determined whether the patient has the inner motivation and desire to enter psychotherapy.

Another college student declared he was in my office because his mother had told him he had to see someone. This needed to be clarified at once. I asked, "So you are here because your mother demanded it? If she had not insisted, you wouldn't be here? As far as you're concerned, you have no difficulties in your life?" If the patient were to say he had no problems of his own, there would be no point in continuing. To enter treatment under these conditions would be a farce. Conceivably, it could be quite therapeutic to refuse to engage in such a ruse. In so doing, the therapist displays respect for the patient, as we never have the right to intervene without direct permission from the patient.

In cases such as this one, the only possible intervention would be to explore the patient's compliance. "So you're telling me you have no problems and no desire to be here, but here you sit. How does that happen? Is this a unique situation or do you have a tendency to comply with others' wishes?" If the patient acknowledges this, the therapist needs to ask, "Do you see this as a problem? Is this something you would like to work on?" Patients must declare that they are in the therapist's office of their own will before the process can proceed.

Maintaining a Focus.   If the patient jumps from topic to topic, the therapist must interrupt and slow that patient down. For example, "Before we go on to this other problem, let's make sure we understand the first problem you mentioned." Similarly, if the patient begins by talking about something that happened when he or she was 3 years old, the therapist must redirect to an inquiry of current difficulties. A statement such as "I'm sure your grandfather's death was an important event in your life and we'll be getting to that, but let's start with what brings you here now." Identifying the current precipitant of the reported difficulties is essential in establishing a context for understanding the nature of the patient's difficulties.

Phase 2.   Defense Analysis

Once an adequate inquiry and survey of the patient's problems has been obtained (which shouldn't take more than 15 or 20 minutes), the therapist moves on to an examination of the patient's defenses. Recalling that the aim of the treatment is to enable the patient to experience feelings "to the maximum degree" the person can bear, all defenses against the experience of feeling must be removed. The defense work can be roughly divided into three steps or stages:

1. Identification and clarification of defenses.
2. Turning the ego against its defenses.
3. Pressure and challenge to give up the defenses.

Identification and Clarification of Defenses.   While conducting the inquiry, the therapist should be noting, and filing away for future use, the kinds of defenses in operation. A patient might have erratic eye contact and have his arms folded across his chest. In response to questions about his feelings, this patient might have the tendency to smile and rationalize. The first therapeutic task in this phase is to identify and clarify the defenses in operation. "As we began to look at your feelings toward your wife, did you notice you were avoiding my eyes, you folded your arms across your chest, laughed, and then offered a rationalization?" The task here is to assess whether the patient is aware or can easily become aware of these defensive behaviors. If so, and the patient says, "Yes, I see that now," then the function of these behaviors must be made clear to the patient. "Isn't this actually a way to avoid looking at the feelings toward your wife?" If the patient can see that he *does something* to avoid feeling, it suggests that his defenses are fairly dystonic.

At other times, patients don't distinguish between what they feel (I/F) and what they do (D) to avoid it (see Figure 1.1). They may be highly identified with the defense and say, "That's just the way I am. I've always been that way," indicating a fairly high degree of syntonicity. In these cases repeated efforts are necessary to identify and clarify the defensive avoidance of feeling in all areas of the patient's life (sometimes referred to as "working the triangles").

Turning the Ego against Its Defenses.   The second part of this phase of the work involves turning the ego against its defenses. This is done by focusing on the cost of defenses, pointing out to the patient the negative, self-defeating consequences of their use.

The following is a fairly typical intervention designed to highlight the cost of defenses and to shift the balance from resistance to alliance. "So now you see that you avoid the experience of your true feelings by laughing them off and going to a rationalization. Let's look at the consequences of maintaining this avoidant stance. First of all, if you're hiding and covering up your true feelings here with me, I can't be of any help to you. Then, you'll carry your suffering with you and be no better off. Is that what you want?" It is crucial that patients see the negative consequences of their defenses. Often, this technique is most effective if patients themselves can outline the negative consequences. If the therapist asks, "What will happen here today if you continue to rationalize, avoid the issue, and skirt around the difficult feelings?" and the patient can say, "I'll be wasting my time," then the ego is already starting to turn on the defense. The therapist is then in a good position to go on to the next step, which is to put pressure on the patient to abandon the defense.

Pressure and Challenge.   Once patients can see that they are defending against feelings and, in so doing, resisting the very work they engaged the therapist to help them with, the stage is set for the phase of pressure and challenge. It is made clear to patients that insight alone is not enough. As soon as patients declare they are defeating themselves by remaining in a defensive position, the therapist challenges them to do things differently. "So why would you want to waste your time? Let's see what you're going to do about this evasion of your true feelings?" This phase of defense work, sometimes referred to as "a head-on collision with the resistance" tends to evoke very strong feelings toward the therapist. The therapist waits for a sign, either verbal (e.g., "I'm starting to get irritated with you") or nonverbal (e.g., teeth gritting and hands clenching the arms of the chair), that the feelings are about to break through and shifts from a focus on defense to direct access of feelings.

Before moving on, it must be emphasized that it would be a grave error to proceed to the phase of pressure and challenge before the ego has been turned against its defenses. In such cases, the patient himself, rather than his defenses, will feel attacked, and a therapeutic misalliance will result.

Phase 3.   Breakthrough of Feelings in the Transference

Keeping a tight focus on defenses and placing pressure on the patient to abandon them stirs up intense mixed feelings toward the therapist, creating an intrapsychic crisis. Pressure is maintained until there is a signal from the unconscious that feelings and impulses are close to the surface. The therapist must remain alert for such a sign and seize it immediately, switching focus from the defenses to the direct experience of feelings in the transference. The therapist challenges patients to be open and honest about the true nature of their feelings and impulses. Any defense against this is immediately identified:

THERAPIST: Do you notice your hand is in a fist? I sense you have a lot of feeling toward me.

PATIENT: Well, I guess I don't like what you're saying.
THERAPIST: You guess? You do like it or you don't?
PATIENT: No, I don't.
THERAPIST: Then could we look at the feeling about that? What is the feeling toward me?

Defenses and resistance increase in direct proportion to the mounting anxiety about the rise in previously forbidden feelings and impulses. In this way, the resistance is not a problem but an indication that feelings toward the therapist, the very key for unlocking the unconscious, are on the rise. It's not an indication to back off, but to proceed to a full breakthrough of feeling, provided that the patient's anxiety is at a tolerable level. During this phase of the work, persistence on the therapist's part really pays off. Backing off de-pressurizes the very conflict these techniques are designed to intensify. Consequently, hesitance on the therapist's part will prolong treatment.

Patients who are able to declare their feelings would then be asked to describe the internal experience of those feelings. In this way, the therapist can assess the level of emotional involvement in the process and detect any remaining area of defense. For there to be a full breakthrough of feeling, all three elements (cognitive, physiological, and motoric) of the feeling must be present (see Figure 1.2).

Once patients indicate they are experiencing the physiological components of the stated affect, the therapist asks about the impulse this feeling mobilizes. "So you are hot and feel revved up. If that energy and heat came out toward me, what would that look like?" It is made very clear to patients that the therapist is not advocating acting on the impulse (a regressive defense) but having an honest look at their feelings and impulses. Fantasy and visualization, sometimes called "portraiting the impulse" (Davanloo, 1990–1991), are techniques used to achieve full expression of the impulse.

Portraiting the Impulse.   To facilitate the process of increasing the patient's access to the full experience of emotion, Davanloo advocates the use of imagery or what he has referred to as "portraiting the impulse." Ferenzi (1924) was probably the first analyst to suggest the use of fantasy as a vehicle to enhance the experience of feelings. He felt that, until the patient's hostile feelings toward the therapist were fully experienced and expressed, no genuine positive transference could develop. He would encourage the patient to have a fantasy about the expression of rage toward the therapist.

In a similar vein, Davanloo makes sure that any sign of negative feeling in the transference is experienced and cleared away rapidly, opening the way for the development of a strong therapeutic alliance. In accordance with Freud's (1949) view that ". . . a patient never forgets again what he has experienced in the form of the transference," (p. 34), Davanloo places the experience of transference feelings at the very center of his technique.

Feelings in the Transference Are Complex. In the most typical scenario, anger is the first layer of feeling experienced, followed by guilt, grief, and the emergence of tender, loving feelings (see Figure 1.5). For example, following a portrait of anger that depicted a violent impulse to rape and strangle the therapist, a patient began to weep. "I feel terrible. I just imagined doing something brutal to you and you didn't deserve it—you're just trying to help me." It is essential that *all* the mixed feelings toward the therapist be experienced and expressed not just the anger, but also the guilt and grief which follow.

The patient is encouraged to experience each layer of feeling in a full and direct way. Davanloo (1988) believes, "It is necessary for the therapist to handle grief and pain in exactly the same way he handles anger, i.e., to challenge the defenses against them in order to bring them to the surface." The therapist might say, "I sense a deep sadness in you and you seem to be on the verge of tears but you swallow it. Why do you want to hide the grief in your heart?" Underneath the pain and grief are love and gratitude. These feelings are also visualized.

THERAPIST: "So underneath the anger is pain and deeper still, your tender loving feelings. How do you feel like expressing that?"·
PATIENT: "I just want to pick you up off the floor and hold you in my arms. I want you to come back."

As you may have already noted, the therapist uses highly charged, emotional language, which Davanloo (1990–1991) feels speaks directly to the unconscious.

Phase 4.   De-Repression of Unconscious Material and History-Taking

The free expression of feelings in the transference is considered the key in the unlocking of the unconscious. Meaningful memories and associations tend to flow quite readily following the breakthrough of affect in the transference. Sometimes patients will make spontaneous links with the past. For example, the man who imagined raping me went on to say, "This is just how I felt with my mother. She was such a difficult woman, always on my case about everything. I just wanted to kill her. But since she died, I am miserable. I miss her. When I was young, we were very close. I was her favorite."

On occasion, there is no spontaneous outpouring of supporting material. In these cases, a brief review of what has just occurred within the transference relationship and a question about who else comes to mind is typically sufficient to facilitate the de-repression of significant memories.

Therapeutic Value.   The experience of intense affect has three major functions:

1. It desensitizes the ego to the experience of previously toxic affects;
2. It leads to a loosening in the intrapsychic system with a de-repression of meaningful memories, dreams, and associations revealing the nature of the core conflicts underlying the neurosis; and
3. It allows patient and therapist to make meaningful links between the triangle of conflict and the triangle of the person (Been & Sklar, 1985).

Developmental History.   Now that defense and resistance have been removed and there is direct access to the unconscious, the stage is set for a meaningful exploration of the patient's developmental history. Davanloo warns that if history is obtained before defenses have been cleared away, the material obtained may well be skewed and inaccurate.

Phase 5.   Interpretation

Once there has been a breakdown in defense and resistance, followed by an intense experience of affect in the transference, with an outpouring of unconscious material, meaningful interpretations are possible. Nearly all Davanloo's innovations have been in the pre-interpretive phase of therapy and pave the way for making accurate and effective interpretations (Malan, 1986).

Interpretations consist of links between the triangle of conflict and the triangle of the person (see Figure 1.1). An example would be, "So now we can see that your smiling—the submissive, compliant attitude you initially displayed with me—was a cover for all the angry feelings you came in with. When you faced that directly, there was an outpouring of grief-laden feeling and, deeper still, we saw the positive feelings and craving for closeness. It then became clear that this was almost identical to all the mixed feelings you have regarding your mother. It sounds like this gets played out in virtually all your relationships with women." This re-analysis of the therapeutic process is essential to drive home the insights obtained and consolidate the process of change. In addition, once these T-C-P links have been made, distinctions between people become clearer. To continue with our example, this patient was able to say, "When you were pressing me, I felt angry and thought you were just like my mother. But my mother was never interested in my real feelings and I feel like you are."

Making a Therapeutic Contract.   Once this process has been completed, a meaningful therapeutic contract can be made. The therapist emphasizes to the patient that this initial work is only the beginning of the process and that therapy will involve hard work. The sense of relief and revival of hope that frequently accompany this initial work is a powerful motivating force for the patient. It is within this hopeful and collaborative atmosphere that a meaningful therapeutic contract can be made. Often the therapist will roughly estimate the expected duration of treatment while emphasizing that the achievement of the stated therapeutic goals will be the decisive factor, and not a prescribed time limit.

Therapeutic Tone.   Throughout this procedure, the therapist should be gentle but firm. The therapist should never argue with a patient but remain mindful to step out of any such interpersonal struggle by redirecting the patient to the internal struggle being experienced. Patients often identify with only one aspect of their conflict and tend to project the other aspect of the conflict onto the therapist, thereby avoiding the tension and discomfort of containing both aspects of the struggle. In ISTDP, we seek to intensify the patient's internal conflict. The following type of intervention is designed to achieve this goal: "Now you want to argue with me. It's not up to me to decide. Only you can say whether you are hiding and covering up your feelings with intellectualization and rationalization. What do you think—is that happening here with me or not?" Again, the therapist is firm but not harsh, and must be ready "to extend the hand of warmth and closeness the moment the patient is ready" (Malan, 1963, p. 76).

SUMMARY

While adhering quite strictly to psychoanalytic theory, Dr. Davanloo has developed Intensive Short-Term Dynamic Psychotherapy, which is designed to make rapid entry into the unconscious. This is achieved by breaking through barriers of defense and resistance and focusing on the patient's experience of painful and conflicting feelings, especially in the transference. This chapter has outlined the metapsychology of the unconscious, defined dynamic concepts in operational terms, and detailed the method for "unlocking the unconscious" developed by Dr. Davanloo.

CHAPTER 2

The Trial Therapy

You need that rite of passage
before you can continue on,
That great self understanding
you can lean your dreams upon.
*Dougie MacLean**

This chapter will outline the process of the trial therapy developed by Dr. Davanloo. The development of this elegant system for assessing suitability for treatment and, when indicated, rapidly entering the unconscious, is surely one of Davanloo's greatest contributions to the field of dynamic psychotherapy. Three cases from my own practice will be used to illustrate some fairly typical responses to the trial therapy. These patients had nearly identical presenting complaints, but the trial therapy revealed different origins to the symptoms and varying capacities for the work at hand, each having distinct implications for treatment.

The trial therapy is a complex and systematic method for assessing the patient's symptomatic and characterological difficulties, determining the unconscious forces behind these difficulties, and evaluating the patient's current ego-adaptive capacity. This extended (2–4 hour) evaluation is, indeed, a rite of passage for both patient and therapist, providing an opportunity for a deep understanding of the unconscious forces responsible for the patient's suffering.

*From "Rite of Passage." Music and lyrics by Dougie MacLean. "Indigenous" Dunkeld, 1990.

ASSESSING SUITABILITY FOR TREATMENT

Patient as Evaluator

Although the therapist assumes a great deal of responsibility for the pace and direction of the initial evaluation, patients must understand from the outset that the process is a two-way street and a collaboration will be required for a successful outcome. Patients are informed that the purpose of the evaluation is to get to the bottom of their difficulties, to understand the driving force behind their problems, and to ascertain whether this particular form of treatment will be useful to them. The therapist must determine patients' suitability for treatment, whereas patients must weigh their own willingness to do the work at hand.

Selection Criteria

In the field of dynamic psychotherapy in general, professionals have paid little attention to developing therapeutic techniques tailored to the specific requirements of the opening phase of treatment. The initial evaluation serves a dual purpose: (a) to determine the factors responsible for the patient's suffering and (b) to assess the patient's ability to benefit from intensive short-term dynamic psychotherapy. Because of the abbreviated nature of this form of dynamic psychotherapy, pioneers in the field (Davanloo, 1978, 1980; Malan, 1976, 1979; Sifneos, 1972) have focused much effort on the development and application of reliable criteria for patient selection.

Some, like Sifneos (1972), are very demanding in the characteristics they require of a patient to be considered suitable for treatment. These characteristics include above-average intelligence, motivation for change, an ability to make meaningful contact with the evaluator, ready access to feelings, and the ability to articulate a chief complaint. In addition, candidates must evidence a willingness to endure hardship and frustration to obtain help. So few patients fit these rigid criteria that the short-term treatment developed by Sifneos has very little applicability.

Malan (1963) and Balint (1957) began their studies on the effectiveness of short-term dynamic psychotherapy with the assumption that only patients with recent, mild, and fairly circumscribed difficulties would be suitable for this type of treatment. When they were unable to find a large enough group of patients to fit their criteria in the outpatient population of their clinic, they reluctantly expanded their parameters for selection and, much to their surprise, found that the majority of those who made substantial and long-lasting gains in brief (up to 40 sessions) psychotherapy had suffered from chronic and debilitating symptoms.

These studies (Malan, 1976; Malan & Osimo, 1992) indicated that the patient's ability to develop a focus within the first four sessions and to respond positively to trial interpretations provided the most accurate predictors of outcome. In this context, "focus" referred to the demarcation of a central theme or conflict that had precipitated the patient's current distress and was linked with similar conflicts from the past. The kind of response to interpretation they were looking for was one in which genuine and deeply felt affect was experienced, leading to new insights. The insight felt to be most crucial involved an understanding of the relationship between the triangle of conflict and the triangle of the person (see Figure 1.1). Follow-up studies (Malan, 1976, 1979) have confirmed that successful outcome is significantly related to the frequency of these very interpretations.

Davanloo (1980), expanding on Malan's notions regarding the importance of the patient's response to trial interpretations, has stated, "No one can tell anything about the patient's likely response without exposing him to some of the important ingredients of the therapy he will receive" (p. 99). Therefore, "The major part of the interview contains exactly the same interventions as are used in the main body of therapy" (Davanloo, 1980, p. 100). In fact, Davanloo asserts that exposure to the vital ingredients involved in short-term dynamic psychotherapy, along with a vigilant monitoring of the patient's responses, is the only reliable way to assess whether the person can withstand the impact of his or her own unconscious material. This is what the trial therapy was designed to accomplish. In addition to, and, in fact, preceding, the use of interpretation, Davanloo has developed a series of pre-interpretive interventions designed to assess a patient's current ego-adaptive capacity and to break through defensive barriers, making previously inaccessible patients open to intervention.

Spectrum of Psychopathology

The first goal of the trial therapy is to obtain a dynamic diagnosis and to place the patient on the spectrum of psychopathology (Figure 2.1).

On the left side of the spectrum are those rare patients who come for help with one narrowly defined problem. Their anxiety is fairly low and is generally channeled into the striated muscle. Their defenses are repressive and typically quite dystonic. These patients erect no barriers

NEUROTIC	CHARACTER DISORDER	FRAGILE EGO
<-->		
Single Focus	Multi-Focus	Multi-Focus
Anxiety in Striated Muscle	Anxiety in Smooth Muscle	Anxiety with Cogniti Disruption
Repressive Defenses	Mix of Repressive and Regressive Defenses	Regressive Defenses
No Defenses against Emotional Closeness	Moderate level of Defense against Closeness	Significant Defenses against Closeness
Defenses Dystonic	Defenses Syntonic	Defenses Syntonic
Highly Functional	Impaired Social & Occupational Functioning	Impairment in Self-Care
Highly Motivated	Ambivalent about Treatment Process	Motivation Severely Compromised

Figure 2.1   Spectrum of Psychopathology

to emotional closeness and tend to perceive the therapist as helpful. They utilize this help, participate actively in treatment, and respond rapidly to intervention. The central dynamic sequence moves with ease to the breakthrough of feeling, usually toward a significant other in their current life, with meaningful links made to figures from the past.

Most often, however, patients come for treatment complaining of several symptomatic disturbances and significant impairment in their social and occupational functioning. These patients, who fall in the middle of the spectrum, are the most frequently encountered in daily practice. In these patients, anxiety is more likely to be of sufficient intensity that repressive defenses alone cannot contain it. Consequently, they resort to regressive defenses (e.g., acting out and externalization). Their characterological defenses, such as helplessness or defiance, quickly erect a barrier to meaningful communication and can become an obstacle in treatment. Although the symptoms presented may be plentiful and fairly severe, they also cause significant distress and interfere with functioning, providing a real incentive to work that milder forms of psychic disturbance do not. This distress can be the therapist's ally.

On the right side of the spectrum are patients with ego fragility, who tend to display some cognitive impairment when anxious and resort to highly regressive defenses such as dissociation. These patients have difficulty distinguishing between feelings and the defenses against them and, even when defenses have been removed, have trouble differentiating between varying affective states. For those individuals, the triangle of conflict is more like a circle of conflict (Celentano, personal communication, 1992) in which anxiety, feelings, and defenses are all confused and lack definition. These patients are not suitable candidates for this kind of rapid uncovering, as their ego is too weak to withstand it. Treatment must be directed toward building ego structures that are more resilient and adaptive than those currently at their disposal.

Contra-Indications

It must be emphasized that no one sign or symptom obtained in the trial therapy can be evaluated out of context or be, in and of itself, a reason for determining suitability or lack thereof. Patients can have episodes of dissociation or severe depression in their history but display a high degree of motivation and prove very responsive to treatment. Contra-indications that are readily obtained through inquiry include evidence of psychosis, major affective disorder, severe impulse control disorder, or active alcohol or substance abuse. Other contra-indications (e.g., a life-threatening condition such as ulcerative colitis) may emerge as the evaluation proceeds and anxiety begins to increase. Any such information indicates to the evaluator that a more supportive approach is required.

Response to Intervention

To assess suitability for treatment, the patient must be subjected to the vital ingredients of the treatment. The central dynamic sequence and the triangles of conflict serve as guides in this process. Each therapeutic intervention is met with a response from the patient that provides data regarding suitability. The therapist takes an active stance, focusing on the patient's inner life and challenging defenses as they arise. Patients are not assumed to be fragile, but rather are challenged to work at their highest level of ability.

In general, there are three categories of response to this intense and focused approach. In the most responsive patients, focusing leads to the production of affect-laden unconscious communications that readily shed light on the genesis of their neurotic conflict. Another frequently encountered response to this approach is increased defensiveness, particularly in the form of transference resistance. Individuals falling into this category are often openly defiant and consciously resistant ("I am not going to answer any more of your questions"). In between these two extremes are those patients who respond with a mix of feelings and defensive attempts to avoid them.

These responses to intervention indicate the patient's current level of ego functioning and serve as a guide to further intervention. In the first case, the therapist can simply proceed to the interpretive phase of treatment. In the second case—fortification of defense and mobilization of resistance in the transference—there is the need for pressure and challenge to the defenses. The third case requires a mix of holding on defense while encouraging the direct experience of the emerging feelings.

Three clinical examples, each representing one of the three categories of response just outlined, will be presented. Various technical interventions and a theoretical understanding of the emerging clinical data will be interspersed throughout the case material.

CLINICAL EXAMPLE

The Manic-Depressive's Daughter

In the following case, the patient proves highly responsive to a focused approach. There are virtually no defenses against meaningful emotional contact with the therapist. Little more than clarification and interpretation are necessary to render defenses against anxiety-provoking thoughts and feelings dystonic and to shift the balance from repression to a full experience of previously warded-off affect. The result is a rapid de-repression of memories and associations that make sense of her current difficulties.

THERAPIST: So, tell me what brings you.

PATIENT: What brings me is the fact that I often have difficulty coping with my oldest son, who is 6. He is, by all accounts, a very difficult child. About a year and a half ago, we took him to see a child psychiatrist.

THERAPIST: Difficult? How do you mean?

PATIENT: Temperamentally. He throws tantrums, is mercurial—a difficult person to live with. He's extraordinarily bright but labile and a behavior problem. He's not of a piece. He's very developed intellectually but emotionally and socially underdeveloped. He was thrown out of preschool for aggressive behavior and then we took him for treatment.

THERAPIST: Is there a diagnosable disorder?

PATIENT: The doctor has had to reassure me about that on any number of occasions because there's a history of mental illness in my family. My mother was a manic-depressive and my husband's father is just a depressive. In many ways, he reminds me of my mother and that's, I think, part of why I have such trouble dealing with him. She was very unpredictable. I never knew what I'd be facing when I came home, and it's the same with my son. When I wake up in the morning, I don't know whether he'll say "Hi, Mommy" or "I hate you." I find that kind of unpredictability very hard to deal with (the patient is becoming tearful).

So far this woman has proved quite capable of articulating her plight in relation to her son and has demonstrated considerable insight by linking this to unresolved feelings toward her mother. The patient was emotionally activated and made excellent contact with the therapist, sitting forward in her chair, maintaining eye contact, and speaking with clarity and specificity. The treatment moved rapidly to an exploration of the feelings toward these two key figures, along with an assessment of the defenses that would inevitably come into operation as these feelings got aroused.

THERAPIST: What do you mean difficult? As soon as you make the link to your mother and what it was like for you growing up, you get tearful.

PATIENT: Yeah.

THERAPIST: What's the feeling?

PATIENT: Well, it's hard to be precise—it's painful.

THERAPIST: Can you describe how you feel that pain inside?

PATIENT: Well, it's almost physical. It feels like a tightness (points to her heart) and I feel like crying. It's a reminder of what was a very painful childhood—one I've done my best to put to bed so I can go on. And I was pretty successful at it (the patient got a scholarship to college, went on to postgraduate study, is highly successful in her career and is married to "a very good man"). Then having a child like this has set me back and prevented me from leaving the past alone.

The patient is clearly in touch with the pain she's feeling. She knows what she feels, how she experiences it, and who the feeling involves. The recent upsurge of symptoms (anxiety and depression) has occurred because her characteristic defenses have failed her. As long as she was able to "forget about the past," she could avoid all the painful feelings associated with that period in her life. The birth of her son, who had physical and temperamental difficulties from the start, evoked intensely painful feelings that could no longer be repressed in her typical fashion. Putting these thoughts and feelings out of her mind no longer worked and she resorted to less adaptive defenses, such as isolation and withdrawal. These defenses were highly dystonic, however, since they were in direct conflict with her desire to be a good mother. This conflict led to symptom formation and motivated her to seek treatment for the first time in her life.

C-P Link

THERAPIST: So these current experiences trigger deep pain from your childhood that you've long been avoiding.

PATIENT: Yes, and my moods are totally dependent on his mood and behavior, which is no good. I want to maintain some equanimity and deal with him more effectively and to do that I can't be so emotionally at one with him.

THERAPIST: The question is how to get there. It sounds like the way you've dealt with trauma in the past, and all the painful feelings that evokes, is to suppress them and try to go on by distancing yourself. You were able to do that as long as there was no external trigger. To detach from feelings you detached from people. To do that now means detaching from your son. You don't seem to want to do that, so instead of detaching and avoiding the feeling, you'll have to go through it.

PATIENT: I want to be free so I can go forward (becoming tearful). I want to be a good mother but it gets so hard. I want to run away or send him away. I've said to my husband, "I can't live with him, I feel like he's killing me" (crying very hard now).

The genesis of the intrapsychic conflict this woman is struggling with has become crystal clear in response to the cost-benefit analysis regarding the defense of emotional detachment. To avoid facing the anger toward her son and the part of her that wishes she was rid of him altogether, the patient has had to detach from him. The emerging grief about the cost of such a defensive strategy is a direct indication that this defense is becoming highly dystonic. This painful feeling will prove a powerful ally to the therapeutic process. In addition to the painful cost of this defense, there is the additional desire to attach to her son and to be a good mother to him. This is another factor in her strong motivation to face what has been avoided.

Her psychological mindedness, intense emotional involvement in the process, lack of resistance, and genuine desire to change indicate that the process can move rapidly to the most painful and anxiety-laden area of the conflict in an effort to get to the core of her difficulties as quickly as possible.

Focus on Anger and Defenses against It

THERAPIST: Could we look at one of those times when you felt like you wanted to be rid of him?

PATIENT: When I had a 3-month-old, was moving into a new house, and he got thrown out of preschool.

THERAPIST: Do you notice you smile as you tell me about this? (Patient smiles again.) I wonder if that's a cover because, obviously, that wasn't funny.

PATIENT: I don't think I'm angry (denial).

THERAPIST: What about the smile?

PATIENT: It's only recently that I've felt like I can't take it anymore.

THERAPIST: It looks like these feelings toward your son are hard to face; you smile, sigh, look away.

PATIENT: I don't remember.

The patient becomes increasingly defensive as the anger toward her son is approached directly. The "slippage" in her memory is especially noticeable, as she was initially able to give a very specific example of a time when she wanted to get rid of her older son. To experience this rage directly is so threatening that the ego is resorting to regressive defenses such as denial and forgetting. The strength of the defenses is in direct proportion to the strength of the anxiety regarding the underlying feelings and impulses. Therefore, the increase in defensiveness is "to be welcomed as an indicator that painful conflicts are not merely being approached but can be brought to the surface and resolved" (Davanloo, 1990, p. 3). Because there are no contraindications for this intensive approach, the conflictual area will be brought to the surface rather than avoided. An attempt to avert her "forgetting" by focusing on her current feelings toward her son will be attempted.

THERAPIST: What about now? How do you feel toward him when you go back to that time?

PATIENT: I don't blame him (rationalization). The school was inept in their handling of him (displacement).

THERAPIST: You see, what gets passed over are the feelings toward your son. Isn't that why you are here—to deal with those feelings?

PATIENT: It's a fear of losing control. I feel like I'm close to beating the crap out of him.

In the foregoing interchange, the therapist calls on the therapeutic alliance to tip the balance from avoidance to facing the feelings of rage toward her son. The pressure to have an honest look at these feelings pays off and the patient reveals her fear of losing control and acting on her rage. The basis of such a fear must always be explored in detail.

Fear of Loss of Control

It is not unusual for patients to report a fear of losing control when strong affect is approached. The basis for this fear must always be explored. If there is a history of impulsive discharge of affect, then the fear is considered "realistic" and the therapist would avoid any intensification of feeling. Any intensification of feelings would not occur until the therapist felt satisfied that the patient was capable of tolerating the internal experience of anger without resorting to impulsive discharge.

If, on the other hand, there is no history of acting on impulses, the fear is considered "neurotic." The patient fears the feelings associated with forbidden action and has failed to make a clear distinction between the two. Gradual exposure to the feared stimulus, the experience of anger, in this case, is required to de-toxify the affect. In essence, the feeling of anger and the anxiety it generates are separated. Consequently, the patient can experience the anger without getting so anxious that she has to defend against it. Then, the affect is available as a source of information to the patient, who can deal with it in a conscious and deliberate fashion. This process increases ego strength, freedom, and adaptability.

In this case, I decided that the direct experience of rage toward her son was too threatening this early in the therapeutic process. I summarized the information already gathered, making a link between the triangle of conflict in the current situation with her son and that in the past with her mother. We returned to the phase of inquiry to see what other conflicts might emerge.

Return to Inquiry

THERAPIST: Any other problems you want help with?

PATIENT: The conflict with my son is primary, but I have some conflict with my husband too. He procrastinates and I get angry.

THERAPIST: Could we look at this anger toward your husband?

PATIENT: With my son, I'm afraid I'll lose control and do harm. With my husband, I couldn't because he can defend himself, but I'm afraid I'll do something I will regret, like smack him.

The same conflict the patient has with her son, over control of her violent impulses and the consequences of same, emerges in relation to her husband. Examining the rage toward him seems less threatening than with a small child, so it is a good place to begin.

THERAPIST: There is a physical impulse to lash out. How do you imagine that? (It is important to make clear we are talking about fantasy and imagination and not advocating that the patient act on impulse.)

PATIENT: Smacking him on the face.

THERAPIST: What else?

PATIENT: Pounding on him. (Patient is waving her hands and shaking her fists, indicating that the impulses have been activated and are being directly experienced.)

THERAPIST: Where?

PATIENT: On his chest. To smack him and punch him.

THERAPIST: That's the full extent of it? You said you were afraid you'd do something you regret.

PATIENT: Do I imagine going down to the kitchen, taking out a knife and stabbing him? No, I don't.

That this last response is a thinly disguised expression of the exact impulse she fears is quite clear. Because the patient has been highly involved and responsive, a touch of humor is used to see if the defensive disavowal of the impulse can be lifted.

THERAPIST: Well, where did that come from? It's pretty specific.

PATIENT: Gee, I don't know. I did lose it once, and I slapped him in the face. We were dating for years and he kept dragging his feet about getting married. One night I got so angry and upset, I hit him. He just held me, like we do with our son when he gets out of control. So, I know what that's like.

THERAPIST: It sounds like there's some real anger toward him but it seems to tap into a reservoir of rage from the past. Who else comes to your mind?

PATIENT: My mother. She was the one who made my life miserable. But, you know, I adored her (Patient starts to sob). She died 20 years ago and I still can't talk about her without crying. I feel very much like a motherless child.

Now the full picture of all the intense and conflicting feelings toward her mother emerges and helps to make sense of why the patient is in such turmoil over similar conflicts with her husband and son. In fact, it is only in the closest relationships, where these feelings get evoked so strongly, that the patient experiences such conflict. Memories of tremendous closeness with her mother emerged. She was an only child, and her parents were divorced when she was 7, leaving her alone with her mother almost all the time. They spent many happy hours together talk-ing, playing, and laughing. Then, her mother would sink into an in-tractable depression and have to be hospitalized or would become manic and bring men into the home for sexual encounters or embarrass her with inappropriate behavior on the street.

As a child, she could not reconcile the intense love and hate she felt toward her mother and withdrew to avoid the anxiety this conflict would precipitate. In the relationship with her son, she felt the same in-tense desire for closeness as well as the same pain, rage, and frustra-tion at not being able to achieve and maintain that closeness with an erratic, unpredictable family member. Facing these mixed feelings di-rectly led to an outpouring of crucial developmental material, making a meaningful exploration of the past possible. Interpretations followed quite effortlessly.

This patient was successfully treated in 25 sessions and reported, in our final session, that she was not only getting along better than ever with both her husband and her son, but that she felt free and truly happy for the first time in her life. She said she felt as though a tremendous weight had been lifted off her shoulders and she could move forward in her life now, rather than running from the past.

The case of the Manic-Depressive's Daughter illustrates a fairly smooth evaluation with a highly motivated and responsive patient. Such cases are the exception in practice. Typically, patients arrive in a highly anxious and defensive state or rapidly become so in response to the thera-pist's focus on painful feelings. In such cases, much more time and effort must be spent on the phase of defense work to turn the patient's ego against the self-defeating defenses that are interfering with the therapeu-tic goal. Working the triangles and focusing on the central dynamic se-quence are guides in this process.

USE OF THE TWO TRIANGLES IN THE TRIAL THERAPY

Davanloo exhorts us not to make assumptions, but to test out our hypothe-ses and to base our diagnostic determinations on the patient's response to intervention. Once a detailed account of the patient's symptomatic diffi-culties is in hand, the therapist begins the inquiry into the feelings in-volved in the situations where symptoms erupted. During this phase of the evaluation, the triangles of conflict and person are used as models for understanding the intrapsychic workings of the patient. In addition, this model provides a structure for assessing the ego's resources and weaknesses and, when followed properly, gives order and coherence to the process of therapeutic intervention.

During the trial therapy, the therapist conducts a three-step analysis of the triangle of conflict. This involves:

1. Assessing each corner of the triangle (anxiety [A], defense [D], and impulse/feeling [I/F]).
2. Determining the extent of clarification and differentiation within the triangle of conflict.
3. Linking the three elements within the triangle of conflict to the elements of the triangle of the person (transference [T], current figures [C], and past genetic figures [P]).

Step 1.   Assessing the Corners of the Triangle

Anxiety.   In most cases, anxiety is the first dynamic factor to be assessed. Exploration of the patient's experience of anxiety should provide the answers to several crucial diagnostic questions. How is anxiety being channeled within the system? Is the anxiety the patient is experiencing realistic (a response to a frightening external event, like getting a diagnosis of cancer) or neurotic (a reaction to the upsurge of conflictual feelings considered dangerous and unacceptable)? Does the patient seem to have a reasonable amount of tolerance for the conscious experience of anxiety? The response to each question indicates something about the patient's level of current ego-adaptive capacity and will guide the process. For example, very high levels of anxiety channeled into the smooth muscle would indicate some fragility and suggest the need for a slow, supportive approach.

Defenses.   The second aspect of the conflict to be examined is the defensive system. Because anxiety mobilizes defenses, the examination of anxiety usually leads quite naturally into the area of the patient's characteristic defenses. What are the patient's typical defenses? Do they seem to be directed internally against the awareness of threatening thoughts and feelings (defenses against impulse/feeling) or externally against emotional contact with others (defenses against emotional closeness)? How varied and flexible are the defenses observed and reported? Of particular importance is the assessment of how syntonic or dystonic the defenses are to the patient.

Impulses and Feelings.   Finally, an exploration of the patient's access to affect is conducted. Assessment of the three elements considered necessary for a full experience of feeling (cognitive, physiological, and motoric) needs to be conducted to evaluate the patient's current capacity for emotional involvement in the process. The range and depth of the patient's emotional involvement should also be noted. How freely can the patient access the affective reactions toward and in response to others? What is the balance between the two? It is fairly typical to observe that patients have good access to one set of feelings but not the other.

For example, a particular patient might experience an internal feeling of sadness regarding a separation in a fairly free and unencumbered fashion, but seem heavily defended against the awareness of the reactive feelings of anger toward the person who left. This type of constellation of feeling and defense is typical in depressives. There are also cases in which the opposite configuration is apparent. In narcissistic characters, there is ready access to anger toward others who hurt or disappoint them, but significant defenses against the internal experience of pain and grief.

The assessment of the three corners of the triangle of conflict yields rich diagnostic data, helps place the patient on the spectrum of psychopathology, and guides the therapeutic process by pinpointing critical areas of conflict or ego weakness.

Step 2.   Differentiating the Corners of the Triangle

Once each element involved in the triangle of conflict has been labeled and evaluated, the therapist must determine whether the patient can distinguish between them. Can the individual distinguish between the experience of a feeling (say, grief), the anxiety it arouses (butterflies and heart palpitations), and the defenses that come into play (intellectualization and isolation) to avoid them? In particular, the clinician should look for any area of fusion between feelings and anxiety, feelings and defense, or anxiety and defense.

For example, if the therapist inquires how the patient experiences anger and the individual describes the physiological experience of anxiety, then there is some fusion between these internal states. Clarification is required to help facilitate the distinction between the two. Failure to make these distinctions can result in an unanticipated and undesirable exacerbation of anxiety when the patient is pressed for the experience of feeling.

Can the patient differentiate between anxiety and the defenses the anxiety calls into play? If a patient tells you about defenses (distancing) when asked about the experience of anxiety, some fusion is suspect. Again, a process of clarification and distinction between anxiety and defense is required until the patient can see (cognitive clarity) and then indicate the ability to experience (emotional) the difference between the two.

Evidence of fusion between feelings and defenses is quite common and is essential to detect early on in the process. Spending some time clarifying the difference between the experience of a feeling like anger, and the defense against it (storming out of the house), pays off in the end. The process leads to clarity and increases ego functioning. Failure to systematically assess and clarify areas of fusion before proceeding to a breakthrough of feeling can lead to an increase in anxiety, symptoms, or defensiveness, any of which can inhibit a swift and smooth therapeutic process.

Step 3. Linking the Corners of the Triangles

The third step in the process of assessing the triangle of conflict is to determine whether the patient, who can distinguish between feelings, anxiety, and defense, can also link them in a meaningful way (e.g., he was angry with his boss, which mobilized anxiety that he dealt with by withdrawing and rationalizing). In addition to linking together the three elements within the triangle of conflict, links between the triangle of conflict and the triangle of the person also need to be made. Can the patient see that the constellation feelings, anxiety, and defenses evident in the current situation are related to unresolved conflicts from the past? Further, can this patient see the same dynamic forces in operation with the therapist?

In the following two cases, a good deal of defense work is necessary for the therapeutic work to begin. Heavy use is made of the triangles (see Figure 1.1) to acquaint the patients with their defenses and render them dystonic.

CLINICAL EXAMPLES

A Gentleman Scorned

The following transcript provides an example of a type of response frequently encountered to the trial therapy. The patient enters the session expressing a conscious desire to participate and to obtain help from the therapist, yet resists any intervention that will evoke painful feelings. Such patients typically provide adequate factual responses to inquiry and are quite "cooperative" as long as you "stick to the facts." However, defensive efforts increase markedly as the therapist begins to focus in on the patient's feelings about the people and events being reported. A focus on the conflict between the part of the person that wants help and the part that wants to run and hide from the pain entailed in the process precipitates the very sort of internal crisis and disequilibrium necessary to enable a rapid entry into the unconscious. Where there has been an external crisis, this intrapsychic disequilibrium may already exist. Patients who are chronically disturbed and highly identified with their character defenses require therapeutic intervention to tip the balance between motivation and resistance.

THERAPIST: What brings you?

PATIENT: An agreement with my wife to remain married but live apart for 6 months, then we'll decide.

THERAPIST: Who instigated the separation?

PATIENT: Mutually agreed, but my wife instigated it.

THERAPIST: She wanted you to see someone as part of the agreement?

PATIENT: I've been in therapy three times. I went to see a friend, who's a therapist, two years ago. I spent 8 hours with him to find out if there was a problem. He asked me, "What do you want?" I realized I had never asked myself that question. To understand that you have to understand my background (begins to rattle off his history with rapid-fire speech) . . .

It is important not to get embroiled in past history or to let the patient diversify before the current difficulties have been adequately explored. Again, the only pressure at this stage of the trial therapy is to maintain focus and be specific.

THERAPIST: I'm sure that's important but let's start with what you're here for now. What are the problems you want help with?

PATIENT: Confirmation of my own health and well-being. I've been exploring what I want and am making changes.

THERAPIST: Like what?

PATIENT: Like a career change.

THERAPIST: So you've made changes in your career, but what have you come here for?

PATIENT: There's a sense of loss regarding the relationship ending.

Exploring the Patient's Feelings in the C

THERAPIST: So you have a lot of feeling about the separation.

PATIENT: Well, when you're married for 25 years and this woman you've loved all along says she doesn't love you anymore (uses sarcastic tone and smiles, to avoid any painful feeling) . . .

THERAPIST: You smile. What is your feeling about this?

PATIENT: Initially, it was devastating, very painful. Now I'm confused and ambivalent. I'm living alone for the first time in my life, and there's a sense of newness and excitement. I've come to terms with the fact that I've held on for 10 years even though it's been very difficult. I was depressed.

THERAPIST: Clinically depressed?

PATIENT: No physical signs, but emotionally down. I didn't care—flat affect.

THERAPIST: You were very detached.

PATIENT: Very detached and just didn't care.

Examining Resistance in the T

THERAPIST: This detachment still seems to be present. We don't get to see what feelings you have. This is what you avoid.

PATIENT: You're assuming. (Resistance in the transference is becoming evident. Now the patient contradicts himself and becomes defiant.)

THERAPIST: Isn't this the problem, that . . .

PATIENT: I don't know if there is a problem.

THERAPIST: You are happy and satisfied with your life?

PATIENT: No.

THERAPIST: It is important for us to look at this. Either you have problems you consider psychological in nature and that's why you've consulted a psychologist, or you are here to appease your wife.

PATIENT: No. If she wanted me to, I wouldn't come. I'm unhappy with the way my personal life has turned out. I invested a lot in a marriage that isn't functional, and I held on for a long time. No one else was surprised.

THERAPIST: Are you saying you have a blind spot? You didn't see it coming when others did?

PATIENT: Yeah. I knew it was bad but didn't . . . chose to ignore it and was very passive.

THERAPIST: You tend to be passive and avoidant and you're concerned about how you let this happen.

PATIENT: Yeah, but since we've decided to separate, all the intellectual pieces are in place. I'm feeling liberated. I'm at ease, at peace.

This pattern of identifying, then denying, an area of conflict or difficulty, continued for 20 minutes. It became increasingly clear that the primary resistance was in the transference. He would rather be damned than agree with me.

This defiance was undermining my therapeutic efforts and had to be eliminated. Despite the high level of defensiveness, some important information was revealed. He reported a lifetime of self-defeating behavior that had affected both his career and home life. At the age of 25, unemployed with three children and a wife to support, he had contemplated suicide. The tendency toward self-defeat was already in operation within the therapy and became the focus of intervention.

Exploration of Self-Defeat in the C and the T

THERAPIST: Let's look at this. Is there a pattern of self-defeat in your life? You keep yourself from being happy and sabotage your own goals?

PATIENT: Until recently I have, and it's all based on being responsible. I got married right out of college and then had three children by the time I was 25. I was so overwhelmed, I seriously contemplated suicide.

THERAPIST: So, how did you get yourself into such a situation?

PATIENT: I could tell you the jokes I lay on others but between then and now I've also had two disastrous business failures in which friends betrayed me. (Now the patient admits a long history of self-defeat which, in fact, continues to the present.) The problem was I trusted people I shouldn't have trusted. Now, for the first time I can say "I want . . ." and if you don't like it, too bad.

THERAPIST: You're better at knowing what you want and declaring it, but for some reason you're having difficulty with that here—to declare what kind of help you want from me. Do you notice?

PATIENT: You're acting very much like my wife and I find this approach very annoying.

THERAPIST: So you're feeling angry with me.

PATIENT: It's the emotion I have the most trouble with.

THERAPIST: Could we look at this?

PATIENT: I was really looking forward to coming here. The experience intrigued me, the 3 hour intensive session, the short-term approach . . .

THERAPIST: So there was a part of you looking forward to it, specifically being focused, intensive, and short-term but obviously there is another part of you in operation because you interfere with that very approach. The element of self-defeat is already in operation here.

PATIENT: Maybe just a self-fulfilling prophesy because I don't see an intensity of problems or emotional distress.

This vignette speaks to the intensity of the conflict this man is experiencing about the prospect of opening up to the therapist. Pointing out the two opposing parts of him and how holding onto the defensive position would defeat him in his goal in coming for treatment was necessary to create an intrapsychic crisis. The patient is mired in ambivalence. He says he wants to get to work and have an honest look at the feelings being evoked but remains evasive. The work must take place in the transference, where the majority of the defenses are being mobilized.

Anger in the T

THERAPIST: You say that, as we go to look at your difficulties, you feel angry with me. How do you experience this anger?

PATIENT: I don't know what the problem is, I feel inadequate (D).

THERAPIST: That's not your anger, could we look at the anger?

PATIENT: The problem is I'm not clicking with you, and I find your approach offensive.

These comments suggest that the patient cannot distinguish between his feeling of anger and the defenses against it (feeling inadequate or finding fault with the approach). This must be clarified before any pressure is brought to bear on the defense. Failure to make such a distinction will lead to a misalliance, as the patient himself, rather than his defeating defenses, will feel attacked or criticized.

THERAPIST: When I ask you about your feelings, you go to your head. Do you notice, from the beginning, when I ask you how you feel, you tell me what you think and give an explanation? You stay emotionally detached, so we don't know what you're feeling inside. Now you say you're angry with me. So, we have a choice, we can have an honest look at your emotional reaction toward me or you can stay detached.

This man's characteristic defenses of sarcasm, defiance, and self-contradiction are very provocative. It is essential not to get caught in an interpersonal struggle, which is just another way for the patient to avoid having to deal with his own intrapsychic conflicts. At this point, I decided to make his options clear and leave the decision up to him. The decision to do the work must be his alone.

Triangle of Conflict in the T

PATIENT: I want to look at it.

THERAPIST: You say you're angry. How do you feel this anger inside?

PATIENT: Just backing off (D). I don't need this.

THERAPIST: That's not the anger, that's the position you take to avoid the experience of the anger—you distance and withdraw. Haven't you been distant and withdrawn this whole time? You stay in your head, are vague and general, you don't look at me when you speak—you erect a massive wall.

PATIENT: I just met you half an hour ago.

THERAPIST: Why do you want to waste more time? You told me you wait passively and hang onto dead relationships. You somehow think you are protecting yourself but we have to look at whether you actually end up wasting opportunities. You don't let me get to know you.

PATIENT: Um . . . (Patient shifts in his chair to face the therapist directly, rubs his chin and looks the therapist in the eye.) I spend a lot of time letting people get to know me and they hurt me a great deal.

THERAPIST: You've been very hurt, and the way you've dealt with that is to withdraw and detach. Now you're hiding behind a wall.

PATIENT: Most people don't notice because I can seem very engaging.

THERAPIST: But if I'm going to be of help, I have to get to know you in a deep and honest way. That's what you avoid.

PATIENT: Right.

THERAPIST: This is a massive conflict.

PATIENT: I don't trust you.

THERAPIST: And, in a sense, why should you? But we also have to ask, why shouldn't you? You have no evidence either way.

PATIENT: I used to blindly trust people and I was a trusting fool.

THERAPIST: Who are you thinking of?

PATIENT: The business partner that stole $25,000 from me.

THERAPIST: So people you trusted have violated that trust. Obviously you have feelings about that, but it sounds like you've gone to the opposite extreme and won't trust anyone. You seem to be saying, "I won't let anyone in."

PATIENT: Oh, I have. It's been a very hard week. I had to tell my sons about the separation and they were very harsh and rejecting, yelling at me.

T-C-P Interpretation

Focusing on the cost and benefit of keeping the therapist at arm's length has finally paid off with increased emotional involvement and meaningful communications regarding the genesis of the patient's difficulties. The recently evoked feelings of grief and anger experienced toward his sons reminded the patient of a similar mix of feeling toward his parents in the past. Upon return from their honeymoon, the patient and his wife had revealed that the bride was already 3 months' pregnant. His parents berated and "disowned" him. This is how his sons behaved when they heard of their parents' separation. So now, as then, he was criticized and rejected by his family at a time when he needed their support. Making these connections and having the opportunity to experience the feelings associated with these events increased the therapeutic alliance and his motivation to do the work, with a marked reduction in defense and resistance. In addition to linking the present conflict with a core conflict from the past, the patient was able to understand his readiness to view me in the same way, as someone who would criticize rather than help in a time of need. This all-important T-C-P link was made by the patient toward the end of the trial therapy, boding well for success. In fact, his treatment was completed in only 10 sessions.

The Woman with Two Failed Marriages

The third example of a response to the trial therapy illustrates what occurs when a patient arrives in a state of resistance that prevents a factual inquiry from being completed. In such cases, the initial phases of the central dynamic sequence must be abandoned. The process must proceed rapidly to the phase of clarification and pressure on the defenses which serve as resistance to any meaningful contact with the therapist.

In the following case, the patient entered the trial therapy with a ready-made transference based on past experiences with other therapists. If feelings toward the therapist are not brought directly to the fore in a speedy fashion, the defenses against these feelings will greatly distort the process. Consequently, an examination of the defenses and the underlying transference feelings must precede inquiry.

Inquiry

THERAPIST: Why don't you start by telling me about the problems you're having right now.

PATIENT: I'm in a major transition in my life and it hasn't been easy. I'm going through a second divorce from a guy who's not unlike my first husband—actually, a carbon copy (smiles broadly). I saw it coming so I left after 6 months.

It should be noted that, although the patient was obviously in a crisis and has serious problems in her life, she was speaking as if she was telling me an amusing story about a day at the beach. Her affect was not at all congruent with the content being reported. I noted this to myself, but tried to proceed with inquiry before addressing the character defenses.

THERAPIST: So it was a very brief marriage.

PATIENT: Extremely brief, and it had a lot of false starts. I know I didn't want to go through this again, the first was so bad. I just wanted to get out quickly. Well, he didn't agree, you know how that is, and it was an extreme case.

THERAPIST: What do you mean?

PATIENT: He's gotten very angry and so when I call, even just to say, "Gee, I can't believe this is happening," and just wishing maybe it could have worked out, or at least we could be amicable, he would go and say I am unbalanced. He'd use a threatening tone.

THERAPIST: Has he actually threatened you?

PATIENT: He was physically abusive so it wasn't a very happy situation (smiles). I just moved back home and I'm not really very excited about therapy by the way (another big smile) because I've been through a lot of therapy with my husband and it was always about how they could make me change, so I'm having a lot of negative feeling about being here.

The patient was not able to provide basic, factual information in response to inquiry. She was vague and overly general in her responses to specific questions and tended to diversity, jumping from topic to topic. Her affect was inappropriate to both the content being discussed and the feelings she reported having about being in the therapist's office.

Exploration of the negative feelings being reported needed to take precedence over the factual inquiry.

Exploration of the Ready-Made Negative Transference

THERAPIST: So you have a lot of negative feelings about being here. Could we look at that?

PATIENT: Yes. I feel a bit defeated (D). I'm put on antidepressants.

THERAPIST: Who prescribed those?

PATIENT: The marital therapist. He said, "Oh, you're depressed, you should go on antidepressants." That was OK because, given the situation a person can become sad or depressed.

THERAPIST: What are you taking?

PATIENT: I don't know. Xanex? Elavil?

THERAPIST: You don't know?

PATIENT: I'm at the point where I don't even care anymore.

THERAPIST: We need to look at this. You complain about how poorly you're treated. Your husbands mistreat you, the doctors mistreat you. You have negative feelings about being here, but here you sit. How do you understand this? Somehow you allow yourself to be used and abused. Do you see that?

PATIENT: It sounds, on the surface, like I allow myself to be taken advantage of but, in a sense, I don't have a choice.

THERAPIST: You don't have a choice about going to a therapist? You are here under coercion or you came of your own will?

PATIENT: No one is forcing me. I came of my own will. But, like with a husband, you don't have a choice. My husband, in his usual state, looks wonderful, he's well-dressed and has a wonderful education, a good job. Then you go into the house and suddenly there's World War III. Do you see what I mean?

Clarification of Defenses

Each attempt at clarification of the patient's current situation results in more defensiveness and confusion. The first issue to be clarified involved the issue of the patient's will to be in therapy. Since she declared that she was seeking help of her own accord, the next step was to assess whether an intrapsychic focus could be obtained. If the patient considered all her difficulties to be externally imposed, then insight-oriented psychotherapy was not what she was looking for. However, if she was able to view her tendency to externalize and assume a helpless, victimized stance as a problem within her that significantly contributed to her recurrent interpersonal difficulties, we could proceed with an analytic focus. This is the central issue at this juncture in the process.

THERAPIST: So you see yourself as helpless.

PATIENT: No, I see myself as out of control. I had to leave, even though I have to come home (she had just returned to her parent's home) and I feel very dependent. If you ever saw me at work, you'd never think I'm helpless.

THERAPIST: No, it's not how *I* see you, it's how you present yourself and you don't seem to be aware of it. I'm sure there is some truth to what you say. Your husbands have mistreated you and therapists are certainly capable of that, but that's not what we're here to look at. We're here to look at how you handle this. We can see, even with the issue of medication, that you take a passive, submissive stance and then feel victimized and taken advantage of. There is a way in which you give up control and allow others to take over. This looks like a pattern, and the question is, do you want to know what is going on inside of you that you should repeatedly let yourself be treated in this way? This is the central issue, do you want to examine what is going on inside of you and get to the bottom of your difficulties?

This last intervention was aimed at clarifying the character defenses of passivity and helplessness evident in the patient's interactions with both the therapist and other significant figures in her current life orbit. The way in which these defenses cost her, by allowing others to use and abuse her, was outlined to bolster her observing ego and encourage an intrapsychic focus.

As this transcript illustrates, these character defenses were highly syntonic and formed a massive resistance to meaningful communication and therapeutic progress. If the patient's tendency to externalize blame and assume a passive, victimized stance in relation to others was not clarified, the therapist would become another abuser in the patient's eyes and the unconscious would remain inaccessible. Therefore, assessing the patient's ability to distinguish between feelings and defenses was essential in determining suitability for treatment.

PATIENT: I thought I should come since I'm at the point of taking medication. I felt so sick I just thought, "Give me something."

THERAPIST: You got sick?

PATIENT: People can get physically ill, you know, physically exhausted (reported with increased sarcasm).

THERAPIST: People? You mean *you* got sick? How?

PATIENT: I haven't been sleeping well, I'm exhausted, I have pains in my chest, pain down my arm, migraines. I'm not doing well. (These complaints were listed in a rapid-fire manner with a decidedly hostile edge to her voice.) So, when a person says, "Here, take this, it'll make you feel better," you take it.

The patient's seemingly intractable defensiveness and list of physical symptoms suggested some ego fragility. Still, until the defenses and resistance in the transference were clarified, one can't be certain. The increase in defensiveness could be driven by a rise in negative feelings toward the therapist. These feelings became the focus.

Mix of Feeling and Defense in the Transference

THERAPIST: Let me ask you how you're feeling right now.

PATIENT: I'm sorry, I'm being very belligerent toward you right now.

THERAPIST: And why is that? There is some feeling toward me.

PATIENT: Yes, there is. It's not you personally (D)—it's easy for a person to say (patient becoming tearful) . . .

THERAPIST: What is your feeling toward me?

PATIENT: You can say, "Take control of your life" (D).

THERAPIST: That's a thought, what's the feeling?

PATIENT: The problem is, I sit here in a therapist's office (more weepiness) and people tell me (D) . . .

THERAPIST: Did I tell you to do anything? We are here to look at your difficulties, and as I inquire into that, you say you get "belligerent." Obviously, you have a lot of feeling toward me.

PATIENT: No feeling toward you personally (D).

THERAPIST: Sure you do, you said you have a lot of negative feelings about being here, and then you realized you were becoming belligerent. That's a behavior. What's the feeling underneath?

PATIENT: (looks therapist in the eye and speaks calmly) Resentment.

THERAPIST: You feel resentment. We should look at this because you didn't declare that to me. First you denied it, then put it into the behavior of belligerence and sarcasm. Then, when I asked you about the feelings directly, you became weepy. The same thing happens here as you say happens with your husband (T-C link). This could be a really crippling problem. Is this a problem in your life, for you to become aware of your feelings and to be able to declare them directly?

PATIENT: Oh, angry feelings get me into big trouble.

This patient presented herself as a passive victim in life, indicating that her character defenses were highly syntonic. In accordance with this view, she identified the source of her problems as external. Such a belief prevents the delineation of an intrapsychic focus and, if intractable, would constitute a contra-indication for ISTDP. A focus on the feelings in the transference, along with an examination of the defenses against them, was an essential step in assessing whether the patient would be able to develop an observing stance. When the angry feelings toward the therapist were finally revealed, the patient changed noticeably. She calmed down, made direct eye contact, and began to give detailed information regarding both her history and current difficulties. Then an accurate assessment of her ability to use this type of treatment became possible. The patient reported a history of psychotic depression with two recent hospitalizations. This information, along with that gathered through the dynamic interaction between patient and therapist, confirmed the diagnosis of ego fragility, a clear contraindication to further uncovering. Medication and supportive treatment were indicated.

SUMMARY

The transcripts from three trial therapies have been used to illustrate some fairly typical responses to the trial therapy. Of note, all three patients presented with similar complaints. Each was experiencing anxiety and depression in response to conflicts in their close personal relationships. The systematic evaluation involved in the trial therapy revealed very different levels of ego functioning in each case. The Manic-Depressive's Daughter proved highly motivated and responsive. The patient arrived with an intrapsychic focus, indicating a high level of ego-adaptive capacity. This assessment was further substantiated as the evaluation continued. The standard technique of pressure and challenge to the defenses with the goal of unlocking the unconscious via a breakthrough of feeling was indicated.

For the Gentleman Scorned, the current problems being described were only the most recent manifestation of lifelong difficulties resulting from the patient's character pathology. His character defenses created a barrier to meaningful communication with the therapist and, left unchecked, would have prevented an intrapsychic focus. Techniques designed to create an intrapsychic crisis were employed as no signs of ego fragility were obtained during inquiry. His response to this challenge was a mixture of increased defensiveness and mounting anger at the therapist. Once this anger was directly expressed there was a decrease in defensiveness, followed by direct and emotionally meaningful communications with the therapist, along with increased motivation. All these factors suggested suitability for treatment.

The trial therapy of the Woman with Two Failed Marriages revealed significant ego fragility, which served as a clear contraindication for dynamic psychotherapy. The patient's defensiveness could have easily masked this fact. She was well-dressed and groomed and reported a high level of education and a responsible, professional career. Failure to address the defenses could have led to an assumption of greater capacity than the patient possessed. The obvious advantage to this method of assessment is the rapidity with which suitability can be determined, preventing the experience of finding out, well into treatment, that the patient cannot make use of dynamic psychotherapy.

CHAPTER 3

Working with Defenses

Slip sliding away
Slip sliding away
You know the nearer your destination
The more you're slip sliding away
*Paul Simon**

Many professionals consider Davanloo's (1980, 1990) technical innovations for handling defense and resistance to be his greatest contribution to the practice of dynamic psychotherapy. The tight focus on defenses from the inception of treatment is also the most controversial aspect of his work. This chapter will review the concepts involved in the mechanisms of defense, will provide a working definition of defense and resistance, and will outline a detailed schema for the conceptualization and handling of these dynamic forces within the treatment setting. The work of those clinicians most directly affecting the development of Intensive Short-Term Dynamic Psychotherapy (ISTDP) will be highlighted.

KEY CONCEPTS IN DEFENSE THEORY

It was during his early work with hysterics that Freud (1894, 1895) first outlined the concepts involved in the notion of intrapsychic conflict—that patients mobilize forces (D) to prevent awareness of painful and anxiety-provoking (A) thoughts and feelings (I/F). He went on to say that the mobilization of these forces, which he called defenses, was a function carried out by the ego.

*From "Slip Sliding Away." Music and lyrics by Paul Simon. Warner Bros. Music, 1982.

The Ego

The ego refers to that aspect of psychic functioning responsible for the observation of and mediation between internal wishes, feelings, and impulses clamoring for expression and the need to control the expression of these "instincts" in accordance with external constraints.

Defenses

Defenses are not psychic entities and cannot be understood in isolation, but only by the functions they serve. Brenner (1976) contends that the entire range of ego functions can potentially be used in a defensive manner. Consequently, no list of defenses can ever be exhaustive. Instead of attempting to catalog defenses as discrete entities, we need to understand defensive functioning within the context of the intrapsychic conflict of which they are a part. In particular, defenses cannot be understood without addressing the anxiety that calls them into action. The second theory of anxiety (Freud, 1926) changed the focus of psychoanalytic inquiry and therapeutic efforts from the realm of id impulses to the functioning of the ego. It is the ego that perceives anxiety and then mobilizes forces to defend against the anticipated danger presented by the uprising of impulses. This theoretical revision also placed greater emphasis on the role of the environment—both the tangible features of the external reality within which the individual is living and the individual's perception of that reality. So the ego is strapped with double duty; controlling internally generated feelings and impulses, and modulating external demands.

Resistance

Frequently, the terms defense and resistance are used interchangeably. In *Interpretation of Dreams,* Freud (1900) stated, "Whatever interrupts the progress of analytic work is resistance" (p. 517). He noted that such resistances were stubborn and required specific technical interventions. He came to feel that the "overcoming of resistances is the part of our work that requires the most time and the greatest trouble." Despite Freud's awareness of the central importance of helping the patient overcome resistance, he developed no specific techniques to accomplish that goal. Instead, he advocated patience, and the slow, judicious use of interpretation. This involved letting patients get acquainted with and really experience defenses and resistance. Then, patients would be encouraged to discover the feelings that fuel these behaviors.

Most analytically oriented therapists have followed Freud's lead, developing a whole rationale for continuing in this slow, gentle manner based on assumptions about the inflexibility of defenses and the fragility of most patients. This has become a self-perpetuating system. The lack of activity on the part of the therapist and the paucity of specific techniques for overcoming the resistance leads to protracted treatments of dubious value, reinforcing the notion that resistances are intractable.

ADVANCES IN DEFENSE ANALYSIS

Anna Freud (1937, 1966) was a pioneer in the study of defenses. She was the first to outline a range of formal operations designed to "avoid painful or unendurable ideas or affects" (p. 42). In addition to repression, she discussed the defenses of denial, displacement, projection, and reaction formation. She also advanced the theory that defenses could be directed toward environmental influences, as well as against instincts and their vicissitudes. "Identification with the aggressor" and "defense against reality situations" (such as dissociation) are examples of behaviors aimed at modifying the traumatic effects of external conditions.

The success with which a given individual navigates between external demands and internal pressures came to define the ego's adaptive capacity. For this reason, Ms. Freud (1937, 1966) advocated examining the defensive system to assess the functioning of the ego. These two theoretical advances—(a) an appreciation that defenses can be directed outward toward anxiety-arousing situations and (b) that an examination of the defensive system provides a vehicle for assessing a patient's current ego functioning—have been incorporated into Davanloo's thinking and have influenced the development of his technique.

Ferenzi and Rank (1925) and Reich (1933) are other clinical theorists whose work on defense and resistance have influenced Davanloo. Their findings converge on a number of theoretical issues and technical maneuvers. Each felt that analysis had become a sterile intellectual exercise. Further, they suggested that defenses needed to be confronted and eliminated to increase the kind of affective involvement in the treatment process necessary for deep and permanent change to occur. To accomplish this goal, they advocated an active approach on the part of the therapist, focusing on an understanding of the contemporary meaning of behavior. References to the distant past were only made once defenses had been eradicated and an affective involvement in the process was palpable.

Although there is a wide area of agreement among these clinicians, each has made individual contributions worth noting. Ferenzi (1924) encouraged the use of fantasy to break through resistance and activate feeling. He also encouraged his patients to openly express their feelings toward the therapist, especially negative and aggressive feelings. These techniques have clearly been incorporated by Davanloo.

Reich (1933) agreed with Ferenzi that resistances must be attacked from the inception of treatment. He focused on what he called "character resistance" or "character armor"; those mannerisms and attitudes that permeate every aspect of patients' functioning, including their posture, gait, and tone of voice. He noted that these characteristic defenses formed a "ballast" around the patient and, unless penetrated, would prevent any interpretation from having a mutative effect. He insisted that it was not enough for patients to remember but they had to *experience* what was remembered. Hence, he was not as concerned with *what* the patient was reporting (content) as with *how* he or she reported it (process). For example, if a patient is remembering a painful and humiliating scene from her schooldays but reporting it in a light and humorous way, the focus would be on the smile and what purpose that served in the current interaction with the therapist. In this case, the patient is avoiding the experience of the pain and outrage associated with the memory and hiding these feelings from the therapist.

Like Ferenzi, Reich felt that the direct expression of resentment, rage, hurt, and longing toward the therapist was an essential step in breaking through a patient's defensive armor. He also felt that negative transference feelings had to be cleared up before any genuine positive transference could develop. If the negative feelings have not been experienced and expressed, then what might look like cooperation and a positive transference would be more likely to represent a defensive compliance on the patient's part. His (Reich, 1933/1987) clinical experience with this technique confirmed what seemed to have been forgotten by most analysts; "that the neurosis itself is contained in the resistance, and that, in dissolving a resistance, we also dissolve a part of the neurosis" (1987, p. 81).

Davanloo's Approach to Defense Work

Davanloo (1980) has incorporated all the preceding strategies and techniques into his system of ISTDP, while adhering strictly to three fundamental psychoanalytic principles: "releasing hidden feelings by actively working on and interpreting resistance or defenses; paying strict attention to the transference relationship; and actively making links between the transference and significant people in the patient's current life and in the past" (p. 45). In so doing, he came to find that "unconscious conflicts emerged in an unmistakable way" (p. 45). Davanloo has built on the foundation of Anna Freud, Ferenzi, and Reich by developing a comprehensive system for combating defenses.

SPECIFIC TECHNIQUES FOR WORKING WITH DEFENSES

The real question for most practicing clinicians is, "How can defenses be rendered inoperable, making treatment rapid and effective?" According to Davanloo, defense work involves three separate but frequently overlapping parts:

1. Acquainting patients with their defenses.
2. Re-structuring the defenses and turning the patient's ego against them.
3. Eradicating defense and resistance through pressure and challenge.

Each aspect of this phase of treatment will be detailed and illustrated.

PART 1.   ACQUAINTING PATIENTS WITH THEIR DEFENSES

In conducting the initial inquiry into a patient's difficulties, the therapist is alert to any signs of defense against clarity, emotional activation, or meaningful contact with the evaluator. In particular, as the therapist probes for feeling, it is important to monitor the balance between defense and resistance on the one hand, and motivation and therapeutic alliance on the other. In this vein, it is important not only to render the resistance inoperable but to release the force toward health buried beneath it.

During this phase of the evaluation, the therapist will begin to make use of the information gathered during inquiry by pointing out the operation of defenses against feelings as they arise. This is a three-step process involving the identification, clarification, and examination of the consequences of those defenses in operation.

Identification

First, the therapist needs to identify defenses as they arise. An example of this would be, "Do you notice that, when I ask you about your feelings toward your girlfriend, you smile, make a joke, and change the subject?" The patient's response will yield diagnostic information and direct the next intervention. If the patient is able to acknowledge that he was smiling and joking, the therapist can proceed to the stage of clarification. If the patient says, "No, I didn't notice that," further examples must be obtained and utilized to increase the observing function of the ego. "It happened again, just now, as you talked about being annoyed with your boss—that smile reappears. Did you notice?" The patient must be aware of the behavior before an exploration of its function will be of any therapeutic value.

Responses generated by the process of defense identification yield preliminary information about the observing function of the ego, particularly regarding the syntonicity of defenses. As such, this exploration quickly alerts the therapist to the direction the work will take.

Clarification

Once a defense has been identified, its function must be clarified and made explicit. "The smile and the joke are not your feelings toward your girlfriend but a way you avoid those feelings. Do you see that?" Once again, the patient's response to this clarification will yield important diagnostic information.

The therapist is assessing whether the patient is capable of distinguishing between the defense and impulse/feeling corners of the triangle of conflict. If the patient can make such a distinction, the defenses are considered "dystonic" or "ego alien." To assess whether the patient can actually distinguish between feelings and defenses, the therapist would then ask, "Now we see the laugh was a cover for your feeling, not the feeling itself. So what was your feeling toward her?" If he can now say, "I was angry," a contrast between the current experience of the anger and the initial report, in which the experience was warded off with the smile, will consolidate this important insight. This type of interaction between patient and therapist highlights how this technique is employed to actually test out the patient's abilities in the session. It is not enough for the patient to agree with the therapist. Some actual demonstration of the ability in question is necessary before moving on to the next phase of work.

So far, the focus has been on highlighting the distinction between feelings and defenses. To complete the phase of clarification, all three corners of the triangle must be assessed and made explicit. Patients will either volunteer or be made aware that, as the therapist begins to probe for feeling and remark on defensive efforts to avoid it, they become increasingly nervous and anxious. In many cases, the patient will volunteer that information. For example, the patient may say, "I dread feeling that sadness." If the anxiety does not emerge spontaneously, the therapist might ask, "We have to wonder why you run from these feelings," or might venture, "You seem terrified to experience your anger." Because it is anxiety about the "danger" involved in the experience of the feelings being targeted that propels the defenses into operation, understanding the role of anxiety in the intrapsychic system is an essential element in the phase of clarification. Davanloo (1990) believes, "The patient needs to be given insight into the ways in which he has been defending himself against his underlying feelings and the anxieties that have led him to do so" (p. 8). Once this understanding has been outlined and it is clear the patient can see how the defenses operate, an examination of the consequences can occur.

Examining the Consequences of Defense

Now the therapist is in a position to summarize what has been learned about the patient's characteristic defenses, as well as the feelings and anxieties that they are designed to avoid. Assuming the patient has indicated a like understanding of these dynamic forces within him- or herself, the focus can shift to an examination of the consequences of these defenses in the patient's life and for the therapy itself. Looking at the consequences of defenses and helping the patient appreciate the cost involved in their utilization has great therapeutic value. For example, the patient would be asked, "What effect will your maintaining this mask of humor have on your goal of getting help with your difficulties?" The ways in which the defenses defeat the patient must be identified.

Responses to Defense Analysis

There are two fairly predictable responses to the examination of consequences. The first, in which patients are deeply involved in the process and are able to appreciate the terrific cost of their defenses, is the experience of grief. This grief becomes a powerful incentive to approach the feelings underlying the defenses. Treatment, in these cases, proceeds quite rapidly to uncovering. The second general type of emotional response to defense analysis is anger and irritation with the therapist. Typically, some compromise between the anger and the patient's characteristic defenses against it becomes manifest. The following case will illustrate the first type of response to defense work in which grief is the first affect to surface.

CLINICAL EXAMPLE

A Grief Response: The Lonely Businessman

THERAPIST: Tell me why you're here.

PATIENT: I've been seeing a marital therapist on and off for 2 years because my marriage has not been good for 3 or 4 years. He helped me with that, but I want to stress I'm not here for the same reason I went there. My own position now is that I expect we'll separate. We have four kids which is why we've stayed together. To all intents and purposes, we're separated but living at the same address.

THERAPIST: But you come now for your own reasons.

PATIENT: One reason we haven't separated is because I've been reluctant to make a change. Some of these are practical reasons, but at least 50% are reasons I have for not wanting to be alone. I've discovered this since separation became a real possibility.

This opening interchange contains a great deal of valuable information. The patient arrives with an intrapsychic focus and makes it clear he has come for treatment of his own accord. He also proves quite insightful regarding the core of his difficulties, the fear of being alone. Intellectually, he's involved and insightful. As he relayed this information to the therapist, he appeared to be choked up. An exploration of his feelings is indicated.

THERAPIST: It looks like you're fighting a lot of feeling.

PATIENT: Yes I am. I've felt that way for 4 to 5 years now, since the marriage started to decline.

THERAPIST: So, once separation became a possibility, you began to confront fears about being alone.

PATIENT: Yes, and I realized that played a large part in staying together and getting together in the first place.

THERAPIST: Any idea what that's about—why you're so afraid to be alone?

PATIENT: No I don't. I'm an intellectualizer by nature, and seek isolation. I'm not a socializer, so it's a surprise to me to find this. I was remembering an event when I was 20 or so (patient is now in his 40s). Before going to college, I traveled for 6 months. I remembered looking forward to traveling and being alone. But then I suddenly realized, midtrip, that I was really depressed and didn't want to go on alone. I beat a hasty path to the airport and went home to stay with my older brother. I only remembered that in the context of the feelings evoked in this situation.

When patients are this insightful, sometimes all that is required is inquiry to unveil the causes of pain and anxiety. In this case, the patient says he doesn't know why he's afraid, but he can recall an earlier time in his life when he got the solitude he thought he wanted but became depressed. He seems well acquainted with and highly identified with his formal (intellectualizing) and tactical (isolation) defenses.

Examination of the Triangle of Conflict

THERAPIST: So there's a combination of anxiety and depression that comes when you're alone and then you want to be reunited with a loved one. Was that the first time, at age 20?

PATIENT: It was the first time I got the isolation I thought I wanted. Many memories before that of looking to escape from people, all very tied up with experiences at boarding school. I thought if I just made it through there and got out, I'd be all right.

THERAPIST: How old were you when you went to boarding school?

PATIENT: Eight.

THERAPIST: Obviously that was traumatic.

PATIENT: Very.

THERAPIST: The way you dealt with that was to go to withdrawal and isolation. Now you find you can physically escape from people, but it doesn't solve the problem. Then you confront the feelings inside.

PATIENT: Precisely. I'm fairly sure that's why I got married, to prevent those feelings about being alone.

Here the therapist ventures the first interpretation of the triangle of conflict—that the anxiety (A) was a response to an upsurge of painful feelings, (1/F) which he attempted to avoid with flight (D). The therapist added that the flight hadn't provided a solution. The painful feelings associated with being left alone were still pressing for expression. The patient's response to these interpretations provided further evidence that he is well acquainted with his defenses, as well as suggesting that they are becoming dystonic.

Exploration of Anxiety

THERAPIST: So let's look at this anxiety. Are you aware of feeling that now?

PATIENT: Yes.

THERAPIST: Where do you feel it?

PATIENT: Emotionally, I suppose I have enough defense mechanisms in place that I don't particularly relish dismantling them.

THERAPIST: We'll get to that, but how do you experience the anxiety?

PATIENT: Some tension but mostly inner guardedness.

THERAPIST: Guarded is a way you avoid these feelings you dread and a way you keep me away from them. But, physically, you feel tense?

PATIENT: Mostly it's a raised heartbeat, stomach tension, and sort of bodily rigidity.

The preceding vignette indicates some fusion between anxiety and defense. His defenses work quite well in containing the anxiety and preventing him from becoming too uncomfortable. As the clarification continues, the patient is able to describe the physical experience of anxiety, which is channeled into the striated muscle. These responses suggest that the patient's ego-adaptive capacity is quite high and that he would be able to tolerate an unlocking of the unconscious.

Anxiety in the Transference

PATIENT: When it's at its height and I'm in an "on the spot" situation, there's an overall feeling of nervousness.

THERAPIST: Like here—being on the spot. You smile.

PATIENT: I've put myself on the spot. I did this intentionally.

THERAPIST: But it makes you anxious. What about coming here to see me today makes you anxious?

PATIENT: I've never been in a situation where someone has put me on the spot and been there, and I don't intend to take refuge in those usual devices (defenses).

THERAPIST: So you've decided to come here and get to the bottom of your problems, but you're terrified to face it and to let me close to you. It raises the issue of intimacy and closeness.

PATIENT: Yes, without question.

The exploration of the patient's anxiety with the therapist leads unquestionably to his fear of closeness. Therefore, the following interventions are aimed in that direction.

Focus on Defenses against Emotional Closeness

THERAPIST: So the question is, will you let me close enough to be of help?

PATIENT: No one has ever been there. I've never really been there.

THERAPIST: You want help but you're running. Are you aware of how you're avoiding me right now?

PATIENT: How I would prevent someone from coming close? I rationalize a lot, but at the same time, I have a distinct feeling people can get there. They get in touch with those things underneath. I actually can't stop them. I'm thinking of boarding school. It was easy, because they were superiors and had authority, to simply invade that space and waste it.

THERAPIST: What do you think brought that to mind?

PATIENT: The feeling that we're already below levels I'm comfortable letting people in.

It is extraordinarily important to clarify at this point whether the patient is beginning to experience an upsurge of feeling about the past or is actually experiencing the therapist as invading.

Cost-Benefit Analysis of Defenses

Whereas Davanloo advocates a focus on the cost of defenses, I believe it is also crucial to acknowledge the benefit and the attempt at adaptation involved in defensive efforts. A good deal of developmental and longitudinal research (Stern, 1985; Vaillant, 1993) suggests that we are continually striving to adapt to our environment to the best of our ability. Although outmoded strategies developed in childhood certainly have self-defeating consequences for patients who are seeking treatment, there is no solid evidence that self-defeat is the motive behind the use of defenses. If the focus remains solely on the cost of defenses, without an acknowledgment of the attempt at adaptation, the patient can feel deeply misunderstood, creating the possibility for a misalliance. Making it clear to patients that their defenses worked at one time, or in a particular situation, while inviting them to examine how well they work now prevents any iatrogenic resistance from developing and increases the therapeutic alliance.

Grief Regarding the Cost of Defenses

THERAPIST: It reminds you of being invaded. Let's make sure I'm not invading where I don't have permission to go.

PATIENT: You're not.

THERAPIST: You keep a safe distance. I'm sure that served you well in boarding school, but here with me, if you stay distant and detached, what impact will that have?

PATIENT: It would have the impact which would be to waste my time and yours, which is why I don't plan to do it, but it's not to say it's going to be easy.

THERAPIST: It's a central conflict. Are you aware you avoid my eyes?

PATIENT: It takes a lot of effort to talk, to verbalize and communicate, to let someone in.

THERAPIST: You're terrified of closeness.

PATIENT: I've always been frightened and so . . .

THERAPIST: I'm sure you have reasons. Initially, it was for protection but now it traps you. It must be terribly lonely.

PATIENT: Yes, I always have been, as long as I can remember. I don't remember ever having anyone there (starts to cry).

Looking at the cost of these distancing defenses, which in this case perpetuate the painful loneliness this man seeks to avoid, results in an outpouring of grief-laden affect. This indicates that the ego is turning on the defense. Now the stage is set for an exploration of the relevant developmental history. The genesis of his difficulties became quite clear. The patient was cared for by servants and then sent to boarding school at the age of 8. All his attempts at contact with his parents were met with rejection. Following the work on defenses against emotional closeness, the deep pain about feeling so alone in the world was easily accessed. However, the reactive anger toward those who abandoned him was still being defended against. Until these defenses were removed, there would continue to be resistance in the transference and possible distortion of the material being reported.

Anger in the Transference

THERAPIST: It sounds like you are making a connection between your mother and me. You're saying that, without ever having established a warm, close relationship with you, she would barge in and demand a response. It sounds like you're saying to me, "Listen lady, I don't know you. You haven't paid your dues. I'll be damned if I'm going to let you in".

PATIENT: That's right.

THERAPIST: So there must be a lot of feeling toward me. Are you aware of feeling angry with me?

PATIENT: Oh yes. I've felt angry for about an hour now.

THERAPIST: How do you experience this anger?

PATIENT: Tension and defensiveness.

THERAPIST: That's not the anger. What happens to the anger?

PATIENT: It says inside, unexpressed.

THERAPIST: Who suffers with it then?

PATIENT: I do, but I don't know what else to do with it.

This last interchange, regarding the experience of anger toward the therapist and the mobilization of the patient's characteristic defenses against it, is very important. It becomes clear that he immediately internalizes his rage and becomes depressed. Insight into the link between the repressed rage and the symptom of depression is necessary to turn the ego against this defense and will further bolster his motivation to face the anger directly.

Turning the Ego against Its Defenses

THERAPIST: So it stays inside and you suffer. It also creates a barrier. To avoid the experience of the anger, you have to keep a distance from me.

PATIENT: Right.

THERAPIST: And then I can't help you. That's self-defeating.

PATIENT: Yes, yes it is.

THERAPIST: Why do you want to do that?

PATIENT: I don't.

The patient now indicates that he is aware of how he is defending against anger toward the therapist and the cost he is paying for it. Further, he declares his will to give up the defense. The therapist will challenge him to put his money where his mouth is. As pressure mounts, the therapist will monitor for signs that the angry impulses are coming close to the surface so they can be immediately tapped.

THERAPIST: So let's look at how you experience this anger toward me.

PATIENT: I don't know how to work it.

THERAPIST: The questions is, how do you experience the anger? Do you notice your hands start going (referring to significant movement in the patient's hands that has just become evident)?

PATIENT: Yes, that's right. I just feel like shaking and strangling you.

Following the breakthrough of the anger toward the therapist, along with the aggressive impulses that accompany it, the patient made spontaneous links to similar feelings and impulses toward both his wife and mother.

T-P Link

PATIENT: I wanted to shake and strangle my mother too, but not to kill her, to wake her up and get a response. Why was she never there for me? The anger is easy compared to the pain underneath. (The patient is crying and clearly in touch with the deep emotional pain he has run from all his life.)

THERAPIST: What is it like to experience this now?

PATIENT: It's a place I've tried to remove as far as possible. There were times I've felt my heart break and I can't handle it (sobs). Nobody cared. It felt like death, in a way.

THERAPIST: It sounds like something died inside. It's as if hope died the night you were sent to boarding school. How could you bear it? It sounds like you killed off the longing to deal with the pain. While you couldn't bear it as a child, you can now. You're able to share it. What is that like?

PATIENT: For the first time, I feel reasonably safe feeling it.

THERAPIST: So as painful as it is, facing it directly and sharing it provides the very kind of emotional connection you've always longed for.

PATIENT: Yes, it's hopeful. It's the only hope. The entrance in was so hard, but now I want to stay there. I get the mental image of a 3-year-old, sitting in a cave. Somewhere, back there, this connection exists.

THERAPIST: There was a real, live, feeling little boy back there.

PATIENT: There's a sense of hope and abandonment at the same time. Loneliness and hope, together. It's painful but not terrifying anymore.

Following the breakthrough of affect and the outpouring of unconscious material, there needs to be a re-analysis of the process to drive home the insights obtained. Initially there was a connection between the therapist and the patient's mother. As the feelings from the past are faced directly and he was able to share them with the therapist, the contrast between then and now becomes clear. This awareness significantly reduces transference distortions.

Another important change occurs subsequent to the direct experience of these previously dreaded feelings. Once they feelings are faced directly, the anxiety that has accompanied them gets stripped away. The patient says it is painful but no longer terrifying to experience these feelings. This leads to the experience of deep relief and to the dawning of hope. Not only have the symptoms of anxiety and depression been lifted, but they have been replaced by a sense of a calm and reasonable hope that, with help and hard work, his problems will be resolved and he will be free of suffering. These changes were evident in the follow-up session, three days later. The patient entered the session ready to work, taking an active role and reporting a flood of memories from his early life, all accompanied by intense feeling.

PART 2. TURNING THE EGO AGAINST ITS DEFENSES

The process of acquainting patients with their defenses, described in Part 1 of the defense work, results in the ego beginning to turn on its maladaptive and self-defeating defenses. For highly responsive patients, this kind of clarification proves sufficient for the ego to abandon its defenses, leading to the direct experience of previously avoided thoughts and feelings. In most cases, however, things do not progress so smoothly. Character defenses are deeply ingrained and, even when patients can see how self-defeating they are, they are resistant to abandoning them. Even Reich (1933), one of the most "radical" analysts in regard to attention to defense and resistance, felt, "We leave it up to him whether or not he wants to make use of his knowledge to change his character" (p. 52). Freud felt we needed to develop a strong lever against the resistance. He suggested that defenses had to be deprived of their value or even replaced by more powerful ones, but he never elaborated on means to accomplish this end. This is exactly what the techniques of pressure and challenge were designed to do. A good deal of ego strength is required (by patient and therapist alike!) to endure the anxiety and intensely conflictual feelings toward the therapist that this technique evokes. In many patients, restructuring of the defenses, which significantly increases ego strength, is a necessary prerequisite to this work. This process will be outlined in detail in the following chapter.

PART 3.   PRESSURE AND CHALLENGE

The technique of "pressure and challenge" was designed to create an intrapsychic crisis, leading to psychic disequilibrium in patients with rigid character pathology. The crisis is developed by the intensification of complex transference feelings and the defenses against them, both of which are aroused by the therapist's active intervention. The patient becomes affectively stirred "within an atmosphere in which he senses, both consciously and unconsciously, that the therapist is directing him toward his most painful buried feelings out of a genuine and compassionate concern, a determination not to spare him pain but to face it, with the sole purpose of freeing him from the self-defeating patterns that have spoiled his life for so many years" (Davanloo, 1990, p. 7).

Pressure and challenge (exerting pressure on the self-defeating defenses while challenging the healthy part of the ego to find freedom from suffering) are the technical elements necessary for creating an intrapsychic crisis. Once the treatment has reached this stage and the therapist has decided to mount pressure on the defenses to achieve a breakthrough of underlying feelings, the clinician must proceed in a determined fashion. This involves relentless attention to each defense as it comes into operation. Interventions must occur in a rapid-fire manner, which frequently involves interrupting the operation of defenses as they arise. The therapist must remain alert to any signal that the underlying feelings are ready to break through into conscious awareness. Once observed, a shift in focus to a full and direct experience of the complex transference feelings can occur. The phase of pressure and challenge seems to be the most difficult technical intervention for most therapists to master, as it is most foreign to them. Davanloo (1990–1991) feels that clinical training and supervision restructure the *therapists'* ego, enabling him to approach anxiety-provoking affects without resorting to his own defenses.

Pressure and challenge can be a "do or die" procedure. When dealing with severely detached patients enmeshed in rigid character pathology, this kind of attack on the defenses is essential. Anything less tends to bounce right off the wall of resistance. A detailed example of the phase of pressure and challenge will be provided.

Goals of Defense Work

The goals of this phase of the treatment, whether achieved through clarification and interpretation in highly responsive patients, or pressure and challenge in the case of more resistant patients, are threefold:

1. De-sensitization of the ego to previously toxic affects.
2. De-repression of memories and associations pertaining to the genesis of the patient's intrapsychic conflicts.
3. Use of this affective and cognitive information to make meaningful T-C-P interpretations and consolidate insight.

Anger in Response to Defense Analysis

It is not unusual for a patient to respond to defense analysis with anger and irritation toward the therapist. Some compromise between the feeling of anger and defenses against it is frequently observed. Although the anger toward the therapist must eventually be dealt with, it is up to the therapist to maintain a focus on the cost of defenses before proceeding to the experience of the anger. At this stage of defense work, anger toward the therapist is most often a diversion from the pain and grief patients have caused themselves by relying on these defenses. Only when patients can see their contribution to the problems they've been experiencing should the transference feelings be explored. Failure to stick with the task of clarification of the defense can distort the transference, such that the therapist is viewed as just another insensitive and demanding individual.

CLINICAL EXAMPLE

The Detached Observer

The following is an account of an early session in which the techniques of pressure and challenge to the patient's character defenses, which had become a major resistance to emotional involvement in the treatment, were used to break through the defensive barrier and gain access to the patient's inner life. This patient exhibited the kind of massive emotional detachment in the treatment setting that had characterized his life. To continue in that way would result in the same sort of sterility and disappointment in the treatment that marked all his other relationships. The self-defeat in operation needed to be addressed directly. As the patient's defenses were repeatedly brought into focus, there was a rise in complex transference feelings. In this case, the first affect to emerge was anger and sadistic rage. It was the direct experience of this anger in the transference that provided an opening into the patient's unconscious.

The patient came for help with the symptoms of anxiety and depression, as well as social isolation and withdrawal. He was 27 at the time he entered treatment and, although intelligent and attractive, was functioned far below his capacity in both social and occupational realms. He repeatedly failed to take advantage of opportunities that came his way, due to his tendency to withdraw in the face of anxiety around contact with others. This central conflict, between the part of him that wanted to get involved with others and the part that would run and avoid such contact because of the pain and anxiety it evoked, became evident in the therapeutic relationship.

The patient entered this, the sixth session, reporting anxiety about coming for his appointment. He claimed he wanted to open up but was nervous about doing so.

His opening comment indicated where he was on the triangles (anxiety in the transference) and provided direction for therapeutic intervention. The increased anxiety in the transference he reported suggested an intensification of complex transference feelings. To access these feelings, which was the goal, all his defensive attempts to avoid the experience of his feelings toward the therapist needed to be rendered inoperable. Pressure and challenge to the defenses were required to achieve the goal of emotional activation and access to the unconscious.

Exploration of Anxiety in the Transference

PATIENT: I'm really nervous about being here. I was thinking about it, and I really want to open up but I get anxious.
THERAPIST: What are you experiencing with the anxiety?
PATIENT: Fidgety.
THERAPIST: Inside?
PATIENT: Tense in my chest and my arms. I'm kind of braced.

THERAPIST: There's lots of muscle tension. Anything else?

PATIENT: I get more quiet.

THERAPIST: That's not the anxiety, is it? You're getting quiet is a retreat in the face of anxiety.

PATIENT: I get the wandering mind too. If I'm with people, especially. That doesn't happen when I'm alone, I notice.

THERAPIST: So the anxiety has to do with being with other people, like being here with me. When did that anxiety start?

PATIENT: A few days ago when I realized I wanted to come here and open up to you.

THERAPIST: So there's something about opening up to me that makes you very anxious and in the face of the anxiety you go to emotional distance—by avoiding eye contact, keeping constricted, even your voice is low and controlled, no emotion, and your mind wanders, you tend to be vague. Are you aware of that?

PATIENT: Yes, pretty much. It comes very automatically.

The last intervention involved an interpretation of the triangle of conflict in the transference with particular attention paid to the types of defenses the patient was using to erect a wall and remain detached. His response indicated that he was able to see that he was backing off in the face of anxiety about close emotional contact but that it kicked in automatically against his conscious will. This indicates that these defenses are still syntonic. As such, some pressure is required to turn the ego against them and render them dystonic.

Examining the Consequences of Detachment

THERAPIST: Right. It's automatic and pervasive. It's not just here with me but you get anxious and then distance yourself from everyone, which has had a devastating effect on your relationships. You end up leading an isolated, constricted life. So if you establish the same kind of detached relationship here with me, we are at an impasse.

This intervention constituted an attempt to examine the consequences of the patient's characteristic defenses, particularly in the transference, and to tie that to the devastating consequences of this stance in his entire life.

PATIENT: Right.

THERAPIST: Is that what you want?

PATIENT: No.

Now that the patient has declared his will to give up the defenses that have perpetuated the pain in his life, the process moves to the phase of pressure and challenge. The patient is pressed to follow through on his declaration of will.

Challenge to the Defense of Detachment

THERAPIST: So then we have to see what you are going to do about the detachment here with me.

PATIENT: (stays silent and looks to the floor).

THERAPIST: You stay silent, look away, sigh—you maintain the distance.

PATIENT: (throws up his hands).

THERAPIST: Now you go to a helpless, defeated position. Do you see the barrier this creates here between you and me?

PATIENT: Yes.

THERAPIST: If you maintain the barrier, what will happen to your goal of getting to the bottom of your difficulties so you can be free of your suffering?

PATIENT: It won't happen.

THERAPIST: More self-defeat. This will be another failure. Is that what you want?

PATIENT: No.

THERAPIST: Then what are you going to do about the detachment that kills off your potential for a helpful relationship here?

PATIENT: (returns to silence and withdrawal).

As pressure is put on the patient to take responsibility and to act on his stated intention to open up, defenses and resistance in the transference increase. One line of defense after another comes to the fore in rapid succession. The patient starts with emotional detachment, then retreats to silence and stubborn withholding. This is a signal that the underlying complex transference feelings are rising. Therefore, a relentless focus on the defense, with an appeal to the part of the patient that wants to be free to directly express himself, must be maintained until the defenses are exhausted and the feelings break through.

Pressure and Challenge

THERAPIST: You look away, sigh, and remain silent.

PATIENT: I don't know what to do.

THERAPIST: That's helplessness. You say you see that you erect a wall of emotional detachment.

PATIENT: Yeah. I know it's there.

THERAPIST: You put it there, and you're the one who can keep it there or take it down. If it stays?

PATIENT: Nothing will get done.

THERAPIST: So it becomes another part of the self-defeat in your life. You come here of your own will to get help but end up sabotaging that by remaining uninvolved—a detached observer. The problem here between us is the same problem that spoils your life—detachment. So the question is, what are you going to do about that?

PATIENT: I don't know.

THERAPIST: You don't know. Now we're in limbo.

PATIENT: Yeah. (There's a decided edge to his voice and a defiant quality to this sequence of the interaction.)

THERAPIST: Where does that get you?

PATIENT: Nowhere.

The "Head-On Collision" with the Resistance

The following sequence demonstrates a combination of interventions that Davanloo refers to as "a head-on collision with the resistance." This is a focused attempt to help the patient confront the strength of his tendency to hold onto self-defeating defenses and to challenge the healthy ego to reassume control. The therapist places responsibility in the patient's lap and refuses either to let the patient off the hook or to do the work for him. The therapist makes it clear she is on the side of openness and honesty, no matter how painful, and will not collude with the part of the patient that wants to skirt the experience of painful feelings and memories. The therapist must be ready to detect and then withstand the full storm of complex transference feelings once they surface.

THERAPIST: Isn't this the problem in your life? Why should we continue in this "nowhere"? Let's have an honest look and you decide—it's up to you. Because, if there is a part of you that has decided, "There is no way I'm going to let this woman into my life," we might as well say our good-byes, because to continue in this way is to perpetuate the misery. Maybe we could have a nice chat but that is not going to help you with your problems. Which is it going to be?

PATIENT: I want to but I don't know if I can change it.

THERAPIST: You want to change, though?

PATIENT: Yes.

THERAPIST: You're not content to remain an observer in life—detached and alone?

PATIENT: No. No.

Again, his conscious will to change is solidified and then pressure is exerted to behave in accordance with that will.

Anger in the Transference

THERAPIST: So what are you going to do about the detachment here with me?

PATIENT: (The patient is silent but physically charged, moving around in his chair and breathing deeply, a sign that transference feelings are close to the surface and can now be tapped.)

THERAPIST: Is there some feeling toward me?

PATIENT: Yeah.

THERAPIST: Which is what, if you don't avoid it?

PATIENT: I can't let it out.

THERAPIST: Could you declare what the feeling is toward me?

PATIENT: It's real anger.

THERAPIST: How do you experience this anger toward me?

The patient was able to declare the anger, indicating a breakdown of the defense against cognitive awareness of his feeling toward the therapist. Now the physiological and motoric elements of the anger must be assessed, and any remaining defense removed, so that the patient can achieve a full experience of the complex transference feelings.

Breakthrough of Sadistic Impulses

PATIENT: I want to but . . .

THERAPIST: But there's another part that fights you, keeps it inside, and the attack is on you. You become more depressed, more isolated, constricted in your life.

PATIENT: Yeah.

THERAPIST: Is that what you want, to let that part rule? Or are you going to decide and take the risk to face this anger with me directly right now.

PATIENT: (retreats to silence).

THERAPIST: This is more avoidance, which is a decision not to let me close to these feelings.

PATIENT: That's because they're almost murderous.

THERAPIST: Very powerful, huh? So there's a murderous rage toward me?

PATIENT: Toward more than just you.

THERAPIST: But, first toward me.

PATIENT: Yeah.

THERAPIST: And if that were to come out, in your imagination, how would you murder me, what is the impulse?

PATIENT: The impulse is to swear at you.

THERAPIST: But that is not to murder me. How would you murder me? Your hands start to move.

PATIENT: Just to strangle you. I'd squeeze your neck with such force, it would come right off. I'd sever your head from your body, take it by the hair and just smash it against a brick wall.

At long last, the patient became deeply immersed in the experience of his angry feelings toward the therapist. To get there, all the defenses he had erected against emotional contact, which triggers these feelings, had to be systematically identified and challenged until they were exhausted. The last-ditch efforts to avoid the direct experience of the rage toward the therapist, including diversifying ("Toward more than just you") and minimizing ("The impulse is to swear at you"), were pushed aside. In a sense, the patient was testing the therapist to see if she would take an easy out at that point.

It is crucial to access all the feelings in the transference before moving to the other figures with whom the therapist is associated. If the feelings toward the therapist are not directly experienced, they are, by definition, being defended against and will contribute to ongoing resistance. In addition, an opportunity for a powerful corrective emotional experience would be lost. As Freud has said, what is learned directly through the transference relationship is never forgotten. Experiencing and expressing the very feelings the patient has dreaded, without encountering any of the anticipated damaging consequences, is a potent corrective experience. So, the resistance is substantially decreased and the therapeutic alliance bolstered by facing these feelings directly. Once the feelings in the transference have been experienced, the genetic figure the therapist has come to represent will become clear.

T-P Link

THERAPIST: So what happens to me? My head is a bloody pulp and my body?

PATIENT: I throw your head down and take your body and break it over my knee. Then I raise it over my head and the blood drenches over me. (The patient is motorically, as well as emotionally involved, going through the physical motions he's describing.) Now I see my mother, only it's more gruesome.

THERAPIST: So as you get in touch with this massive rage toward me and the impulses that come with that, you get a picture of your mother?

PATIENT: Yeah. Only it's worse with her. I break every bone in her body. I target her fingers and break them one by one. It was those fingers, all that twitching and crazy shit she did with her hands, I target that. The sounds are deafening. (Patient begins to tear up.)

THERAPIST: As you face this rage toward her, other feelings seem to come. This is a horrendous scene.

PATIENT: I don't think it's horrendous

The patient was very involved in the experience of anger but did not seem ready to move to the underlying guilt and grief. As our time was up, I summarized what had occurred in the session, linking the triangle of conflict in the transference with that in the past with his mother. He entered the next session noticeably changed. There were no signs of anxiety, and rather than being quiet or hesitant, he started speaking right away, declaring that he still felt angry. This provided evidence of character change.

De-Repression of Memories

PATIENT: I'm still really pissed about the last session.

THERAPIST: I think it's very important that we examine what happened and what your reactions are.

PATIENT: I'll tell you what I've been thinking. I thought I'd come in here and lay it on you but then it got transferred—you were my mother, you were her. Because I felt like it was an attack and it felt unprovoked, it was similar to what I got with my mother. It had nothing to do with what I did, she would just come at me.

THERAPIST: So, as you began to face the feelings toward me for what felt like an unprovoked attack . . .

PATIENT: It went right to my mother. I said, "For 17 years (she died when he was 17) I was right in front of you and you basically ignored me." The only attention I got was "You're a lazy bum," "Why don't you go out and make friends?" shit like that. And then she bought a dog. It was for her, because she felt lonely . . . (getting choked up with emotion) . . . and I was right there. I hated that fucking dog. I know, when she died, we kept that dog. I'd open up the door and it would fucking growl at me. That dog was just like her. The only person it cared about was her—wouldn't let anyone next to it. I used to beat that fucking dog sometimes. And I wanted to beat her.

THERAPIST: The rage toward her is a reaction to all your needs to love and be loved being repeatedly thwarted.

PATIENT: I don't understand it because, you know, I tried to be the best I could, I was good, I don't cause trouble. (In fact, the patient was an A student and star athlete while his mother was alive). So what was it? It was her.

THERAPIST: But that doesn't make it any less painful. You tried to be so good, but she still couldn't respond and would sometimes lash out in an unprovoked way?

PATIENT: That leads to another thought I had. We're in a padded room and I'd just keep slapping her, to stop this ranting and raving (his mother appeared to have a serious mental illness, with tics, phobias, and paranoid ideation), just keep slapping her (arms waving) until she'd stop all this wild talk and these crazy body movements and she'd just look at me—just see that I need her, I need her love (begins to cry and is clearly grief-stricken).

Now the full range of intense feelings toward his mother, which had been precipitated by the uprising of complex transference feelings, comes pouring out. This was followed by the de-repression of significant memories shedding light on the very real trauma this man experienced in relation to his very disturbed mother. This material also provides an example of the direct relationship between the extent of the trauma to the early attachments, the intensity of the reactive anger and sadism, and the strength and tenacity of the defenses erected against them. When the full intensity of this man's rage and the horrendous trauma that gave rise to this rage became apparent, it was fairly easy to see why such massive defenses had to be erected to contain it all. When the feelings were experienced directly, the patient's adult ego had another chance to put it all in perspective. Although initially there was a direct connection between the feelings and perceptions of the therapist and the patient's mother, by the end of this session, clear distinctions were made. Even though I had, in fact, put pressure on him and repeatedly pointed out the ways in which he was avoiding me and rendering me useless to him, I did not attack him personally as his mother had. In addition, my motive was to help him, not berate him. He made these distinctions spontaneously, and they were accompanied by a feeling of gratitude toward me for going through all this with him. The direct experience of anger toward the therapist did not result in feared death and destruction, but actually led to relief, a greater understanding of himself, and a genuine feeling of closeness with and gratitude toward the therapist. This is the essence of a corrective emotional experience.

SUMMARY

In most cases, patients arrive for treatment in an ambivalent state and tend to become increasingly defensive as painful areas of their life are explored in depth. Because these defenses create resistance to the treatment, they must be eradicated as quickly as possible if treatment is to be efficient and effective. In rare cases, a focus on the high cost of the patient's defenses evokes deep grief, which is sufficient to shift the preexisting psychic equilibrium. Such was the case with the the Lonely Businessman.

To deal with more intransigent defenses, Davanloo has developed a whole series of interventions designed to break through the barrier of resistance, rendering patients who had been poorly motivated and inaccessible to intervention open to genuine involvement in treatment. In the case of the Detached Observer, a heavy dose of unrelenting pressure and challenge was required to shift the balance from resistance to accessibility.

CHAPTER 4

Restructuring
Regressive Defenses

Tell me and I forget
Teach me and I remember
Involve me and I learn

Benjamin Franklin

As has already been demonstrated, many of Davanloo's techniques are employed pre-interpretively, to prepare the patient to withstand and then effectively utilize material from the unconscious. Intensive Short-Term Dynamic Psychotherapy is quite demanding on both cognitive and affective levels and can only be successful if both patient and therapist are deeply involved in the process. In rare cases, patients come for the initial evaluation with the motivation and ability to become freely involved and make use of this focused and intensive approach. More often than not, however, patients arrive in a resistant state or become resistant as painful areas are approached. This resistance prevents the kind of emotional involvement necessary for a successful outcome. Davanloo (1980) has developed a standard technique for handling highly resistant patients, in which "pressure and challenge to the resistance are steadily increased and are not relaxed until the patient directly experiences the complex transference feelings" (Davanloo, 1987, p. 77). Following this experience, there is an outpouring of unconscious material that not only provides a deep understanding of the genesis of the patient's difficulties but dramatically increases the unconscious therapeutic alliance. This process was illustrated in the case of the Detached Observer (see Chapter 3). The patient's resistance was massive and prevented any meaningful contact between patient and therapist, as he was keeping the innermost part of himself sealed off from view. Because all the initial interventions indicated a strong ego, the standard technique of applying unremitting pressure and challenge to the defenses was employed. The outpouring of memories and associations following the breakthrough of complex transference feelings confirmed this assessment.

RESTRUCTURING

Indications for Restructuring

The standard technique involving pressure and challenge to the patient's defenses is contraindicated in those cases where patients suffer from depression, functional disorders (e.g., headaches, irritable bowel syndrome), panic, or impulsive discharge. Common to all these disorders is a deep-rooted inability to distinguish between the elements involved in the triangle of conflict. Most often, various defenses are mistaken for the impulse itself. With this type of fusion, challenge to the defenses, with pressure to experience the underlying impulses, will result in an exacerbation of symptoms and/or unmanageable anxiety. Modifications to the standard technique are required in these cases. The technical requirements involved in restructuring and clinical examples of this process will be detailed in this chapter.

The Technique of Defense Restructuring

The technique of restructuring defenses involves the systematic and repetitive reworking of the triangle of conflict in both the transference and the patient's current relationships. Restructuring involves the following elements:

1. Clarification and differentiation within the triangle of conflict.
2. Gradual exposure to the direct experience of feelings and impulses.
3. Cognitive re-analysis of the process.

The goals of this phase of therapeutic intervention are directed toward an increase in the adaptability, flexibility, and strength of the ego. This is achieved by:

1. Increasing insight into the link between repressed impulses and anxiety or other symptoms.
2. Decreasing the patient's reliance on regressive defenses.
3. Reducing the intensity of anxiety that accompanies the direct experience of affect.

All this work must occur before attempting any access to unconscious impulses and feelings toward central figures from the patient's past.

Working the Triangle of Conflict in Current Relationships

During the phase of inquiry, special attention is devoted to the examination of recent episodes preceding depression, panic, or exacerbations of psychosomatic complaints. As these episodes are explored, slow and repetitive work on the triangle of conflict begins.

It is essential that patients become aware of the mechanisms by which they have avoided particularly painful impulses and feelings. Since these patients are typically very identified with their defenses and don't distinguish defenses from feelings, repeated clarification is required to achieve this insight. A clinical example will be used to illustrate this process.

RESTRUCTURING WITH DEPRESSIVES

Patients who are currently experiencing depression require a phase of defense restructuring that follows inquiry and must precede any pressure or challenge to experience the feelings they typically avoid. A detailed inquiry should cover all areas of symptomatic disturbance, history of previous episodes of depression, including severity and duration, examination of past treatments, and assessment of current ego functioning and character structure. When depression is severe or is deeply embedded in a patient's character, patients cannot participate actively in the treatment process. Their slowness, passivity, and helplessness form a barrier of resistance in the transference that must be addressed from the outset. Clarification of the self-defeating nature of this resistance in interactions with the evaluator, as well as in other areas of the patient's life, is necessary to turn the ego against these ego-syntonic character defenses.

Davanloo's (1987) work with depressives has demonstrated that a reliance on the defenses of repression and internalization is a central and overriding feature of this disorder. Fosha (1988) has stated:

> Thus, Davanloo conceptualizes the phenomenological hallmarks of depression—the withdrawal, the self-reproaches, the passivity, the helplessness, the sense of inferiority and inadequacy—as the result of regressive mechanisms used not only to defend against sadistic impulses but also to avoid the experience of the associated painful feelings, such as guilt and grief. (p. 189)

This last point is very important. Depressives are defending against guilt and grief as well as aggressive impulses. The following clinical example will illustrate several of these crucial factors.

CLINICAL EXAMPLE

Woman on an Emotional Roller Coaster

THERAPIST: Why don't you start by telling me about the problems you came for help with.

PATIENT: First of all, I got cancer. My marriage is falling apart and I'm about to leave. I have one child still living at home who doesn't know yet. One older child has known since last year. I have been disconnected from my parents for three years, so they don't know. I have a boyfriend, lover . . .

THERAPIST: You're telling me about events but . . .

PATIENT: You want feelings.

THERAPIST: Well, how is this causing you a problem?

PATIENT: Pain, I'm on an emotional roller coaster.

Exploration of Anxiety

The patient began by presenting a list of highly traumatic events in a rather businesslike fashion. Before the therapist could complete her first intervention, the patient took over, indicating a strong tendency to be compliant with what she imagined was expected of her (in this case, a focus on feeling). At this opening stage, what needed to be delineated were the problems in her current life. The patient reported the onset of anxiety attacks and depression 9 months prior to our meeting. An exploration of the phenomenological experience of the symptoms and exploration of the precipitating events follows.

Exploration of Depression

THERAPIST: So let's look at how you experience this anxiety and then we'll look at the depression.

PATIENT: It's like hot flashes, but they're emotionally precipitated. So I become flushed and sweaty and feel anxious in the pit of my stomach.

THERAPIST: And this started?

PATIENT: After my husband left and my older daughter went back to college.

THERAPIST: So you realize the anxiety is a reaction to emotion.

PATIENT: When I contemplated leaving or talked about the separation.

THERAPIST: The anxiety was a reaction to the feelings about separation.

The patient was able to give a good account of the physical experience of anxiety and indicated an awareness that anxiety was a response to an emotional trigger. Her ability to distinguish, yet meaningfully link, anxiety and a rise in unpleasant feelings indicates a fairly high level of insight into her own inner workings.

PATIENT: Separation anxiety, yeah. Depression was about ambivalence. I want to break loose, but there's a loss. In part I want to re-do adolescence; drive a motorcycle, have sex; but I also want to be secure with my family around.

THERAPIST: Clearly, the cancer diagnosis created an internal crisis and you began to reevaluate your life.

PATIENT: That, and midlife, and the kids taking off with their own lives. Even the youngest doesn't need me as much, so the loss of the role of mother. And I lost my mother too, and when you're in pain, you want to call "Mommy."

THERAPIST: What's that about?

PATIENT: I disconnected from my parents. I was an abused child and had a difficult childhood. I always tried to be good, to work hard to try and please them and, on a very erratic schedule, I'd manage to do that. So, I kept trying, but just as often I'd get slapped down and I became very rebellious and I began to believe what they said about me.

C-P Link

THERAPIST: So this recent separation, and the ambivalence about that, brought all these unresolved feelings from the past close to the surface. On the one hand, wanting to be good and pleasing to secure the attachment but then enraged about having to win their love, which goes into rebellious behavior. You say, "To hell with you." So there's a sense in which this emotional roller coaster is not just about now, which is traumatic enough, but stirs up unresolved feelings from the past. How do you understand it?

PATIENT: I was trying to be tough and independent to survive it on my own, but cracks in the armor that covered the pain started to show. I think there is tremendous anger (getting weepy) because I spent 25 years of marriage being a good girl, good wife and mother, and he was conditionally loving.

Both the precipitant to the recent crisis and a meaningful link between that and an unresolved conflict from the past emerged rapidly, making sense of the patient's intense struggle. To work the triangle of conflict, the process moved to an examination of the current conflictual relationship. While the relationship between anxiety and affect had been established, the exploration of defenses was just beginning and needed to be solidified by a repetitive process of examination.

Triangle of Conflict in the C

THERAPIST: You were angry with your husband and how did you deal with that?

PATIENT: By leaving.

THERAPIST: So you run (D) in the face of your anger (I/F).

PATIENT: And the other is to go into manic behavior (D)—exercising, buying and spending, like $2,000 on clothes, having an affair.

THERAPIST: Characteristically, you don't let yourself experience what you're feeling. You suppress it, are compliant, the good girl, then get angry and fed up and channel the anger into rebellious behavior. The anger goes directly into behavior.

PATIENT: Yeah, I went to this tough stance and shut down my feeling, went to being self-sufficient. I'm not sure what triggered the actual breakdown, but when my husband left, I felt I didn't want to get up anymore. I had been rebellious, the bad girl, and then went to helplessness. I liked being rebellious better.

THERAPIST: You go to various positions, rebellious or helpless, but these are not the feelings themselves.

PATIENT: Yeah, I was running away.

THERAPIST: Right. It was a way to avoid feeling.

This work provided evidence of some fusion between feelings and defenses. The internal experience of angry feelings was avoided by acting on the feelings in some external way; either passivity and compliance or rebellious behavior. Such acting out would trigger guilt, and she punished herself by becoming depressed, helpless, withdrawn, and fairly nonfunctional. Her responses to this phase of the work indicated that she now had a cognitive understanding of how feelings were being avoided. She spontaneously commented that she had dealt with her anger toward her parents in the same way—by cutting them off. However, in that situation, it was more accurate to say she provoked a rejection. This interaction was explored to re-work the triangle of conflict and increase her capacity to experience the feelings themselves in a direct manner.

Triangle of Conflict in Relation to Her Father

PATIENT: I wrote to my parents to ask for a "hearing" in which I could tell them what I really thought about them. I knew they would put me down but I thought that surviving it and telling them what I really thought would be cathartic.

THERAPIST: You thought that this action—telling your parents what you really thought—would lead to a resolution of your own conflicted feelings toward them?

PATIENT: Yes, but my father said, "No, it'll be two adults against a child whose memories are warped." He was furious and wanted to know why I had to cause trouble. So I sent them a letter. It wasn't a poisoned pen letter but it was accusatory. They each wrote me separately saying nasty things and that they wanted nothing to do with me. That was it. I got really manic in my behavior. I was furious.

THERAPIST: So you were furious (I/F) with them but channeled it into manic behavior (D).

PATIENT: I didn't know what to do with it.

THERAPIST: You immediately want to do something with it but the first question is, how do you experience this fury toward your parents? When was it most acute?

PATIENT: When my father called and said he didn't like the idea.

THERAPIST: How did you experience this anger toward him?

PATIENT: I started crying (patient gets tearful).

Restructuring the Depressive Mechanism

THERAPIST: But crying isn't your anger. It's just like what's happening now. You get tearful as we look at your anger.

PATIENT: If I have a good crying jag I feel relieved.

THERAPIST: Is this the anger or the way you avoid it?

PATIENT: That's how I get angry. (This response indicates fusion of feeling and defense.) If I have a good crying jag, I feel better.

THERAPIST: For the moment, but what happens to the anger?

PATIENT: I act on it.

THERAPIST: How adaptive is that?

PATIENT: But I'm scared of it (getting weepy). I don't know what else to do or how to feel it, because my mother is an extremely angry, hostile person, and when I feel that kind of rage and fury toward someone, that she so easily expressed, it scares the hell out of me and I don't want to be like her so I try to do something else.

THERAPIST: You are terrified (A) of your own anger (I/F). We can see it here. There's some rise in your anger (I/F) but that mobilizes a lot of anxiety (A) and you go to weepiness (D).

PATIENT: But then it gets back under control.

THERAPIST: But at what price? Does this work for you, or is it a very self-defeating way of dealing with your anger?

PATIENT: I suppose, but I'm not convinced. I'm ambivalent. I like to go into high gear. I just don't like getting depressed.

Turning the Ego against Character Defenses

The preceding work was designed to turn the patient's ego against these regressive and self-defeating defenses. They are quite syntonic, and the patient openly expresses her hesitance to give them up. The manic behavior, in particular, is hard to relinquish because it provides some immediate gain. These defenses work by fending off depressive affect and by providing revenge on those she's angry with. These defenses must be rendered dystonic before any more anger is evoked; otherwise, the acting out will accelerate.

THERAPIST: They are flip sides of the same coin. You either swallow it or spit it out, but in neither case do you really let yourself experience the anger, know who it's toward and decide the best way to deal with it. But, you're saying maybe you don't want to because it's very gratifying to feel pumped up. It's gratifying in a direct way to act on these feelings and indirectly by getting back at others.

PATIENT: It's also the way I punish myself for feeling something bad. I'm my own judge, jury, and executioner. I make myself suffer.

This is an extraordinarily important communication from the patient, signaling the turning of the ego, the easing of the resistance, and

an increase in the unconscious therapeutic alliance. She goes on to solidify her determination to do things differently.

THERAPIST: How?
PATIENT: By embarrassing myself, wearing myself out.
THERAPIST: So it is self-defeating and you end up suffering. You don't want
to . . .
PATIENT: I really don't. I want to be an autonomous person.
THERAPIST: So do you want to take this opportunity to have an honest look
at your feelings, to get to the bottom of what drives you?
PATIENT: Yeah, I really do. I don't have a chance to be happy if I don't.
Otherwise I'm on this roller coaster, always mildly manic-depressive.

Cognitive Re-Analysis of the Process.   To consolidate the insights
obtained by clarifying and differentiating the triangle of conflict, a period of cognitive re-analysis should follow each gradual increment toward a full experience of affect. This phase of the work is aimed at
strengthening the observing function of the ego.

Two rounds of this work have been conducted thus far. The patient's responses indicated she was clearer about the distinctions between feelings, anxiety, and defense. Further, she was beginning to
acknowledge just how self-defeating her defenses have been, motivating her to approach directly the feelings behind the defense. A third
round of work was required to highlight these distinctions and prepare
the way for a direct experience of her mixed feelings toward others. We
proceeded to examine her feelings and reactions to Drs. who gave her
the cancer diagnosis.

Triangle of Conflict in a Current Relationship

PATIENT: It took two weeks to get an appointment with the OB-GYN.
Halfway through the exam, my doctor, a female, was called out on an
emergency C-section. They asked if I wanted to reschedule or have another doctor finish the exam. I didn't want to wait, so I said, "Send in
another doctor." In came this Oriental male who, without introduc-
ing himself, just said, "Lie down, I'm going to do a pelvic." I thought
to myself, "I'm here for a breast exam but he must just want to do a
Pap smear." So I lay down, but by the time he was through, I felt as if
I had been raped (patient is tearful). I was already really angry with
him, and then I started crying right there on the table. Then he asked
if the Nurse Midwife could come in and have a look. I thought, "Why
should she come in? Oh, maybe it's just a lactating cyst." So I said it
was OK. Then he said to her, without ever speaking to me, "You

wanted to feel a tumor, right?" She was so patronizing! She said, "Did you find this yourself? Aren't you good to do your self-exam and aren't you brave to come to the doctor." I really felt like smacking her! I just wanted to punch her out, so I started crying.

There are several important points to be noted in regard to this last segment of the transcript. The patient is describing an incident in which she was, in fact, treated very poorly. While this must be acknowledged, the therapist should guard against getting caught up in personal feelings about such incidents and stay focused on the task, which is to point out the operation of regressive defenses against feelings that interfere with the patient's optimal functioning. This can be a tricky task. When patients are highly identified with the victim role, they are likely to respond defensively to any attempt at exploring their own role in their victimization. Tact and precision are absolute requirements to achieve this end. The following interventions will illustrate the therapist's attempt to direct the patient's attention toward an examination of the self-defeating nature of her characteristic defenses against anger.

THERAPIST: Just like now. You cry, but what was the feeling inside? Already you have waited a long time for the appointment. Then your doctor is called out. You're quick to be understanding, she has an emergency, OK, but it doesn't mean you don't have feelings about it. Then this man comes in who treats you in a highly impersonal, even cold, manner. What was your feeling toward him?

PATIENT: Why couldn't he . . .

THERAPIST: That's a question. Your feeling?

PATIENT: Helpless.

THERAPIST: That's a position you take but the feeling?

PATIENT: Angry.

THERAPIST: You were angry. You don't like to be treated this way, so how did you deal with that?

PATIENT: It was quiet resentment.

THERAPIST: You kept it inside, stayed quiet, and behaved in a compliant manner. This is for you to look at. Somehow you allow this, like you did for the first 25 years of your marriage. You were the good girl—quiet and subservient—but all the anger and resentment were building until you explode.

PATIENT: I don't think I was even in touch with those feelings. It all happened so fast.

THERAPIST: And that's the problem. It's not the interaction that happened so fast but these automatic mechanisms you employ to stuff your feelings. Because you do not allow yourself to know what you're feeling and to use that information in your own behalf, you make yourself vulnerable to mistreatment. Do you see what I mean?

PATIENT: Yes, but in general, I'm not passive.

THERAPIST: I don't know about in general, but in this situation.

PATIENT: It's with anger.

THERAPIST: And what's the purpose of anger? It has a self-protective function. If you don't have access to it you can't protect yourself. (Patient nods.) So you can see, with the doctor, that you were angry but went to tears and took a victimized stance. Then you look foolish and no one pays attention to your outburst. Pretty self-defeating.

PATIENT: I agree with that. It is a way I defeat myself. Still, I don't like to hear it.

THERAPIST: So this is what you want help with? (Patient nods.) The problem is clear then, but you don't like to look at it. You must have a certain feeling toward me, as I point it out to you.

Graded Pressure and Challenge

As defenses are identified, clarified, and rendered dystonic, graduated pressure is placed on patients to experience their feelings directly. The initial aim is to increase insight into the mechanism by which patients turn feelings and impulses into anxiety, depression, or symptomatic disturbances. This woman turns her anger into tears and takes a helpless stance in the face of her violent rage ("I just wanted to punch her out, so I started crying").

As soon as patients indicate a clear cognitive understanding of the link between the repressed impulse and the symptom being targeted, the focus shifts to the experience of the feeling itself. Patients are encouraged to face their feeling without resorting to defense and to compare this new experience with that which they had previously mistaken for the feeling.

This step-by-step approach is more horizontal than vertical. The process moves from example to example in the patient's current life orbit and then expands to include the therapist. There is no attempt to break through to the unconscious and expose the genetic links at this juncture, as there would be in the standard technique. Each small breakthrough of feeling into conscious awareness is highlighted and compared with past examples. This process is one of consolidation in which these distinctions become increasingly clear to the patient. The therapist continually looks for direct evidence that the patient can now experience anxiety-provoking affects without resorting to regressive defenses.

Similarities to Systematic Desensitization

This carefully graded approach to the experience of affects that have been avoided in the past is quite similar to the kind of graded exposure used in the process of systematic desensitization. The difference lies in the stimuli that are being targeted. In behavioral treatment, feared external stimuli are gradually approached. Here, the focus is on the gradual exposure to the internal experience of feeling. Such exposure is designed to reduce the anxiety that's been associated with these affects, thus reducing the tendency to automatically avoid or defend against them. Once the feared stimulus, in this case the experience of angry feelings or impulses, is approached and experienced without the feared consequences coming to pass, the patient's perceptions change. In fact, the direct experience of feelings that had previously been avoided constitutes an experience of mastery. This is typically followed by a deep sense of relief, a new understanding of oneself, and a feeling of closeness with the therapist, all of which are profoundly reinforcing.

Goals of Restructuring

To summarize, the goals of restructuring include:

1. Undoing the regressive defense.
2. Re-directing the pathway of impulse and feeling into consciousness.
3. Building the ego so that these feelings and impulses can be experienced directly.

To achieve this, a phase of cognitive re-analysis of the process must precede the breakthrough of feeling. This incremental process begins with a low level of intensity that is steadily increased until the patient indicates a tolerance for the direct experience of affect. Each round of work is followed by systematic re-analysis, leading to consolidation of insight within the session. Ultimately, direct experience of the complex transference feelings is achieved.

To return to the present clinical example, this repetitive work on the triangle of conflict in the current situation with the Gynecologist was required to consolidate the insights already obtained. This phase of the work was persued until the patient provided clear evidence that she understood the link between repressed impulses and symptoms and indicated a desire to give up these defenses. The statement that she now sees her defenses as self-defeating was followed by several other examples which indicated real insight on the patient's part and not mere compliance. She also signaled the therapist that she was ready to approach the feelings being evoked in the transference by saying that she "doesn't like to hear it."

Triangle of Conflict in the Transference

THERAPIST: What is your feeling toward me, as I point this out to you?

PATIENT: I know the answer should be "I don't like you" but . . .

THERAPIST: "I don't like you" isn't a feeling.

PATIENT: Anger. I guess I feel annoyed.

THERAPIST: How do you feel that inside?

PATIENT: Kind of a tightening—wanting to rip tissues.

THERAPIST: There's a mix of anger and anxiety. You want to discharge it by ripping the tissue, but the feeling is toward me.

PATIENT: Right.

THERAPIST: What's going to happen if we skip over this?

PATIENT: I'll stuff the feelings, I won't trust you, I'll cry a lot and be manipulative.

THERAPIST: So what effect would that have?

PATIENT: But people don't like the anger.

THERAPIST: You have a terrific problem with your anger and you come to me for help with that. Don't you want to see if I'm capable of helping you with it?

PATIENT: I don't think we should avoid it, but it won't be easy.

THERAPIST: Who said it would be easy? How do you feel this anger toward me, if you don't look away?

PATIENT: Feels like a growing pressure pushing up (motions with her hands).

THERAPIST: And if that came out toward me, in your mind, what would that be like?

PATIENT: It would be ugly and show all this bad stuff I have inside.

THERAPIST: What do you feel like doing?

PATIENT: Be sarcastic, imitate you, be prissy, just be mean.

THERAPIST: To be mean is to put it into behavior. How would you declare this anger?

PATIENT: (voice raised) Stop pigeon-holing me.

THERAPIST: You're pleading. That isn't declaring your anger toward me. Do you see that your arms and legs are going?

PATIENT: A lot of power.

THERAPIST: What's the impulse in your hands?

PATIENT: It's growing. Like strangulation, if I let it go. Get off your high horse, leave me alone, let me be. You don't know me. (The patient is deeply involved in the emotion and is motorically activated, making strangling motions as she speaks.)

THERAPIST: With this anger is an impulse to strangle me and shut me up. What happens to me?

PATIENT: You'd go "Ahhhhhh" and faint.

THERAPIST: Faint?

PATIENT: Or pass out and then I'd get scared and try to revive you. I'm getting dizzy; it's like it's happening to me.

Techniques to Lower Anxiety

Every attempt is made to engage patients in the process of treatment at their highest level of ability. If no anxiety is being experienced, there will be no therapeutic movement. On the other hand, if the anxiety getting aroused by a focus on affect becomes too high, patients cannot function to their highest level of ability. In fact, if patients become overwhelmed by anxiety, they may resort to highly regressive defenses such as projection, which will have a corrosive effect on the treatment process. Therefore, it is essential to be familiar with fairly simple and direct techniques to rapidly reduce anxiety and prevent the mobilization of regressive defenses.

There are three direct methods for lowering anxiety: (a) switch the focus to an exploration of the physiological manifestations of anxiety; (b) return to phenomenological inquiry; or (c) switch focus on the triangle of person; for example, from the transference to a figure in the patient's current life. Once the patient's anxiety has been lowered to a tolerable degree, a cognitive re-analysis of what has occurred is necessary before returning to the feeling in question.

This is a crucial point in the therapeutic interaction. The patient in our example was beginning to experience directly the intense rage she had always avoided. When the impulse to strangle the therapist began to break through the repressive barrier, there was a sudden and intense spike in anxiety with an instantaneous internalization of the impulse. This had to be analyzed immediately in order to interrupt the defense and consolidate the insight into the link between the repressed impulse and the symptoms. In this case, the link between the repressed impulse and the symptom was very specific; she did to herself what she wanted to do to me. Once this crucial insight had been achieved, it was essential to return to the moment of the surge in anxiety to see clearly what was previously too frightening to comprehend.

T-P Link

THERAPIST: Exactly. This is it, right here. You do to yourself what you want to do to me. (Patient nods.) You barely let yourself experience this impulse to strangle me before you internalize it, and then you're the one who is dizzy.

PATIENT: And I feel all choked up (puts her hands to her throat).

THERAPIST: What happened is, you've been working really hard and you begin to let yourself free to experience this anger toward me. You got further than you've probably ever gotten before (patient says "yes") and got to the point of getting in touch with an impulse to strangle me, but there's something about that which is so threatening, so terrifying, that you get flooded with anxiety. In an instant, that impulse is redirected from me to you—you get dizzy and choked up. It makes me wonder what happened at that moment when you got in touch with the impulse. I wonder if someone else came to your mind?

PATIENT: Yeah, my mother.

Several rounds of work on the triangle of conflict in a number of current relationships have resulted in an increase in the patient's capacity to face her true feelings without resorting to regressive weepiness and helplessness. This done, feelings in the transference were approached. There was a sudden surge of anxiety as the repressed impulse came into consciousness. After lowering the patient's anxiety to a tolerable level, cognitive re-analysis of the process solidified the insight into the link between the repressed impulse and the self-attack. Following the breakthrough of sadistic rage toward the therapist, a direct link was made with the generic figure she had come to represent. Then, feelings of guilt, grief, and longing emerged.

De-Repression of Feelings and Memories from the Past

PATIENT: Yes, my mother (starts to cry), when she was younger and prettier. She choked me and I felt helpless. Anytime I'd express anger . . .

THERAPIST: Do you have a memory?

PATIENT: Being enraged and wanting to choke her when she was choking me.

THERAPIST: This actually happened?

PATIENT: I was 12 and she was 36 and pretty but she was livid, enraged, with hate-filled eyes, like she wanted to kill me. And I wanted to kill her but I couldn't raise a hand—Father was outside the door. She had me by the throat and was knocking my head against the tiles.

THERAPIST: She did literally?

PATIENT: Yeah, and calling me names and saying I was bad, ruining her life and driving her crazy.

THERAPIST: So your mother would completely lose control.

PATIENT: Usually she would tell my father and he would take out his belt, but sometimes she would be physically abusive herself.

THERAPIST: Here's a situation where she's out of control. You are feeling both terrified and enraged. If that rage came out?

PATIENT: I'd be punished, get it four-fold.

THERAPIST: But even now, you punish yourself. The feeling is toward her. Can we look at that or are you dizzy?

PATIENT: No, I'm OK.

THERAPIST: In your mind, if you had taken over?

PATIENT: I would have smashed her against the medicine cabinet window and watch her bleed.

THERAPIST: Her head smashes on the glass?

PATIENT: Glass shatters, her head bleeds.

THERAPIST: That kills her?

PATIENT: No, it wouldn't. I'd take a piece of glass and drive it into her heart (makes stabbing motion).

THERAPIST: In her heart?

PATIENT: Make her bleed. In a pool of blood on the floor.

THERAPIST: What do you feel toward her when you see her dead on the floor?

PATIENT: OK—still feel hatred and some relief.

The patient has been able to directly experience rage toward her mother but is avoiding feelings of guilt and grief. All the complex, mixed feelings must be directly experienced, or defense and symptoms will return. The therapist must be persistent in order to achieve this goal. Here, it was accomplished by returning to the scene and intensifying emotional involvement by looking closely at her mother's face (use of visualization).

THERAPIST: Initially relief. What does her face look like?

PATIENT: It's soft, soft and blank, her eyes are rolled up, she's powerless (becomes teary).

THERAPIST: It looks like there's feeling there.

PATIENT: All the anger had gone out of her, drained. Then I'd want her back some other way (deep sobbing). . . . See, being brutalized by my mother, it didn't start that way. I loved her so much when I was little. She was gorgeous and had a beautiful voice. She would sing me lullabies and read me stories. I want her back that way—soft and cuddly and warm.

THERAPIST: So beneath the anger toward her, there is tremendous grief about the loss of closeness with her. There's also tremendous love for her.

PATIENT: Yes, I thought she must be good and I was bad.

THERAPIST: How did this happen?

PATIENT: My sister was born when I was 3½.

The origins of the patient's core conflict were revealed following the experience of complex, mixed feelings toward her mother. The patient's mother was not always an angry, hostile person, as the patient had initially described her. It was only once she got in touch with the rageful feelings and murderous impulses toward her mother, that the underlying pain and grief about love lost could be experienced. Now an accurate developmental history could be obtained.

The restructuring in this case was largely completed within the 3-hour initial evaluation. Because we were able to achieve a breakthrough of feeling in the transference, with an outpouring of memories from the past, the core neurotic structure was readily exposed. This patient proved highly responsive to these interventions and left the evaluation tired but relieved and hopeful. Treatment was completed in two 12-session blocks. The first segment of treatment focused on the current crisis. After a 6-month break, the patient came back to therapy to work on the relationships with her parents and children. Of significance, she became re-involved with her parents and was both surprised and delighted by their responses to the changes in her.

RESTRUCTURING WITH PATIENTS SUFFERING FROM FUNCTIONAL DISORDERS

As in the case of depressives, patients who suffer from functional disorders display a marked inability to distinguish between the three corners of the triangle of conflict. Physical symptoms function as a defense against the awareness and experiences of anxiety-laden feelings. There is frequently a direct, one-to-one correspondence between the repressed sadistic impulse and the particular symptom the patient experiences. As such, the symptom contains both expressive and defensive elements. The symptom expresses the impulse but disguises the aim through displacement. In addition, suffering oneself what was wished on another serves as a punishment for the disguised act of sadism. Great economy is involved in such symptom formation.

CLINICAL EXAMPLE

The Woman with Headaches

This single woman in her mid-30s entered treatment because she was unable to decide whether to marry her current beau. Inquiry revealed a history of anxiety, depression, and headaches going back to childhood. The patient's mother was seriously ill throughout her childhood, was frequently hospitalized, and almost died on several occasions. Her father was a brutal man who beat both his wife and children. The patient and her older brother seemed to bear the brunt of her father's uncontrollable rage.

Course of Treatment

The patient presented a whole host of intellectualizing defenses. Isolation of affect was especially prominent. She was intelligent and insightful, but almost completely shut down on an emotional level, which contributed significantly to the difficulties with her boyfriend. Because this woman instantly internalized any experience of anger, becoming depressed or sick with headaches, restructuring was required. In the following session, the patient came in complaining of a headache that, as she described it, "is killing me."

Exploration of the Symptom and Its Trigger

PATIENT: I don't know what to talk about today. It's been a non-week. I've had a headache all week which is killing me right now.

THERAPIST: You mentioned the last time that you haven't had headaches for some time now (since therapy had begun, some two months earlier).

PATIENT: But this one has been for 2 weeks now. I'm not sure why.

THERAPIST: Could you describe what it feels like?

PATIENT: Behind my eyes. I've been diagnosed with ocular migraines, although the Neurologist couldn't confirm that. There's throbbing from my eyes to temples, a pounding that even wakes me up at night. It can even hit my stomach with vomiting (the patient is squinting and appears to be in considerable pain).

THERAPIST: When did it start?

PATIENT: I've had headaches since I was a child.

THERAPIST: But this particular one?

PATIENT: About 2 weeks.

THERAPIST: What was going on then?

PATIENT: I went home to visit, and I had it when I came back.

THERAPIST: So you got it when you were down there, visiting your family?

PATIENT: I didn't really want to go. I was there to see my mother but I was really angry with my father. He was tense. I was too. I had to run around and visit all the relatives (sighs). I couldn't relax. And my big brother, at dinnertime (smiles)—I could just smack their heads together. I think I've told you how my mother turns on the radio at dinner so she doesn't have to listen to silence. Then my brother or father starts to complain about it. I turned it off. There was tremendous tension. My father is glaring at my brother with complete hatred because he's eating too much and my father resents him living at home.

THERAPIST: You're telling me this story, but you seem very emotionally detached. What was it like for you sitting at the table?

PATIENT: I was angry (I/F), I get tense (A). It's like an automatic response when I go back there—angry and tense.

Inquiry into the Situation Surrounding the Symptom

The patient entered the session complaining about a painful symptom. Exploration of the conditions preceding the flare-up of the symptom provided clear clues regarding the underlying impulses. The patient recalled going to her childhood home for a recent visit and readily acknowledged feeling angry with her father. However, there was no indication that she was actually in touch with the experience of the anger. The last response in the previous vignette suggests a lack of differentiation between the experience of anger and that of anxiety. The patient described increasing tension as her anger mounted, which culminated in a massive tension headache. This lack of differentiation within the triangle of conflict required clarification.

THERAPIST: So there's a tremendous anger and then tension. Do you think the tension is from trying to keep the anger in check?

PATIENT: Yeah, because I just want to flail my arms and send the plates flying.

The distinction between the anger and the tension, with an emphasis on how the tension is designed to rein in the anger, had the effect of loosening its grip and the patient became animated and involved in the process. Her voice, which had been very soft and slow up until this point, became suffused with energy. However, there was still evidence of defensive displacement, as the patient talked about wanting to throw plates, when she had already declared she wanted to smash heads.

THERAPIST: But you had said, "Smash their heads together." Whose?

PATIENT: My brother—he's manipulative—and my father. My father hates him but I blame my father.

THERAPIST: So let's look at it, what's the impulse as you sat at the table, viewing all this?

PATIENT: I want to push the table away and them away. I feel trapped by the table.

Linking the Symptoms with Repressed Feelings

It is essential that all three components of affective experience (cognitive, physiological, and motoric) be clearly in evidence before proceeding to pressure and challenge. At the start of the session, the patient was able to cognitively label her feeling toward her father, (anger) but she was completely detached from the physiological and motoric aspects of the feeling. These elements were instantly internalized, with a headache and depression as the end product. As she began to get in touch with the physiological experience of anger and the aggressive impulses they mobilized, she started to lose the cognitive focus—in that the anger was getting displaced from her father onto inanimate objects. She was clearer about *what* she felt and *how* she felt it but lost sight of *who* she felt this rage toward. All three elements needed to be present simultaneously for the patient to be considered in touch with the experience of her feelings. In addition, evidence of all three elements of feeling is a prerequisitive to moving onto the phase of increased pressure and challenge.

Internalization is really just one aspect of displacement in which the rage toward another is displaced onto the self. Given depressives' reliance on the defense of displacement, it is not unusual to find that they also have episodes of explosive temper tantrums in which they displace rage from the actual target to an inanimate object or less threatening figure. All elements of displacement must be removed so that the patient can have a full and direct experience of their rage.

THERAPIST: So you want to push the table away and then?

PATIENT: My father is glaring at my brother. His table manners are horrible and he eats like a baby, but so what? Big deal. My father is glaring at him . . .

THERAPIST: And the feeling inside you?

PATIENT: Hatred toward my father and disgust with my brother.

THERAPIST: How do you feel that inside?

PATIENT: With my father, it's just this cold . . . I'm so disgusted I just want to push him and smack him.

THERAPIST: But you go cold?

PATIENT: It feels like a cold hatred. If icicles could come out of my eyes and pierce, I would give it to him that way.

THERAPIST: How?

PATIENT: I would send daggers out to pierce him, make puncture wounds.

THERAPIST: Where?

PATIENT: I don't know, now my eyes hurt (patient hangs her head and rubs her eyes).

Reemergence of the Symptom

Throughout the process of restructuring, the therapist must vigilantly monitor for any signs of undue anxiety or an increase in symptoms will result. In the previous sequence, the use of the word "cold" to describe her intense hatred toward her father, and the slow quiet manner in which she was relating to me, suggested that she was detached from the actual experience of anger. The crucial question here is, where does that go? The clinical material suggests that it flows into the well-worn path of internalization, which causes an exacerbation of symptoms. In this case, the flare-up in eye pain was both good news and bad news. The reemergence of the symptom at that moment suggested that the impulse had intensified and was threatening to break through into consciousness. That was the good news. The upsurge of feeling was experienced as dangerous, so the defenses, which were driving the symptoms, came marching back with a vengeance. Left unchecked, that would certainly be the bad news. The mechanism of internalization had to be undone to prevent any further exacerbation in symptoms. Reducing the patient's reliance on this defense would also increase the functioning of the ego so that she would be able to tolerate the direct experience of rage. To accomplish this, insight into the link between the repressed impulse (to pierce and wound her father) and her symptoms (piercing pain in her eyes) had to be reinforced.

THERAPIST: See, isn't that what happens? Do you see this connection? Inside, there is this terrific rage toward your father with an impulse to pierce him and wound him, but you keep it inside and you get it—you suffer the very thing you wished on him—the piercing in your eyes.

There is a one-to-one connection. You want to smash their heads, but you get the headache. You want to pierce and puncture him, but you get the stabbing pain in your eyes.

PATIENT: I didn't even think of that.

THERAPIST: Do you see it now?

PATIENT: Yeah. We're talking about heads and eyes and that's what's hurting.

THERAPIST: So you end up experiencing the pain you wanted him to feel.

PATIENT: But I don't know why.

The patient's attention, curiosity, and desire to understand herself were evident. She was making direct eye contact with the therapist, and the alliance felt strong. Rather than respond directly to her query about why she would internalize this pain or make an interpretation about it, I continued to explore with her what would happen if she directly expressed the impulse. The information to emerge would allow the patient to answer her own question.

THERAPIST: Let's look at what you imagine would happen if it came out toward *him*.

PATIENT: I'd smash him. I'd go for my father, smash him in the face.

THERAPIST: Do you feel the anger inside or are you still cold?

PATIENT: Inside, I feel my muscles tense. This is funny, this always happens, I go cold.

THERAPIST: At one time, it was all you could do; you were a child.

PATIENT: I was trying to survive.

THERAPIST: But now, shutting down and going cold doesn't help you survive, it leads to suffering. Now the enemy is inside. You keep yourself trapped in the suffering.

PATIENT: I keep trying to picture it, but it doesn't go anywhere.

THERAPIST: The feelings drive the picture, and you don't let yourself feel it. This has been inside you for 35 years. As much as it costs you, you're terrified to experience this rage.

Cost-Benefit Analysis of the Defense of Internalization

The preceding interventions were aimed at turning the patient's ego against these highly syntonic character defenses. It was acknowledged that these defenses may have helped her at one time but are presently outmoded and self-destructive. Focusing on the cost of the defenses will help turn her against them.

PATIENT: To really face it, I'd have to let it go. Maybe I could if I felt better.

THERAPIST: But the two are intimately connected. Only by feeling it emotionally will the symptoms be relieved, because you turn an emotional pain into a physical one.

PATIENT: I used to scream at the top of my lungs. Last week, I beat up the car because I was so angry. It was a rage.

Again, there is evidence of both an increase in the patient's ability to get in touch with the experience of her rage (as evidenced by a rise in her voice, sitting up in her chair, and an angry look in her face) and of displacement from her father onto the car. Now that the feelings and impulses are mobilized, the therapist will try again to see whether the defenses can be removed so the patient can experience the anger toward her father in a direct way.

THERAPIST: The rage was toward your father?

PATIENT: Yes. I wanted to kill him, wanted to kill him.

THERAPIST: Now you feel it *and* can imagine it? It was *him* you wanted to beat and kill?

PATIENT: Yes. I want to face the rage toward him, but there's a loop inside my head and it keeps derailing and I run in a circle. I can almost see it in my head, getting away.

The cyclical process involved in restructuring is quite evident in this transcript. We were making incremental steps toward the full experience of the warded-off feelings and impulses. The loop was getting progressively smaller and the diversions fewer and fewer as we progressed in the hour.

THERAPIST: What would happen if you let out toward him all that rage that came out toward the car?

PATIENT: I would lose. He's stronger than me. When I was 14, I started to fight back but he would overpower me, then lock me in the bathroom. If my mother was around, I felt I had to protect her because if she tried to intervene, he would go after her. As a child, it was unbearable. I would rather be beat up, otherwise I would feel it was my fault, that I caused her to get hurt.

Although the emergence of this new material certainly shed light on the very real predicament she had faced as a child, at that moment in the session it served as a diversion from the anxiety she was feeling about facing her own rage now. Rather than getting caught up in a discussion about the past, focus was maintained on the current feeling welling up in her and the defenses against it.

THERAPIST: So you wouldn't just want to provoke him. You said you'd kill him.

PATIENT: What entered my mind was a knife. I can't watch movies with knives, anything entering people.

THERAPIST: Like the daggers.

PATIENT: I never thought of that, but yeah. I'm seeing it in the kitchen again, there are knives in the kitchen. I could plunge it into him, in his chest, over and over, in a frenzy, with lots of strength. It would even get stuck sometimes (making stabbing motions), it's that deep. It's my Tazmanian devil, I'd go berserk. Then he can't fight back. He's on the floor, white as a ghost, blood all over. I'm sweaty, that's how much energy, like running 30 miles. I can see him on the floor, all bloody, but I don't care. I almost want to see him get up again so I could do it again.

THERAPIST: You don't want him to die so soon.

PATIENT: Yeah, I want to torture him.

THERAPIST: Let him see what it was like.

PATIENT: Well, he knows because his father tried to kill him a few times. He was an alcoholic. He set the house on fire once with all the little kids inside. He tried to throw him out an apartment window when he was 18 and had joined the service. My father won't talk about it, but once I said to him, "You're doing what Grandpa did to you."

Davanloo (personal communication, August 1990) has suggested that there is a direct relationship between the severity of the suffering involved in the symptom and the severity of the sadistic impulse being repressed. In this case, the sadistic rage the patient has felt toward her father was enormous and was a direct response to his brutal attacks on the patient herself, her siblings, and her mother. Killing him didn't seem like enough. Very often, in cases where patients have been severely abused, their reactive rage takes on the form of an impulse to torture. There is often a desire to respond in kind with the same mal-treatment they suffered.

In this case, when the impulses came into consciousness, a deep feeling of sadness over all the damage done emerged. Although there was relief in facing the reactive sadism, there was no satisfaction in it. In fact, the patient began to experience some empathy for her father's pain. This empathy should not be confused with forgiveness. The patient still has a great deal of anger toward her father for the very real pain and damage he inflicted. However, these feelings were now conscious and integrated with feelings of sadness. After these conflicted feelings were summarized, the therapist inquired about the patient's headache. She smiled and said, "Isn't that funny—it's gone away." The fact that a headache which had persisted for two weeks and proved intractable to medication should lift within the hour that her repressed feelings of rage toward her father were faced directly, seems to provide compelling evidence for the psychodynamic factors implicated in symptom formation.

SUMMARY

The process of restructuring in patients with regressive defenses, such as depression and somatic complaints, has been outlined and illustrated. Patients who rely on regressive defenses—including depression, panic disorder, and functional disorders—demonstrate a deep-seated inability to distinguish between feelings and the defenses against them. Consequently, a significant rise in feeling is accompanied by increases in regressive symptomatology. Therefore, any strategy designed to intensify affect would be clearly contraindicated. Davanloo has developed a method for restructuring defenses in these cases. This circular process builds the ego in order to increase the patient's tolerance for the direct experience of feelings and the unconscious material associated with these feelings. Patients must be able to link their symptoms to the feelings and impulses being repressed before any further uncovering can occur.

Detailed clinical examples were given to illustrate this important innovation, making ISTDP possible with patients who had previously been considered unsuitable for most forms of short-term dynamic psychotherapy. It should be noted, however, that in cases such as The Woman with Headaches, treatment often takes 40 sessions.

CHAPTER 5

Facilitating Grief

*It's a necessary condition of human
health to be able to bear what has
to be borne, to be able to think
what has to be thought.*
Semrad (1980)*

Patients come to us because they are suffering and want to get well. For patients to achieve health, they must experience the thoughts and feelings they have considered unbearable and unutterable. That which has been buried in the shadows must come to light. The process through which previously inaccessible feelings, memories, and ideas are de-repressed and made available for re-working will be the focus of the next two chapters.

This chapter describes how to facilitate the experience of grief-laden feelings through specific techniques designed to deepen affect. Chapter 6 will discuss techniques for working with positive and erotic feelings.

THE CENTRALITY OF AFFECT

Wachtel (1993) succinctly summarized the psychodynamic view of the cause and cure of neurotic suffering when he wrote:

> The patient's problems are understood as deriving most funda-
> mentally from his having learned early in life to be afraid of his

---

* Ranko, S., & Mazer, H. (1980, 1983). *Semrad: The heart of a therapist.* Northvale, NJ: Aronson.

feelings, thoughts and inclinations, and the effort to help him overcome his problems is focused very largely on helping him reappro-
priate those feelings and incorporating them into a fuller and richer
sense of self and of life's possibilities. (p. 32)

While most in the psychodynamic community would agree with this
statement, the methods for achieving this goal vary considerably from
therapist to therapist.

Davanloo (1990) takes an uncompromising stance on the central
importance of affect in intensifying and accelerating the process of dynamic psychotherapy. Emotion is the lifeblood of existence—the fuel of
all our endeavors. For those patients who repress their feelings, life becomes a sterile and mechanical exercise. In addition to the deadening of
inner life that accompanies extensive repression of emotion, repression
keeps patients blind to the source of their pain and prevents resolution
of the underlying problem. Therefore, Davanloo (1990) advocates tenacious work on the defensive (repressive) barrier to achieve a breakthrough of feelings into consciousness. Once the feelings penetrate the
repressive barrier, all the memories and traumas they are associated
with flow freely. This process provides the affectively charged material
required to make meaningful interpretations about the repetitive dynamics operating in the patient's current life, in the interactions with
the therapist, and in the past, with significant others.

THE PHENOMENON OF DE-REPRESSION

The outpouring of unconscious material from the past, following an emotionally charged reliving of recent events within a therapy session, has
been referred to as "de-repression" (an alternative to the phrase "undoing of repression" used by Freud in 1917). This process, also referred to
as "uncovering," seems to be facilitated by the patient's affectively
charged involvement in the therapeutic process. "Since in most instances,
anxiety is most strongly attached to a complex configuration of cues in
which verbal, affective, cognitive, and motoric elements are prominent,
verbalizing without the other cues being present is unlikely to have much
therapeutic value." (Wachtel, 1977, p. 94). Davanloo's technique of applying pressure to the defenses and challenging the patient to be affectively, cognitively, and motorically involved in the process seems to
effectively achieve this end.

There is some agreement in the psychodynamic community (Alexander & French, 1946; Ferenzi & Rank, 1925; Gill, 1982; Strupp & Binder, 1984) that the most rapid and accurate route to the core conflicts underlying patient's symptoms and complaints is achieved through a focused examination of the patient's *current* affective experience. This is contrasted with an approach that begins with a long and detailed past history, only understanding the patient's current difficulties within this historical framework. To acquire historical data early on in treatment, when anxiety and defenses are high, could lead to a highly distorted picture of past events. For this, and other reasons already outlined, clinicians like Davanloo have championed the view that it is essential to bring the patient's current experience, especially that with the therapist, into focus at the inception of treatment. Only those memories that surface as the current emotion is being experienced are deemed dynamically significant. This insight seems to get "discovered" and then forgotten repeatedly, as clinicians get caught up in a seemingly random search for memories about the past.

Ferenzi and Rank (1925) were the first clinical theorists to encourage an approach in which feelings and defenses currently in evidence are the focus of dynamic inquiry. Their work seemed to have little impact on mainstream psychoanalytic theory and practice at the time. Years later, Alexander and French (1946) expanded on this early work, re-emphasizing that a focus on contemporary experience, particularly in the transference, is the most powerful tool for achieving rapid therapeutic change. More recently, Strupp and Binder (1984) have concluded, "Current evidence of transference is primarily a beacon guiding the therapist toward interpretive reconstruction of childhood patterns of conflict." The treatment model being delineated here shares this view and endeavors to work in the present, only making links to the past as they emerge spontaneously from the contemporary experience of affect.

RESEARCH SUPPORT

In addition to the accumulating clinical evidence (Been & Sklar, 1985; Strupp & Binder, 1984) that the most rapid and effective route for obtaining access to the unconscious is through the direct experience of affect, empirical data on state-dependent learning also supports this hypothesis (Bower, 1981; Della Selva, 1991). State-dependent learning refers to the fact that subjects are most likely to retrieve a memory when in the same affective state as when the memory was encoded. Therefore, anything we can do to help patients experience their feelings as fully as possible should speed the process of memory retrieval. Once these memories become conscious, patients have a fresh opportunity to understand what has happened to them and how these recalled events have affected them throughout life.

INTEGRATING COGNITIVE AND AFFECTIVE MODES OF EXPERIENCE

As important as the free and unencumbered experience of affect is for the process of psychotherapy (as well as for life itself), this is not an end in and of itself. Rather, affective activation is an effective means for gaining rapid access to core conflicts. Once these conflicts come alive within the session, they can be dealt with directly. This provides a pathway for achieving deep cognitive understanding of emotionally felt experiences, a vital combination in facilitating rapid therapeutic change.

Those therapies based almost solely on the expression of affect (Janov, 1970) often ignore the vital role of defensive processes, irrational beliefs, and perceptual distortions of self and other that accompany these affects. Other, more cognitively based therapies, often give short shrift to affect. But even Aaron Beck (1976), the father of cognitive therapy, has acknowledged the vital role of affective involvement for successful outcome. Dealing with just one or the other—cognition or affect—is insufficient in most cases to achieve therapeutic success.

According to Strupp and Binder (1984), who have conducted years of research on the process of change in short-term dynamic psychotherapy, the key to therapeutic change is "conceived of as the affective experiencing and cognitive understanding of current maladaptive patterns of behavior that repeat childhood patterns of interpersonal conflict" (pp. 24–25). This is the essence of what Malan and Osimo (1992) have referred to as the T-C-P link. Their research, as well as that of others (Trujillo & McCullough, 1985) investigating the effectiveness of STDP, has generated data corroborating the hypothesis that successful outcome is highly correlated with the frequency of affectively meaningful T-C-P links.

There is a rather wide consensus in both the clinical and research literature that the most effective and efficient method for the facilitation of deep change is a two-pronged approach: (a) mobilize intense affect, and (b) examine the thoughts, memories, and beliefs associated with these feelings as they emerge through the affect-laden communications from patient to therapist. As affect is experienced and memories surface, the perceptual distortions of self and other that accompany them become available for re-working. Again, many forms of therapy seem to focus on one to the relative neglect of the other. A large part of the power and grace inherent in the systems of short-term dynamic psychotherapy developed by clinicians like Malan (1976, 1979), Malan and Osimo (1992) and Davanloo (1978, 1980, 1990) is derived from the ways in which the cognitive and affective spheres of experience are integrated and interwoven within each session.

TECHNIQUES FOR ACTIVATING AND DEEPENING AFFECT

There is accumulating clinical and empirical evidence that creating an emotionally charged atmosphere in the treatment setting is a rapid and reliable route for facilitating therapeutic movement. Short-term dynamic therapists have developed a whole host of tools and techniques for achieving this goal. These include (a) focusing on detail and specificity; (b) using imagery; (c) dealing with defense first to remove barriers that may block the activation and expression of affect; (d) acquainting the patient with the physical sensations accompanying affect; and (e) providing therapist empathy. Each of these techniques will be briefly described. Although all these techniques are useful at times, specificity on the therapist's part is equally important for successful outcome. For some patients, focus and specificity is sufficient to evoke affect. For others, defenses prevent this and therefore must be confronted. Finally, there are patients who are so out of touch with their feelings that they require an introduction to emotion which is roughly parallel to the process of acquainting patients with their defenses. In these cases, a focus on feelings and sensations in the patients' body is the place to begin.

Focusing on Detail and Specificity

The ISTDP therapist conducts a tightly focused interview in which patients are expected to be quite specific about the people and events being discussed. The therapist is actively involved in a dialogue with the patient from the outset and asks clarifying questions when indicated. Any vagueness is challenged. If the patient speaks in generalities, the therapist asks for recent and specific examples of the issue being discussed. This procedure facilitates recall and tends to increase affective involvement in the process, both considered necessary ingredients for intensifying and accelerating the therapeutic process. Recent research (Bucci, 1985; Geiselman, Fisher, MacKinnon, & Holland, 1985) strongly confirms the notion that memory retrieval is enhanced by a tight focus on specific and concrete details.

Using Imagery

One technique for enhancing and intensifying affect is the active use of imagery. This technique is equally useful for facilitating the recall of emotional significant memories and for the expression of previously repressed feelings. Davanloo refers to this technique as "portraiting." The patient is asked to "paint a picture" of the memory or impulse being discussed. This frequently includes (a) physical and temporal details, (b) the thoughts and feelings experienced by all the central characters in the memory or fantasy, and (c) the sequence of events. This technique provides an avenue for experiencing and re-living events in an emotionally meaningful way, without resorting to repression or acting on the feelings and impulses involved.

Encouraging patients to immerse themselves as fully as possible in their own experience provides an emotionally powerful tool for the reworking of traumatic situations from the past. In addition, a focus on the sights, sounds, smells, and sensations associated with a particular feeling seems to aid the integration of the experiencing and observing functions of the ego.

The case of the Woman on an Emotional Roller Coaster (see Chapter 4) is a good example of this process. It was the breakthrough of complex transference feelings, achieved through a portrait of the patient's hostile impulses toward the therapist, that ushered in the long repressed memories of these same mixed feelings toward the patient's mother. The memory of an especially traumatic incident, accompanied by all the terrifying feelings and impulses involved, came rushing to the fore in a clear and dramatic fashion as the patient was asked to portrait her angry impulse toward the therapist. This provided the patient with a new opportunity, as an adult, to deal directly with a situation that had been too overwhelming to deal with as a child. In addition, this revelation made clear what the central dynamic forces have been in her life. Then it became possible to work on the central conflict directly, at the source, eliminating the need to unconsciously recreate the situation with her husband, daughter, therapist, and friends. This method of rapid uncovering greatly reduces the likelihood of acting out and further repetition, and speeds the process of working through.

Dealing with Defense before Feeling

Rather than "fishing for feelings" in those patients who defend against the experience of affect, Davanloo advocates a focus on the defenses first. This preliminary work is designed to render the patient's defenses dystonic, to mobilize intense and complex mixed feelings toward the therapist, to facilitate the direct experience of these feelings and, in so doing, promote the development of a full partnership in the therapeutic process.

Anger is often the first layer of feeling to surface. It is important to emphasize that, in practice, dealing with defenses against anger is rarely sufficient to expose the complex system of mixed feelings toward significant others. On occasion, the experience of previously repressed rage leads quite directly to the pain, grief, and longings for closeness that lie beneath it. More frequently, the therapist encounters defenses against the experience of guilt, grief, and longing as well. In fact, defenses against the painful affects involved in mourning and the bittersweet nature of tenderness and joy can be quite tenacious and must be dealt with directly. Patients often want to revert to anger as a way of avoiding these other feelings. It is essential that the therapist be able to follow the process and not get diverted by defensive anger at such times.

Again, the goal of this intensive treatment is to enable patients to fully experience all their mixed feelings toward others by increasing their capacity to bear them without resorting to splitting or other regressive defenses. The question is how this is accomplished.

Acquainting Patients' with the Experience of Affect

For some patients, the previous techniques prove insufficient to activate affect. If the patient's detachment is the result of defense over a conflict, the techniques described tend to be successful at evoking strong feeling. What happens when there is a deficit in affective attunement and discrimination? When such patients say, "I don't know what I'm feeling," they may be making an accurate statement. As one patient said, "You keep asking me how I feel. How do I feel? I have no idea. I am not keeping anything from you, it's just that I have spent so much of my life ignoring and numbing myself to feeling that I don't know myself." In these cases, keeping pressure on defenses would be an error. Instead, the therapist should alert patients to subtle changes in their posture, tone of voice, and facial expression. In the case just described, the therapist noticed sadness in the patient's face as she talked about how little she feels. This was pointed out and was followed by an exploration of the bodily sensations that accompanied the dawning awareness of the emotion of grief. The patient noticed a slight heaviness in her chest. At the end of the session, the therapist suggested that she continue to notice her bodily sensations and use them as cues to what she was feeling. The patient found this very helpful. She began to "tune in" to her physical feelings and use them as information regarding the emotions involved.

Providing Therapist Empathy and Encouragement

Once the unconscious is accessible and communicating freely to the therapist, pressure and challenge to defenses are no longer required. In fact, such an approach would be contraindicated. Instead, maintenance of a focus on affect through gentle but firm encouragement, along with occasional interpretive links between past and present, will usually suffice to keep the work moving apace.

The techniques of pressure and challenge, so useful in the early stages of defense work when resistance in the transference is at its height, are not helpful once an alliance is in place and the unconscious is more freely available. At this stage, should defenses resurface, they can usually be brushed aside with relative ease, as the therapist has the unconscious therapeutic alliance to call on for assistance. For example, when resistance returned in the case of the Woman on an Emotional Roller Coaster, all that was needed to get her back on track was gentle encouragement ("You've been working really hard, let's not stop now") followed by a question about what else came to mind when the impulse to strangle the therapist came into consciousness.

THE UNCONSCIOUS THERAPEUTIC ALLIANCE

The breakthrough of feeling into consciousness seems to be the key in facilitating rapid de-repression. In addition to "unlocking the unconscious," this process solidifies what Davanloo (1986) has referred to as "the unconscious therapeutic alliance." The unconscious therapeutic alliance is just that—an alliance based on communication between the therapist and the patient's unconscious. This alliance comes into operation once the resistance is in abeyance. According to Davanloo, these forces exist in inverse proportion to one another. When resistance is high, the unconscious therapeutic alliance is low and vice versa.

This type of alliance should be distinguished from a conscious therapeutic alliance (Greenson, 1967), which depends on patients' intellectual curiosity about themselves, as well as conscious positive feelings toward the therapist. Since negative transference feelings block the development of a conscious therapeutic alliance, traditional psychoanalysis is impossible in such cases. This is not necessarily so with ISTDP. If a patient enters treatment with negative transference feelings, they become the first order of business. All the patient's feelings toward the therapist are dealt with in a direct and straightforward manner from the inception of treatment. The ways in which the patient attempts to avoid the full experience of these feelings are also addressed, until the resistance is broken through and a genuine therapeutic alliance based on the revelation of the unconscious determinants of the patient's feelings and behaviors is possible. Conducting a trial therapy is the only certain way to assess the patient's ability to establish an unconscious alliance with the therapist. This alliance is the strongest weapon we have against the return of resistance and, hence, lends speed and clarity to the process.

KEEPING THE THERAPEUTIC GOAL IN MIND

The goal of ISTDP, like all dynamically oriented treatment, is to gain access to the unconscious forces driving the patient's maladaptive behavior. Despite agreement on the goal, the therapeutic approach advocated here is quite the opposite of the traditional psychoanalytic method. The therapist is active in questioning patients and encouraging them to have an honest look at the painful and anxiety-provoking feelings they typically avoid. In fact, any avoidance is noted and challenged. According to ISTDP, the spontaneous offering of memories, dreams, and associations are a signal to the therapist that the unconscious is open and accessible. Interpretations about the meaning of symptoms and behaviors only occur after the feelings involved have been directly experienced and the memories that surface on the heels of them come to light. This eliminates the need for the therapist to guess what the possible meaning of a defense or symptom might be, as the emotional truth is clearly revealed through the process of affective activation and de-repression. Patients frequently make their own interpretations at this point.

GRIEF WORK

> I dreamed I was sad and sometimes cried. But through the tears and the melancholy, inspired by the music of the verse or the beauty of the evening, there always rose upwards, like the grasses of early spring, shoots of happy feeling. . . .
>
> *William Trevor (1991)**

Thus far, the importance of achieving a high level of affective activation and involvement for the speed and effectiveness of dynamic psychotherapy has been reviewed.

In the following section, specific techniques for working with grief, and the defenses against it, will be examined and illustrated. As was demonstrated earlier, patients enter treatment in a state of ambivalence. They want relief from suffering but dread facing the painful thoughts, feelings, and memories involved in the psychotherapeutic process. In ISTDP, the patient's defenses, which become a resistance in the treatment, are rapidly identified, clarified, and exhausted as the patient is encouraged to have an open and honest look at his or her emotional life. In many cases, the first emotion to surface is anger at the therapist for challenging and pressuring the patient to get actively involved and to face what has been vigorously avoided. In other cases, particularly those in which defenses against emotional closeness are prominent, grief over loss is the first emotion to surface. In most cases, the outpouring of grief is complex. There is grief for those who have been loved and lost, but there is also grief over the ensuing loss of freedom to re-attach. Patients become acutely sad over the lack of close relationships in their current life.

Many of the patients who seek psychotherapy, regardless of their initial presentation, complain of an inability to experience joy in their lives. As William Trevor (1991) suggests in the quoted verse from the novella *Two Lives,* warded-off grief is often found beneath this lassitude. Unless the acutely painful feelings of grief and mourning are directly experienced, no joy or happiness is possible. As therapists, our job largely revolves around helping patients face pain and grief and to render the experience tolerable, reducing their need to resort to pathological defenses against these affects.

To design a therapeutic intervention that will aid the grieving process when it has been distorted or derailed, we must understand the natural course of mourning.

* From *Two Lives* by William Trevor.

THE GRIEF PROCESS

Freud's Contribution

Freud was the first psychotherapist to discuss grief in clinical terms. In *Mourning and Melancholia* (Freud, 1917), he outlined four features characteristic of mourning the loss of a loved one: (a) a profoundly painful feeling of dejection; (b) an abrogation of interest in the outside world; (c) the loss of the capacity to love; and (d) inhibition of activity. The tasks involved in mourning include facing the harsh reality that the loved one is gone and then withdrawing "libidinal cathexis" from the deceased so that this emotional energy will be available for further attachments.

Freud has outlined the two areas of functioning—the cognitive and the affective—that must be addressed to complete the process of mourning. Exactly how to tackle these problems clinically was not addressed, however. What Freud did suggest was that the patient become conscious of every hope and memory "which bound the libido to the object" to achieve detachment from the deceased. Only then would the ego be free to attach again. It was assumed that a healthy individual should be able to complete the mourning process in a fairly rapid and complete fashion.

Subsequent theorists have suggested that these notions, based on drive theory and the hydraulic model, are out of keeping with the current evidence. For example, studies (Goin, Burgoyne, & Goin, 1979) of those who have successfully navigated the mourning process suggest that a strong attachment to the deceased is maintained over time. What distinguishes successful from pathological mourning is the nature of the attachment. In successful cases, attachment to the deceased is generally positive and provides a sense of unity and comfort. In cases where the bereaved do not fare as well, attachment to the deceased is typically hostile, highly ambivalent, or guilt ridden. Still, the effects of loss are devastating in any case. There remains a tendency to "underestimate how intensely distressing and disabling loss is and for how long the distress, and often the disablement, commonly lasts" (Bowlby, 1980, p. 8). Bereavement can literally be fatal, with widowers being at particularly high risk (Jacobs & Ostfeld, 1977; Parkes, Benjamin, & Fitzgerald, 1969). In this sense, the feeling that one can't go on without the beloved has some basis in fact.

Lindemann's Work

Dr. Lindemann's pioneering work on grief following the Coconut Grove fire that occurred in Boston in 1942 is widely heralded, yet his interest in adjustment to loss predated this event. In his work with patients suffering from ulcerative colitis, Lindemann (1945) discovered a clear link between the loss of a loved one and the onset of the disease. Of particular importance was the finding that patients suffering from ulcerative colitis were detached from their emotional reactions to the loss. In these cases, "Adequate mourning is replaced by an impaired mental state combined with a visceral disorder" (Lindemann, 1979, p. 45). In addition, "The course of the ulcerative colitis was strikingly benefited when this grief reaction was resolved by psychiatric technique" (Lindemann, 1979, p. 70). The patient's avoidance of the psychological suffering integral to the grieving process manifested itself in gastro-intestinal symptoms. As the patient was helped to face the grief directly, the need to avoid it through such somatic discharge lessened considerably.

Because of his work on the link between loss and physical illness, Dr. Lindemann was primed for the study of acute grief reactions after the Coconut Grove disaster. Hundreds were killed in a nightclub fire, leaving many more to confront the sudden and traumatic loss of their loved ones. For the first time, a major study was undertaken to examine the process of grief as it occurred. The findings from this report (Lindemann, 1944) indicated:

1. Acute grief is a definite syndrome with specific somatic and psychological symptomatology.
2. This syndrome can occur immediately after a loss, or be delayed, exaggerated, or apparently absent.
3. In place of the typical syndrome, a distorted picture may appear, such as ulcerative colitis or an exaggerated identification with the deceased.
4. With the application of appropriate techniques, these distortions of the mourning process can be transformed into normal grief so that the reactions can be resolved.

The Acute Grief Syndrome

Lindemann (1944) outlined five features he considered characteristic of an acute grief syndrome:

1. Somatic distress, including tightness in the throat, deep sighing, a heavy feeling in the chest and abdomen, and an overall feeling of muscular weakness.

2. A preoccupation with the image of the deceased.
3. Guilt.
4. Anger and hostility.
5. Restlessness.

What he found most compelling about mourning was not only the number and variety of symptoms involved, but the way they tended to conflict with each other. For example, the desire for reunion coexists with anger at the deceased. Anguished cries for help occur alongside rejection of any attempts at comfort. Helping someone grieve requires a great deal of skill as well as sensitivity to all the complex and conflicting emotional states involved.

Kübler-Ross's Findings

Elizabeth Kübler-Ross (1969) has been a pioneer in the study of death and dying. She has focused most of her attention on the experience of those facing their own death, rather than the bereaved they leave behind. Still, her work with dying patients has relevance to our understanding of the grief process. She has outlined five stages of the process: (a) denial; (b) anger; (c) bargaining; (d) depression; and (e) acceptance. She has found that those close to the dying patient go through very similar stages of adjustment. In addition to those stated, guilt is often prominent in the bereaved. For the dying, there is an end. For those who remain, grief is a long and difficult process, which frequently feels endless. According to Kübler-Ross, the greatest help for the bereaved is human contact—providing the support necessary to render the emotional turmoil bearable.

Her work with the families of dying patients supports the notion that it is the defenses against the experience and shared expression of the feelings around the impending loss that cause most of the difficulties in the end. "If they had been helped before the death of their partner to bridge the gulf between themselves and the dying one, half of the battle would have been won" (Kübler-Ross, 1969, p. 143).

Bowlby's Contribution

Bowlby (1980), who studied the effects of separation and loss, mostly in children, repeatedly focused on the "long duration of grief, on the difficulties of recovering from its effects, and on the adverse consequences for personality functioning that loss so often brings" (p. 8). He identified four phases in the mourning process: (1) numbing, (2) yearning and searching accompanied by periods of sobbing and angry outbursts, (3) despair and disorganization, and (4) reorganization.

Numbing.   C. S. Lewis (1961) described many of these experiences in his personal account of the grief he suffered following the loss of his beloved wife. He starts off by describing the numbing and restlessness characteristic of the early phases of grief. "No one ever told me that grief felt so like fear. I am not afraid, but the sensation is like being afraid. The same fluttering in the stomach, the same restlessness, the yawning. I keep on swallowing" (p. 1). Here he also describes the somatic distress so characteristic of grief. He then goes on to say, "At other times it feels like being mildly drunk, or concussed," which seems to describe that state of numbness so characteristic of the initial stage of grief.

Yearning and Searching.   Bowlby contends that yearning is a powerful and highly painful affective state in its own right and can't be reduced to guilt or fear of retribution, as classical psychoanalytic theory might hypothesize. Others (Shand, 1920) have focused on the survival value of yearning and searching during the early phases of mourning. Since the irretrievable loss of an attachment figure during childhood is such a statistically rare event (a parent can only die once, and in most cases, the "lost" figure returns following separation), feelings and behaviors that get mobilized during unwanted separations are the first to appear when a loss is confronted. The yearning and searching, so highly adaptive in prompting reunion following separation, only wane slowly as the reality of the loss is accepted. In addition, these feelings and behaviors tend to elicit strong caretaking responses in others during a time when the mourner is most in need of support. Kübler-Ross has emphasized the crucial role of social supports for the survival and adaptation of the bereaved. Because our highly technological society tends to isolate the dying from the living, people today are often ill prepared to deal with the reality of death.

Despair and Disorganization.   As the phase of yearning and searching subsides and the full impact of loss begins to be felt, despair and a state of disorganization set in. In this regard, Engel (1961) has pointed out that normal grief involves not only acute suffering but impairment in the person's ability to function for days, weeks, or even months. Left alone, those who mourn are at high risk for death themselves. An active and responsive support system that supplies basic care is crucial for the survival of the bereaved.

The Process of Reorganization. What is required for the process of grief to proceed to resolution? Many feel it is essential for the bereaved to endure the emotional upheaval involved:

> Only if he can tolerate the pining, the more or less conscious searching, the seemingly endless examination of how and why the loss occurred, and anger at anyone who might have been responsible, not sparing even the dead person, can he come gradually to recognize and accept that the loss is in truth permanent and that his life must be shaped anew. (Bowlby, 1970, p. 93)

Many in the field have emphasized what a long and grueling process this is and that we tend to underestimate the time mourning requires.

PATHOLOGICAL MOURNING

Lewis (1961) wrote, "Aren't these notes the senseless writhings of a man who won't accept the fact that there is nothing we can do with suffering except to suffer it? Who still thinks there is some device (if only he could find it) which will make pain not be pain" (p. 38). Most agree that the differences between normal and pathological grief are relative, based on degree and intensity of reaction. No clear line between normal and pathological can be drawn. Bowlby (1980) has suggested that pathological mourning is an exaggeration or distortion of normal behavior due to defensive efforts that have interrupted or distorted the normal course of mourning. Because defensive processes always accompany grief, it is not the defenses themselves that suggest a pathological course, but the "scope, intensity and tendency to persist" (Bowlby, 1970, p. 35) that derail the successful completion of the grief process.

Any mental process that minimizes or avoids the pain of grief can be considered a defense. All mourners resort to such strategies at times, but if these defensive attempts at excluding painful thoughts and feelings become rigid and fixed, the mourning process will be distorted, resulting in symptoms. The most important factors in differentiating normal from pathological grief are the flexibility within the defensive system and the individual's awareness of behaving in ways that temporarily avoid the pain of mourning. Flexibility and awareness are hallmarks of adaptability. Conversely, rigidity and a lack of awareness suggest pathology.

Frequently, the defenses adopted against the painful feelings of grief get encrusted and prevent future adaptation. Consequently, the patient seems to get stuck in one phase of mourning, say numbness (chronic detachment) or despair (chronic depression and hopelessness). Fixation at one phase of mourning prevents the patient from moving through the process required to achieve acceptance and resolution. When this occurs, the characteristic defenses against mourning take on a life of their own and come to resemble character pathology, as they effect all areas of the patient's functioning. This was the case with the Detached Observer (Chapter 3), who became immobilized in the phase of numbness and detachment. The patient's chronic avoidance of grief prevented him from becoming emotionally attached to anyone.

Davis (1988) has called pathological mourning "the great deceiver," as it rarely appears in a clear and direct form and is often disguised as an affective disorder, anxiety and panic, or a psychosomatic disturbance. Others have suggested that post-traumatic stress disorder may be a form of pathological mourning (Horowitz, 1979).

Susceptibility to Pathological Mourning

Most in the field (Bowlby, 1980; Lindemann, 1944) agree that the following three factors greatly influence susceptibility to pathological mourning:

1. Premorbid personality adjustment.
2. The nature of the relationship to the deceased.
3. The manner of death.

In other words, someone with a fragile or depleted ego will be more likely to succumb to a pathological course of mourning than someone with a strong, flexible ego. Disordered mourning is also more likely to occur in cases where lives have been "deeply intertwined" (Bowlby, 1980), or when the death is traumatic and/or untimely (Parkes, 1970, 1975). Any combination of these factors greatly increases the likelihood of a pathological outcome (Parkes, 1975).

Davanloo's Studies on Pathological Mourning

While a psychiatric resident in Boston, Davanloo studied with Dr. Lindemann and was profoundly influenced by his work on grief and mourning. He has continued to be very interested in the phenomenon of pathological mourning, and his own studies (Davanloo, 1988) have identified six factors that predispose individuals to a pathological course of mourning:

1. A highly ambivalent or hostile relationship with the deceased.
2. A sudden, unexpected death.
3. A feeling of responsibility for the death.
4. Witnessing a death by accident.
5. Low ego-adaptive capacity.
6. Ego depletion due to caretaking prior to death.

IMPLICATIONS FOR TREATMENT

Lindemann (1944) has suggested a tightly focused approach to grief work. The therapist guides patients to review their relationship with the deceased in detail, focusing on both positive and negative feelings and impulses. In so doing, patients are encouraged to face and accept, rather than avoid, the emotional pain of bereavement. In addition, patients need to become aware of the maladaptive defenses they have used to avoid the experience of grief. This is especially important in increasing patients' ego-adaptive capacity (i.e., to respond flexibly and realistically) and preparing them to endure future losses without resorting to pathological defenses. In the end, patients should be able to acknowledge all their mixed feelings for the deceased and have a new perspective from which to view their life and death.

Bowlby (1970) has found that "only to a non-judgmental companion who shows himself sympathetic and understanding are these latent responses likely to be expressed" (p. 239). Obviously, this need not be a therapist. Isadora Duncan lost both her children in a car crash. She had a friend who, rather than offering platitudes, encouraged her to talk about her children, review her memories, bring out pictures, and cry over the untimely loss (Moffat, 1986). In her autobiography Duncan (1927, 1955) wrote, ". . . for the first time since their death I felt I was not alone." Such experiences allow the intense grief and anger of mourning to be directly felt and shared and seem to prevent a lapse into despair.

Pathological mourning often presents itself in subtle and disguised forms. It can masquerade as anxiety, depression, psychosomatic illness, or character pathology. Because of the hidden nature of the problem, traditional analysis has had very little success in treating this disorder (Davis, 1988). Davanloo has suggested that the same defenses employed to ward off the pain involved in the grief process are also used in the therapeutic relationship to keep the therapist at an emotional distance. Davanloo's techniques of defense analysis and rapid identification of the transference pattern of behavior create psychic disequilibrium. This greatly increases the likelihood of transforming pathological mourning into acute grief (Davis, 1988).

In fact, much psychotherapy, even that not explicitly directed toward resolution of grief, is concerned with undoing the denied losses experienced throughout life. As the patient faces the impact of these losses, all the disavowed feelings of anger, despair, and longing can be directly experienced. A feeling of liberation from the past is frequently the result of this therapeutic work.

Stark (1994) believes that most of the resistance encountered in therapeutic work is the result of the patient's unwillingness to face grief. In her opinion, "the defended patient, the resistant patient, is someone who has not yet grieved . . . (p. 123). By activating mourning in the therapeutic setting, patients are given the opportunity to deal with the reality of painful losses and the effects these have had on their life. Through this process, patients abandon chronic detachment and regain the capacity to make emotional contact with others and to experience joy in living.

CLINICAL EXAMPLES

The Man in a Fog

In the following case, the patient arrived for treatment complaining that he was preoccupied and "in a fog." This 30-year-old married man reported a significant decrease in his ability to focus or concentrate at work. Consequently, his job performance was suffering. His gait and speech were slow, and his physical movements were stiff and restrictive. He struck me as being among the "walking wounded." Inquiry quickly revealed that the onset of these symptoms coincided with the death of his dog. He had decided to carry the dog into the vet's office and hold him while the lethal injection was administered. As this experience was explored, the patient reported that his first child, a son, had been still-born some 3 years earlier. This information was communicated in a detached and "matter-of-fact" tone.

Within the first 10 minutes of the initial interview, it became clear that the primary therapeutic task would involve focusing the patient's attention on the painful events involving the death of his son. The sudden, unexpected, and untimely nature of this death was a predisposing factor to a pathological outcome. Many studies have confirmed that the death of a child is among the most devastating losses anyone can face (Bowlby, 1980; Friedman, Chodoff, Mason, & Hamberg, 1963). In the case of a stillborn, the baby is often whisked away quickly, depriving the parents of the opportunity to face the reality of their loss (Peppers & Knoff, 1980). This also prevents the couple from sharing their grief. Marital and sexual difficulties frequently result (Raphael, 1983).

In this case, the patient's use of defensive detachment, used to avoid the experience of grief over his son, became a way to defend against emotional closeness with anyone. If the pathological course of mourning were not to be translated into acute grief, this detachment could harden into character pathology. Reviewing the painful events surrounding the baby's death while in an emotionally detached state would be of little therapeutic value. The first step of treatment involved the identification and clarification of all the patient's defenses against closeness with the therapist. He was then guided to focus on the consequences of maintaining such a stance.

The defenses of detachment were directly linked to his presenting complaint of being in a fog and unable to function. Linking these defenses with his presenting complaint increased his motivation to approach the painful memories and feelings he had previously avoided.

As the patient's ego began to turn against its defenses, the therapist was able to capitalize on the strengthened therapeutic alliance and guide the patient, gently but firmly, toward the most painful aspects of the loss. Imagery and visualization proved powerful tools in this process. Once the avoidant defenses were punctured and the sadness and grief begin to be felt, the therapist asked what picture came to the patient's mind. Now mind, body, and emotion were all activated and involved, contributing to a deep experience of grief.

Feelings of Sadness

THERAPIST: So now we see that you have never faced the feelings about your son.

PATIENT: I've had a hundred feelings but never faced them. The first feeling is sadness.

THERAPIST: You feel that now?

PATIENT: Yes, I feel a lot of sadness. Usually I wouldn't think about myself. I'd think about my wife.

THERAPIST: You have sadness too. What's the image that comes to your mind?

PATIENT: One that comes back most is seeing the baby in the blanket when it was all over. He definitely looked like me.

THERAPIST: Could you describe his face?

PATIENT: It's hard to describe a face. A baby is a baby.

THERAPIST: But you said he looked like you. You knew it wasn't just any baby, but yours.

PATIENT: I remember his eyes. His lips were all red, very red, like lipstick, almost purple. The color was definitely not right. I can remember (arms shaped as if holding the baby) feeling him and he was warm—after the delivery, you know. Then I felt like, maybe he's sleeping and he's going to wake up (tearful). I know it's stupid and doesn't make sense to feel that, but inside you want to believe it. I think that's natural. I remember his eyes being closed and wishing he would wake up.

THERAPIST: His lips tell you something is not right. The pain and grief are so intense you want not to believe it.

PATIENT: Everyone said he looked like me. That made it more real—that this was my child. This happened to me.

THERAPIST: What's the feeling inside now?

PATIENT: I want to keep the baby. I don't want to let him go. I want to keep him forever but I can't. I just feel that loss (cries). I think about the future—the things that will never be (more tears).

THERAPIST: The loss of all those hopes and dreams.

PATIENT: Feeling of wanting to hold on was so great—the hardest thing was to let go (makes grabbing motions with his hands and is crying).

This material is very sad, almost heartbreaking. I was gentle but persistent in my focus on the patient's painful feelings of grief. Painting the scene and returning to the delivery room were techniques used to heighten the patient's awareness of his own affect. The specificity and detail, especially of the baby's face, were especially important in bringing the experience to life in the here and now. It was so moving, in fact, that the therapist's eyes filled with tears. At that point, the patient seemed to physically recoil and he fell silent. He had previously mentioned an inability to cry at the time of his son's death, fearing that his grief would intensify that experienced by his wife. His hypersensitivity to the therapist's reaction suggested a link between the two (C and T) that was vital to expose and work through rapidly. The following excerpt will illustrate the shift in focus to the patient's experience of the therapist and her emotional reaction.

Feelings and Defense in the Transference

THERAPIST: It looks like you're having a reaction to my welling up with tears.

PATIENT: I wasn't thinking of anything. I'm just trying to get myself together.

THERAPIST: Why now? It seems to be a response to my emotion.

PATIENT: I guess if I were to share this with the average person, they'd tear up too.

THERAPIST: What comes to mind?

PATIENT: I guess I think I feel your sorrow, your reaction, and maybe it stops me from going on.

THERAPIST: Yes, I sensed that. You stop and pull back. It's as if my having a reaction frightens you.

PATIENT: It's like how my wife felt. I tried not to think about myself. I didn't want to lose it because then she would lose it.

THERAPIST: That fear, of the woman losing it, gets in the way of sharing the grief. You stay alone with it.

PATIENT: Yeah, I guess you're right—it's not necessarily desirable to keep it all inside (long pause). I feel cold. My whole body feels cold. I'm going back to the hospital (starts to cry).

This brief vignette is very important. While the affective shifts are not readily apparent in the transcript, on videotape there was a noticeable change in this man's demeanor when he saw the therapist's emotional reaction. He stopped crying, sat up in his chair, and said he was trying to get himself together. By examining this interchange, the patient gained insight into the parallel between his reaction with the therapist and that with his wife. As he evaluated the cost of this strategy (emotional detachment and interpersonal distance), his position shifted once again from avoidance and repression to connection and activation. He spontaneously returned to the scene in the hospital, signaling the therapist that he was ready to resume the work.

Resuming the Portrait

THERAPIST: We ended with the feeling that you didn't want to let go. You go cold, like the baby. Did you let him go or did they take him?

PATIENT: The doctor took him and I handed him over.

THERAPIST: But what you wanted to do?

PATIENT: Hold on.

THERAPIST: Can you put it in words?

PATIENT: I was so shocked I didn't have words.

THERAPIST: But now?

PATIENT: "You can't have him, he's mine." I hold him tighter (clutches his chest) and say, "Stay away, he's mine, you can't have him." I just want to hold onto him (more tears). I felt so helpless—I wanted to change the situation.

THERAPIST: What's it like to hold on? How does it feel to say no?

PATIENT: Maybe the more I hold on, the harder it will be to let go. The emotions get stronger and stronger. I wouldn't let anyone near him. Maybe I'd think crazy things like the baby is OK and it was all a mistake. I just couldn't believe it.

This communication suggests that the patient has learned to be afraid of intense emotion and equates it with going crazy. His feelings and reactions need to be normalized and put into context.

THERAPIST: Their coming in so quickly interfered with the process—for it to become a reality to you.

PATIENT: But my poor wife—to have to physically go through that—giving birth. I guess I was really concentrating on her (very tearful). I was devastated. She was even more. I wish I could spare her that pain.

DISPELLING PATHOLOGICAL BELIEFS

To aid the process of working through, we must deal with the pathological beliefs that accompany the affect-laden experiences our patients have had. Stern (1985) has hypothesized the operation of an innate drive in humans to form and test beliefs about their interpersonal world. Research findings suggest that infants regulate their behavior according to these beliefs about reality. It is the babies' interpersonal reality, their interaction with primary attachment figures, that supplies this vital information. Because infants are totally dependent, they must adapt to parental demands and expectations or their very survival will be threatened. As Wachtel (1993) has put it, a child will "trim his sails to meet the prevailing winds."

These ideas have been confirmed by Emde (1989) and Weiss (1993), both of whom have gathered data supporting the hypothesis that we are powerfully motivated to unconsciously assess external reality in terms of safety and danger before commencing with action. In other words, people take action to master their environment and optimize the chance for a successful outcome, and not simply to express an impulse, defense, or compromise between the two. Yet these things affect a person's ability to reach that goal of mastery. Defenses can impair the accurate assessment of reality and predispose people to failure and frustration.

This research has direct relevance for understanding the therapeutic process. It is not enough to reactivate the painful emotions involved in the memories that surface during the treatment process. The pathological beliefs associated with them must be elicited and corrected as well (Weiss, 1993). Weiss has developed a rationale for therapeutic intervention based on Freud's (1920) theoretical shift from an emphasis on centrality of the pleasure principle to that of the reality principle. This shift was accompanied by the suggestion of the operation of a motive toward mastery—not just of our inner drives and instincts, but the external world. In *An Outline of Psychoanalysis,* Freud (1949) wrote, that man, "after taking its bearings in the present and assessing earlier experiences, endeavors by means of experimental action to calculate the consequences of the courses of action proposed" (p. 199).

Our patients frequently suffer from distorted and pathological beliefs acquired in early life and need to be assisted, through fresh experiences, to change these beliefs. This is most likely to occur within the therapeutic relationship (Strupp & Binder, 1984; Wachtel, 1993). In fact, "Most people who have undergone psychoanalysis feel that they have learned and gained from the contact with their analyst, from the kind of person he or she is and the way the analyst functions" (Pine, 1985).

These theoretical revisions, and the research data that support them, have not been adequately translated into standard practice. ISTDP attempts to do so. The type of intervention being suggested here is multi-faceted. The initial focus on defense liberates affective expression, leading to the rapid de-repression of memories, ideas, and beliefs acquired early in life. This process facilitates the uncovering of unconscious conflict, increasing the unconscious therapeutic alliance and decreasing reliance on maladaptive defenses. Further, this work increases the patient's tolerance for the experience of strong mixed feelings toward significant others. As the process unfolds, working models of self and other become more realistic, complex, and multidimensional. Past and present, although clearly linked, also become distinct.

Three Sessions Later

The patient entered this session reporting that feelings of grief were welling up spontaneously now. He also noticed that other feelings, including happiness and joy, were beginning to emerge. He was noticeably lighter and brighter in appearance. I asked if he was able to share these feelings with his wife, and he said he was still keeping the sad feelings to himself. We began to explore, in greater detail, where he got the idea to share feelings is to burden someone.

Examination of Distorted Beliefs about Self and Others

PATIENT: Feelings have been coming up all week. It feels good to release it.

THERAPIST: And were you able to share it at all?

PATIENT: No, I'd only let it come up when I was alone.

THERAPIST: What we've learned about this so far is that you tend to be very protective of others. You've gotten the idea that your emotions are a burden to others. You're afraid to burden them so you keep the feelings closed up.

PATIENT: It's hard to get away from that. Part of me wants to open up but I'm still afraid and hold back.

THERAPIST: Where did you get this belief? It must have come through experience.

PATIENT: I'm sure. What comes to mind is my grandfather. He passed on, and I thought I shouldn't let my upset show because my mother was so devastated I didn't want to add to her sense of loss.

THERAPIST: So you were just a boy?

PATIENT: That was just a few years ago.

THERAPIST: But wasn't there an earlier loss?

PATIENT: Oh, that was my grandmother, but I don't remember much about that.

THERAPIST: Wasn't your mother also very upset then?

PATIENT: Oh, definitely. She had a nervous breakdown.

THERAPIST: What happened?

PATIENT: I was about 7. My grandmother was sick and we expected her to die. I remember feeling really sad but not crying because my mother was so upset. My father never showed any feeling—especially in those situations. He'd try to be light and say, "It's all for the best."

THERAPIST: But your mother was very upset? What's the picture?

PATIENT: I can see her sitting in the chair with a tissue—bawling and sobbing. She let everything out—crying really hard. It was too much to control.

THERAPIST: How do you feel going back to that?

C-P Link

PATIENT: Sad that she had to go through that—to experience all that pain. I wish I could help her. I felt helpless, like I did with the baby.

THERAPIST: So there it is all over again. You have your own loss—your grandmother and your son—but you are so preoccupied with the sadness of the woman and feel such a pressure to do something that you don't experience your own grief.

PATIENT: Maybe it gets me away from my own grief. I was confused. My mother was so upset and then my father, not at all. I thought that was the male role. All the men in the family were like that.

THERAPIST: Then your mother couldn't bear it. What kind of breakdown did she have?

PATIENT: She was hospitalized and had shock therapy. They took her out to Long Island and we would visit. I was hoping she'd come home soon.

THERAPIST: So right after losing your grandmother, you lose your mother to depression and hospitalization.

PATIENT: I can feel my body tense. I feel a reaction in my body but I'm not sure what it is. I feel like I want to do something physically—like reaching out.

THERAPIST: That separation is gut-wrenching. Again, you don't want to let go. What's the feeling?

PATIENT: I didn't want her to go. I see myself as a little boy by the screen door (very tearful). I'm sad and confused, feeling so helpless.

In this case, the mother, wife, and therapist were initially linked. They were all viewed as women who might break down in the face of grief and abandon him. As the work progressed and the patient dealt with his feelings toward his mother directly, he was able to see how he had been misperceiving women over the years. The therapist and the patient's wife were then seen more accurately, as women who could feel grief but not decompensate. Changes in the patient's characteristic mode of attachment followed.

EFFECTS OF LOSS ON SELF-IMAGE

Bowlby (1970) and others (Stern, 1985) who have studied the effects of early relational patterns on the formation of a self-image, have paid particular attention to the effects that separation and loss have on the child's ongoing sense of self. Mann (1973) has placed special emphasis on the relationship between the patient's current and chronically endured pain regarding separations, losses, and disappointment in relationships and a persistent negative self-image. He has stated, "I came to understand that the repetitive series of separations and losses that every human being endures forms the outline of the self-image that each person constructs" (Mann, 1991, p. 18).

Engel (1961) has stated the opinion that the loss of a loved one is, in and of itself, traumatic. Multiple losses result in cumulative trauma and grossly affect the individual's sense of self and the world. "The affective result of trauma blurs a person's perception of time, which in turn increases negative affect, which increases the sense of hopelessness" (Mann, 1991, p. 28). Even those in the mental health field often grossly underestimate the devastating effect of loss on our patients and how long and difficult the path to resolution really is.

In this case, the material suggests that the patient learned to be afraid of strong affect in himself and others. In his mind, intense feelings lead to breakdown, hospitalization, and loss. The patient remarked that his mother was never the same after the shock treatments, so there was a sense of loss even after physical reunion with his mother.

The patient was given a new opportunity to understand the impact of these early experiences on him and thus to appreciate how they affected his reaction to subsequent losses. Now he was free to evaluate, as an adult, whether strategies developed as a child were currently required. Again, the experience of affect was a necessary but insufficient step to achieve permanent change in his adaptation to loss. We also had to expose and then critically assess the accuracy of the distorted and pathological beliefs that accompanied these experiences.

It became apparent that this man's tendency to keep his feelings to himself and to assume a caretaking role for others, especially the women in his life, was a strategy adopted at an early age to prevent further loss. Although this strategy is maladaptive in adult life, it was adaptive when the patient was a child since his mother was quite fragile and couldn't bear any additional burden. He was now in a position to consciously evaluate whether this strategy was helpful or harmful in his relationships with women in the present, such as his wife and his therapist. He was now able to see that neither one of these women needed to be shielded from his grief. On the contrary, he found that sharing grief increased his feelings of closeness with them.

A Man with Sexual Difficulties

While evidence of pathological mourning was readily obtained in the case of the Man in a Fog, in many cases it is more difficult to ascertain. In the following case, a middle-aged man was referred for psychotherapy by his Urologist, who could find no organic basis for the patient's erectile dysfunction. Inquiry revealed an 18-month history of anxiety and depression in addition to the erectile failure he specifically wanted help to remediate. When asked what was going on at the time his difficulties began, he reported that his mother, a chronic psychiatric patient, had died. The patient attached no significance to this "coincidence." There is no therapeutic value in trying to convince a patient, on some rational level, that symptoms have symbolic meaning. The emotional significance of his mother's death was the very thing he was defending himself against. Thus, the focus became the patient's emotional detachment. By linking the patient's presenting complaint (lack of sexual desire and an inability to maintain erections) to the defenses in operation (emotional detachment), the defenses became dystonic. The avoided affects were then approached. Only if the patient is able to engage on an emotional level will deep change be possible.

The first several sessions of treatment were spent acquainting the patient with his defenses against emotional closeness. He reported being afraid of letting himself feel because the most prevalent emotion in him was that of anger, and he worried about losing control. The session being recounted here began with an exploration of this issue.

Anger toward His Boss

PATIENT: I have two feelings when it comes to anger—I either tense up and keep it in or it erupts.

THERAPIST: So what you're saying is that when you feel angry, the aggressive impulses that come with it are so strong, you're afraid, if you don't squelch it, you'll act on it. To keep yourself in check, you don't let yourself feel the anger.

PATIENT: With the exception of the last month, since coming here. I've been able just to talk to certain individuals and say "I'm angry"—be firm and to the point and it works out well. But these people are reasonable to begin with.

THERAPIST: But when someone is unreasonable, like your boss, you become enraged. There's no dealing with this guy—words don't work.

PATIENT: That's true. And it's worse right now. Others feel this way about him too and are losing their cool.

THERAPIST: So you're not the only one. The anger is stronger than ever.

PATIENT: Yeah.

C-P Link

THERAPIST: So, if this came out, in your imagination?

PATIENT: If I ever let go, I would hit him and beat him, continue to beat him with my hands in his face and continue to beat him until he says he understands and would change.

THERAPIST: How likely is that?

PATIENT: Not at all. But that's what I picture—just hitting him until he stops acting the way he acts.

THERAPIST: So what point would that be?

PATIENT: Probably kill him because it never worked with my mother so why should it work with him (puts his head in his hands and rubs his eyes).

THERAPIST: That's who comes to your mind?

PATIENT: Yeah. I wish I had killed her 20 years ago—maybe I wouldn't have the problems I have today.

Facing the Rage toward His Mother

THERAPIST: So as you get in touch with the impulse to beat this man, you see your mother and realize you had a murderous rage toward her. He's another unreasonable person you just can't get through to in any civilized way. You feel so enraged you want to kill him. Where would this take place with your mother?

PATIENT: In the apartment next door.

THERAPIST: Where?

PATIENT: In the dining room where she would sit smoking. That's where I'd try to talk to her but I couldn't get through. I imagine talking to her quietly and trying to resolve problems but she would talk, talk, talk, but make no sense, jumping from subject to subject. In fact, it's just like this guy—he's just like her.

THERAPIST: So as you think about this, you're trying to talk but you can't get through and the feeling of anger rises. If those feelings came out toward her?

PATIENT: Yeah, I feel it (voice up, hands mobilized). I'd start hitting her and choking her and punch her and, if I was smart, I'd kill her.

THERAPIST: How?

PATIENT: I'd just beat her until she stopped talking. You couldn't stop her talking. I'd punch her and choke her until she couldn't say anymore, until she was dead so she would just shut up.

THERAPIST: How do you see her?

PATIENT: Laying on the floor dead.

THERAPIST: What does she look like?

PATIENT: A poor soul, at rest now.

Facing the Guilt and Grief

THERAPIST: Physically?

PATIENT: Her face would be swollen, she'd be bleeding, and like a jerk, I'd feel sorry about doing it.

THERAPIST: So there are feelings of remorse?

PATIENT: Sure. I don't know why I should . . .

THERAPIST: But you do.

PATIENT: Yeah, I do (tears up).

THERAPIST: There's a deep feeling of sadness that comes over you.

PATIENT: Yeah, because she had a shitty life—she did (starts to cry). And then to end like that would make it worse.

THERAPIST: So there are tender feelings underneath all this.

PATIENT: Yes, but I resent those feelings.

THERAPIST: But they are there—angry as you have been with her.

The preceding is an example of staying with feeling and brushing defense aside without returning to the phase of pressure and challenge. The feelings of pain, sorrow and grief are evident, but the patient wants to consciously resist coming to terms with them. He would rather stay angry with his mother than face the pain over the tragedy of their life together. The therapist follows the feeling and encourages the patient to let himself experience the emerging grief and underlying tenderness toward his mother. Utilizing fantasy facilitates this process.

THERAPIST: But they are there. As angry as you have been with her, you also feel for her. So what would you do with her body?

PATIENT: I don't know, it would depend. I could picture myself sitting down and thinking it through. Would I admit it or hide it? I would probably cover it up.

THERAPIST: So you would bury her yourself.

PATIENT: If I could get away with it (laughs).

THERAPIST: What's funny?

PATIENT: I see myself burying her behind the house in the woods. I see myself covering her up with dirt. I'm only laughing because, through the years, she would make comments about how she didn't want me to go to any fuss when she died and I'd say, "Don't worry Mom, I'll just dig a hole in the back and throw you in."

THERAPIST: So there's some truth in that.

PATIENT: I guess so (laughs again).

THERAPIST: You're saying that for 20 years, at least, you've been enraged with her. She was such a pain in your neck, you just wanted to kill her, dig a ditch, and throw her in it. When the anger is spent, then sadness comes. You don't like it, you want to resist that feeling, but it's there. So to face throwing this lifeless body of your mother into a ditch . . .

PATIENT: At this point my main concern would be to cover up what I did.

This response is a clear indication of the ways in which this man's guilt and need to cover up what he is feeling have interrupted the grief process. It also underscores how this strategy has resulted in his anxiety, depression, and withdrawal from others. If he's hiding a secret and trying to cover his tracks, how can he let anyone close to him?

Linking Repressed Grief and Guilt with Symptoms

THERAPIST: But what happens to these sad feelings?

PATIENT: I think it would bother me a lot. If I covered it up, I wouldn't get a guilty conscience and confess later but I'd suffer internally with my own guilt.

THERAPIST: So what would that be like, to suffer internally?

PATIENT: Phew (big sigh). I don't know, it would bother me for the rest of my life. I'd think about it all the time and my stomach would bother me—you know the way my stomach gets—and I would never have any peace.

THERAPIST: So, let me ask you, isn't this exactly what you've been experiencing inside? Ever since she died, you've been filled with anxiety and guilt and there's been no peace for you. You've isolated yourself, and no one knows what you're suffering inside.

PATIENT: That's true.

The source of this man's suffering now becomes quite evident. He considered himself a murderer and had been punishing himself ever since his mother's death. Once he became consciously aware of the link between his repressed guilt and grief and his symptomatic suffering, he was able to reassess his relationship with his mother and whether the punishment fit the crime. In fact, he had been an extraordinarily dedicated son to his seriously disturbed mother. All in all, he left the session feeling good about the way he had treated his mother and very sad about the suffering she had to endure because of her illness (she was alternately diagnosed as having paranoid schizophrenia or manic-depressive illness).

What also became evident was that the patient's mother had accused him, since childhood, of wanting to kill her. She was seriously mentally ill, with paranoid and manic episodes. He had internalized her voice and was afraid to admit his murderous feelings, lest he prove her right. Now he was able to distinguish between feelings and actions and to understand that these wishes were a reaction to the real neglect and abuse he had suffered at his parent's hands. The eventual compassion he was able to have for his mother, he was also able to feel for himself. The harshness in him softened. Others at home and at the office commented on how approachable he had become.

A pervasive sense of guilt and the assumption of a caretaking function for his mother throughout life were two of the factors that had predisposed this man to a pathological course of mourning. By activating acute grief, he was able to acknowledge and integrate his disparate feelings toward his mother. This led to changes that were fundamental and far-reaching. His whole demeanor and characteristic way of dealing with his own feelings and interacting with others changed significantly as a result of this work.

The Woman with Panic Attacks

The following case is another in which pathological mourning was initially disguised. This middle-aged mother of two entered treatment because of anxiety and panic that had plagued her since moving from her hometown to a new city. The move was necessitated by her husband's employment. Not only were they in a new city, but her husband, who had been a teacher and had been home a good deal of the time previously, had changed his profession and now worked long and erratic hours. The patient would become anxious and panicky when her husband was gone for long periods. She was also increasingly angry with him for leaving her alone. The patient wondered whether these separations were especially difficult for her because her mother had always been sick and was in and out of hospitals most of her life. She died when the patient was 12. All this was reported in a highly detached manner. The patient said she had no memory of her mother's death.

The therapeutic work began in the transference, highlighting the defenses of detachment and the self-defeating nature of these for our work. The patient became an active collaborator in the process and was especially motivated to face all the mixed feelings toward her husband, which she viewed as the source of her anxiety. In this, the sixth psychotherapy session, the patient reported an incident in which her husband arrived home considerably later than expected. She reported feeling furious but, as soon as he came in the kitchen door, she was filled with anxiety and retreated behind a newspaper in the living room. Our focus was on the experience of anger toward her husband.

Anger toward Her Husband

THERAPIST: How do you experience this anger toward him?

PATIENT: I start seeing myself pushing him but then it goes away. I start to get real upset and then I stop (getting tearful). I don't see the point of this.

THERAPIST: You don't seem to let yourself really feel the anger. You have a thousand ways to avoid it. There is nothing more terrifying to you than experiencing your own rage.

PATIENT: (nods in agreement). Yeah, I'd like to get rid of my own rage (smiles).

THERAPIST: But you're so terrified that as soon as it starts to rise you bury it and then the tears come.

PATIENT: Then I'm up all the time and I try to figure everything out and then I'm going to leave . . . I can't stand it, I just can't stand it.

THERAPIST: So do you want to bury it or look at it?

PATIENT: Let's look at it!

THERAPIST: So if this anger came out toward him, what would this look like?

PATIENT: I see me pushing him (motions with her arms) on his chest.

THERAPIST: And you're in the kitchen?

PATIENT: Now I think about a knife. I push him until he falls down and I think about (brother). The kitchen made me think of the knife.

THERAPIST: Who has the knife?

PATIENT: If I could, I would probably take the knife and stab him (voice up, hand making a stabbing motion)!

THERAPIST: Where?

PATIENT: In the heart . . . because I don't want things the way they are.

THERAPIST: This is very frightening to face and I'm sure it runs deep—thoughts of your brother came.

PATIENT: But I don't want to talk about that. I told my husband I don't want to talk about my family and the past. I just want to know why these things happen to me now.

THERAPIST: But I'm sure there's a link. It's as you face your anger toward your husband that your brother comes to mind.

PATIENT: Well as a kid, he wanted to kill me—he slashed my wrists with a knife.

THERAPIST: That was a terrifying experience, no doubt, but it looks like that also evoked a reactive rage in you toward him which is equally frightening. How much are you going to take until you strike back? It's the same pattern with your husband. You put up with his being late, breaking promises, leaving you alone with the children and your anger toward him builds and builds.

PATIENT: Yeah, it's true, but it's scary because if I'm going to react I'm not going to mess around. I'm saying I wouldn't want him just hurt.

THERAPIST: So what happens?

PATIENT: He's dead. If he's dead, he's dead.

THERAPIST: How does this happen?

Sudden De-Repression of Past Trauma

PATIENT: I push him, then stab him. How he's lying on the floor. He's flat on his back.

THERAPIST: How does he look?

PATIENT: Quiet. Dead. White. No, orange. I don't want to see orange (becomes agitated and highly distressed, shaking her head and covering her eyes). I want to talk about something else (breathing rapidly, eyes darting around). I don't want to see. I want to go home now.

THERAPIST: Tell me what's happening inside right now. You seem to panic.

De-Repression of Mother's Death

PATIENT: I see my mother in the coffin—lying on her back, dead. Her skin is orange, her fingers are black. She doesn't talk to me. Well, I just want her to talk to me (uttered in a childlike voice). But dead people can't talk (starts to cry), and I don't want my husband to be dead because I want him to talk to me.

Lowering Anxiety

THERAPIST: Let's look at what happens inside.

PATIENT: I'm scared.

THERAPIST: You seem to panic.

PATIENT: I'm just scared right now, and I don't want to be around anybody.

THERAPIST: What happens physically? You hyperventilate.

PATIENT: I can't breathe.

THERAPIST: What else.

PATIENT: I get shaky. I don't want to be bad, I wanna' be good (crying). I wanna' stay married. I don't want to go away.

THERAPIST: You think your mother went away because you were bad?

PATIENT: She went away because she wouldn't go to the doctor. By the time she went it was too late—it had gone through her body.

This very powerful, and unexpected, de-repression of feelings and memories regarding her mother's death surfaced spontaneously as the patient faced the anger she was feeling toward her husband who, like her mother, left her alone repeatedly. On what turned out to be the last visit to her mother in the hospital, the patient reported feelings so angry that her mother wouldn't wake up and talk to her that she stomped out of the room saying, "If you won't talk to me, I'm never coming back to see you again." The next thing she knew, her mother was dead. The feelings of guilt were too much for her to bear alone as a child and she repressed the entire series of events surrounding her mother's death and funeral. Now the memories returned and she was able to assess the situation from the viewpoint of an adult. She was now able to see that she had nothing to do with the death and that it was, in fact, the result of her mother's fear of doctors and refusal to get treatment. She was able to feel compassion for the little girl who had to face her mother's death alone and had no one to talk to about her guilt and grief.

Following the grief over the death of her mother, she was able to face all the grief she experienced while her mother was alive but chronically sick and unavailable. The impact of the psychological loss of support and connection that many of our patients faced as children cannot be over-estimated. Death is not the only kind of loss that needs to be mourned.

Grief work can be nearly as difficult for the therapist, as the patient. We must be able to bear the sorrow of our own losses and disappointments if we are to help our patients deepen their own experience of pain and grief. If we defend against these painful feelings, we'll keep a distance from the grieving patient. Conversely, the attuned therapist's compassionate attitude in the face of grief can often, in and of itself, deepen the patient's experience of painful longing. We often overlook the fact that repressed pain and sorrow are frequently triggered by being gratified. When patients find the understanding they always longed for but never received (Schnarch, 1991), the contrast between past and present responses intensifies affect.

Saying Goodbye

The tenaciousness with which we want to hold onto loved ones can prevent us from coming to terms with loss and moving on to new relationships. Helping our patients say good-bye to loved ones once they have experienced all their mixed feelings toward the deceased can be a very freeing experience. Following this work in therapy, patients sometimes find their own highly personal and meaningful ways to say good-bye and pay tribute to their loved ones.

In the case of the Detached Observer (Chapter 3), the patient had a dream about a young boy riding down a river on his mother's coffin. This dream clearly depicted his enduring attachment to his mother and inability to say good-bye to her. A young woman, with arms outstretched, was waiting at the shore. He wanted to jump off the coffin and swim to her, but he felt he couldn't leave his mother. He was holding on, not just to spare himself the pain of loss, but to spare his mother her fear of being alone. This dream graphically depicted the price he was paying for holding onto his mother (i.e., he was unable to attach to available women and remained alone).

The Detached Observer

THERAPIST: It looks like you've never said good-bye to your mother. You're like the boy on the coffin, drifting. It's a barren scene, but you're still holding on.

PATIENT: It's a hard thing for me to see. To say good-bye to someone you never knew is what makes it harder.

THERAPIST: It means facing all the regrets. It looked like you had a reaction to something I said. Was it the image of the little boy on the coffin? (Patient nods and starts to cry.)

This is a common phenomenon observed in clinical practice. It's not those who have had a good relationship with a parent that can't seem to let go, but those who didn't have enough of the good. At one point in the session, he said it very precisely: "There just wasn't enough good to hold onto." As he got in touch with the grief and the resistance to saying good-bye to her, I asked him to imagine talking to her about his struggle.

THERAPIST: Can you imagine telling your mother about all that's been lost and how you've been holding on for dear life to a corpse?

PATIENT: (crying). I can't imagine telling her.

THERAPIST: What happens?

PATIENT: I can see her, like, in heaven. Not how she was here but I can see her up there, fully aware of everything I've been going through and how sad it makes her. That she wishes she could help . . . but, she can't.

It is illustrated again here, how, once the unconscious is open and fluid, minor defenses can simply be ignored. When first asked to imagine talking with his mother, the patient says he couldn't do it. The therapist simply continued with another question ("What happens?"), and the patient responded with a spontaneous image of his mother in heaven.

THERAPIST: What's that like for you, to get an image of your mother as calm, knowing what's happened, and feeling for you?

PATIENT: Well, it's a connection, seeing me and feeling for me.

THERAPIST: She can't actually do anything, but what is it you think she wishes for you?

PATIENT: Oh shit (head in his hands), . . . to be happy and get what I want.

THERAPIST: What happened just now?

PATIENT: That feeling that she would want me to be happy. That's something I never felt from her—that it mattered how I felt.

THERAPIST: But why the "Oh shit"?

PATIENT: For her to want me to be happy even though she wasn't. That's sad.

This material speaks to the patient's identification with the deceased. For this man to embrace life, there needs to be a change in the quality of the maternal introject, from depriving and frustrating, to warm, nurturing, and gratifying. Even though he did not have interactions of this kind with his mother to build on, the interaction with the therapist provided an experience he could use to imagine what it would have been like had his mother been healthy and emotionally available. In a sense, imagining her wanting him to be happy gave him permission to move on and develop satisfying relationships. He had been remaining connected and loyal to his mother by staying alone or choosing women who were like her—cold and aloof. Following this work, he found himself attracted to women who were outgoing and affectionate.

Survivor's Guilt

Those who have assumed a caretaking role for the deceased seem to have special difficulty in saying good-bye. There is a kind of survivor's guilt (Weiss, 1993) that prevents them from embracing anyone who might in some way replace the deceased. In this case, the guilt was overcome by imagining that his mother would approve of his happiness. In this scenario, he doesn't have to choose between loyalty to his dead mother or the arms of a warm, available woman. He can imagine she wants that for him, so no conflict exists. When the parent has actually been possessive and jealous and has demanded exclusive loyalty, this transition is much more difficult (just such a case will be presented in Chapter 6).

SUMMARY

These rather diverse cases demonstrate both the magnitude and variety of psychological sequelea stemming from unresolved grief—from symptoms such as panic attacks and sexual dysfunction, to ingrained character patterns of isolation and detachment. In addition, techniques designed to transform pathological mourning into acute grief were demonstrated. It was repeatedly emphasized that helping patients get in touch with the experience of guilt and grief is a necessary but frequently insufficient condition for permanent change in defensive patterns and character style to take place. To achieve those ends, the pathological beliefs that have accompanied the feelings and memories associated with loss must also be examined and re-worked; allowing a fuller, more complex and contemporary view of self and other to evolve.

CHAPTER 6

Working with Positive and Erotic Feelings

Deep oh deep is grief,
but deeper still is joy.

Goethe

One of the central goals of any psychodynamic psychotherapy is to increase patients' awareness of and tolerance for a mix of strong and conflicting feelings toward significant others. In Intensive Short-Term Dynamic Psychotherapy, the therapeutic process typically proceeds in a kind of spiral from the outer layer of defenses against emotional closeness, to anger, underlying pain and grief, and finally, longings for closeness. The goal of treatment is to enable patients to acknowledge, contain, and integrate the full range of human emotion. All the layers of feeling must be accessed, experienced, and woven together in such a way that patients can see themselves and others clearly. This integration is a pre-requisite for what is sometimes referred to as "whole object" relationships, in which both gratification and frustration are expected and tolerated. Basic needs for attachment and closeness are met without compromising the need for autonomy. Ultimately, an inner sense of personal freedom and a renewed or expanded capacity for joy should be evident.

ANXIETY AND DEFENSE IN REGARD TO POSITIVE AFFECTS

The process of de-repression reveals the factors that have been responsible for the avoidance of strong internal feelings and close emotional involvement with others. Anger and grief are not the only affects that are capable of evoking anxiety and, hence, fueling avoidance. In many cases, there is considerable anxiety, guilt, shame, and inhibition around the experience and expression of warm, tender, loving, and sexual feelings. What is responsible for this? There is a great deal of debate about this matter. On the one hand are the drive theorists who view difficulties with closeness and the experience of positive feelings largely as an epiphenomenon (the result of defenses against reactive sadism and unresolved grief). This view posits that, to contain the forbidden feelings of anger and the painful feelings of grief, the patient maintains an emotional distance from others—for it is close contact that evokes these frightening affects. Because warm, tender, loving feelings lie beneath these other emotions, they get lost in the process. Davanloo seems to fall into this camp.

There is no indication in Davanloo's writings, clinical case reports, or presentations that he believes positive feelings can be directly associated with anxiety. With the oedipal situation, for example, Davanloo (1990–1991) contends that anxiety and inhibition regarding sexual feelings, impulses, and fantasies are secondary and indirect. It is not the sexual feelings themselves that are forbidden, he has argued, but the murderous feelings toward the rivalrous parent accompanying the sexual longings that are taboo. Therefore, working through the anxiety and guilt associated with the sadistic impulses should be all that is required to free the patient's sexual inhibitions.

Other theorists (Fairbairn, 1954; Winnicott, 1965), who have expanded and revised classical psychoanalytic theory to include theories of attachment and object relations, have suggested that affects are not *intrinsically* good or bad, safe or dangerous, but are *deemed* so as the result of direct experience with primary caretakers in early life. Those affects that were freely expressed and responded to are more likely to recur than those that met with punishment and censure. In some families, rather harsh and violent behavior is sanctioned, whereas warmth and tenderness are forbidden. Children raised in such an environment would be expected to express anger and hostility with relative ease but to become anxious, defensive, and avoidant when positive feelings are aroused. Similarly, sexual feelings and behaviors can be actively encouraged or prohibited, with direct consequences for the child's sense of comfort or anxiety in the presence of such feelings. If this is true, then dealing only with anger and aggression would not necessarily strip sexual feelings and impulses of their attendant anxiety, nor render their expression more likely.

Although a fusion of sexual and aggressive feelings is often discovered in patients who have serious difficulties with intimacy and closeness, my clinical experience suggests that dealing with anxiety and defense against aggressive feelings is insufficient for achieving ease and comfort with one's sexuality. To accomplish this, all the prohibitions against sensual contact must be explored. An integration of sexual and loving feelings does not necessarily emerge spontaneously, as these are actively kept apart in some cases. Direct therapeutic intervention aimed at achieving an integration of the two is usually required. The case of the Man with Primary Impotence (in this chapter) will illustrate this type of work.

SEXUAL FEELINGS IN THE THERAPEUTIC RELATIONSHIP

Although longings for closeness and tenderness will most likely emerge following the experience of reactive rage and grief, their full expression may still be defended against if the danger associated with them is not exposed and critically evaluated. Again, the interaction with the therapist, which is a living example of the patient's characteristic mode of attachment, will provide the most direct information regarding those feelings, impulses, and fantasies that have become fraught with anxiety and dread.

The Early Emergence of Sexualized Feelings

Sexualized feelings can emerge very early in treatment. When this occurs, it either indicates fairly severe pathology or that sexual feelings are being used as a tactical defense. On several occasions, male patients have raised the issue of their sexual attraction to me in the opening phases of defense work when pressure toward closeness is beginning to be exerted. The patient might say, "Well, I can't discuss that with you because you're an attractive young woman." Tactical defenses such as these must be immediately targeted with a statement such as, "What does my appearance have to do with this? You are here because of your difficulties, and to help you, I have to understand the problem. Now you tell me you can't go into it. How can I be of help to you?" In most cases, this approach is sufficient to turn the patient's ego against this defense. Inquiry can continue, and the sexualized content typically disappears.

Occasionally, however, the patient's focus on sexual impulses is strong and indicates a primary area of difficulty. In one such case, a young man came to treatment because of serious difficulties in relationships with women, most of which had a sado-masochistic quality. He reported feeling very anxious and upset to find that I was young and attractive. He had hoped I would be "old, heavy, and unattractive" so that he would not have to struggle so directly with his conflicts over sexual impulses. Inquiry revealed that his concerns were warranted. As an adolescent, he sexually molested his sisters, was caught breaking and entering the home of a young woman he planned to molest, and was expelled from college for writing a threatening note (in blood) to a classmate who had insulted him. This historical information, along with the anxiety and disorganization apparent in the session when we addressed his attraction to me, all indicated serious deficits in ego functioning and were contraindications for this type of treatment. He was referred to a male psychiatrist who specialized in the treatment of sex offenders.

Positive Feelings during the Midphase of Treatment

Positive feelings toward the therapist, marked by a heightened desire for closeness, frequently have an erotic and sexualized flavor. These feelings typically emerge during the mid-phase of treatment, as reactive anger and grief get worked through. The therapist is often a target for these feelings, just as he or she had been for anger and grief earlier in the process.

It should be emphasized that warm, tender feelings are sporadically present from the early stages of treatment. It is not unusual for patients to comment on the relief and gratitude they feel toward the therapist at the end of the evaluation process. Facing thoughts and feelings that had long been avoided results in a feeling of mastery and a sense of safety within the therapeutic relationship.

As treatment progresses and reactive anger and grief get worked through, positive feelings and longings for closeness emerge more clearly. If these feelings and impulses are not frightening to the patient, they will get expressed freely and reports of greatly improved interpersonal relationships will follow. Little, if any work is required in the transference in these cases. However, where anxiety and defense accompany positive and erotic feelings, the therapist will become a target for the working through of these conflicts.

In this form of treatment, positive and sexual feelings are dealt with in the same direct and matter-of-fact manner as feelings of anger and grief. The patient is encouraged to face them directly, experience them fully, and "portrait" the impulses these feelings mobilize. In addition, getting such longings out in the open prevents the development of resistance, dependence on the therapist, and the development of a transference neurosis.

CLINICAL EXAMPLES

The Detached Observer: Part 2

The clinical material to follow is suggestive of an oedipal conflict. As already detailed in previous chapters, The Detached Observer required a period of intensive pressure and challenge to facilitate a shift from a highly resistant stance to one of affectively charged involvement in the treatment process. During the mid-phase of treatment, the patient was able to get in touch with highly charged erotic desires for the therapist, which were linked with similar feelings toward his mother. Rivalrous feelings toward the therapist's husband, as well as toward his own father, were also experienced. As the triangular relationship conflicts were addressed, the pre-existing diadic problems with both his mother and father emerged. Then the ways in which the pre-oedipal situation affected the patient's adaptation to these intense and conflictual oedipal feelings became clear.

The Emergence of Longing and Desire

The case of the Detached Observer, first presented in Chapter 3, proceeded in a fairly straightforward manner from pressure and challenge to the patient's defenses against emotional closeness to a breakthrough of reactive sadism. This was followed by deep grief over longings for closeness with his mother that were never met.

Many sessions were spent on grieving not only the ultimate loss of his mother by death but, even more so, the loss of what would have been possible had she been emotionally available when alive (see Della Selva, 1993, for a detailed account of this phase of the work). This patient tended to be attracted to women who were cool and aloof, as his mother had been toward him. As treatment progressed, he became interested in women who were warm, friendly, and responsive. He wanted to date but found that, as soon as his desire for physical contact started to rise, he would get anxious and withdraw.

A similar pattern was discernible in the therapy sessions. As soon as we would begin to explore his sexual feelings and impulses toward women, he would become anxious and avoidant. His defenses against sexual feelings were becoming a resistance in the transference, suggesting the presence of these forbidden longings for the therapist. When asked, the patient acknowledged that he had been having warm, loving feelings toward the therapist. As with other feelings, the therapeutic focus began with the actual experience of these feelings and desires.

Defense before Feeling

THERAPIST: You want to be with me, not to be separated. What is that yearning like inside?

PATIENT: I have these feelings, but what good will this do? I'm not going to have all the things I want from you, so why is this a good thing?

THERAPIST: Let's look at the effects if we don't examine these feelings. How is this any different from your angry feelings, for example? Now, obviously, we were not going to enact them—you were not actually going to sever my head and smash it against a brick wall, but the feelings were there and if we didn't get to them and face them, they would become another brick in the wall. So, there's a big difference between experiencing a feeling and acting on it.

PATIENT: I draw a parallel to my mother. I couldn't touch her either.

THERAPIST: There's a desire to touch me.

PATIENT: Yeah.

THERAPIST: How?

PATIENT: To hold you on my lap. Your arms are around my neck and your head is on my shoulder.

Patients will attempt to rationalize their avoidance of loving, sexual feelings. In this case, the fact that these longings would not be gratified was used as an excuse to avoid the whole topic. The therapist dealt with this defense by pointing out that these feelings are no different from any other. By focusing on his past success in dealing with previously dreaded feelings (sadistic rage, in this case) and noting the disadvantages of avoidance, the resistance was successfully diminished and the work continued apace.

The images that accompany loving feelings and impulses are just as important as those that accompany anger and grief. These spontaneous images frequently contain direct links to the past, as will be revealed in the next vignette. Such images contain a wealth of unconscious meaning and are by no means arbitrary.

NEXT SESSION—DANGERS ASSOCIATED WITH SEXUAL LONGINGS

PATIENT: The last time we were talking about sexual feelings and I left feeling very agitated. Then at night I had strong thoughts of someone breaking in—coming right through the glass doors with machine guns to get me. I also had thoughts of me having my own gun and blowing them away—it would be a fight.

Aside from the content being reported, which is of great significance, the ways in which this man relates to the therapist are also of note. As is characteristic of patients in ISTDP, he takes the initiative in sessions and gets right down to work. The patient is fully involved, not only within sessions, but in between meetings, coming prepared with important material to work through. Because of his high level of involvement, the patient was encouraged to make his own interpretations about what is emerging.

THERAPIST: What do you make of it?
PATIENT: I related it to our session—talking about sex. It's like it's dangerous. It's life or death—kill or be killed. There's no scaring away. Even if I have the edge, if they turn around, I'll shoot them in the back so there's no coming back.
THERAPIST: So who are these men who are after you?
PATIENT: There are two. It's my father and, I guess, your husband.

Transference First

As a general rule, feelings, impulses, and fantasies regarding the therapist should be the first order of business. Often, therapists collude in the avoidance of the transference (the most anxiety-providing area for therapist as well as patient) by moving too rapidly to genetic figures (Gill, 1982). Failure to attend sufficiently to the transference has several consequences. First of all, feelings that are evoked but not expressed are, by definition, being defended against and will contribute to increased resistance over time. Conversely, dealing directly with the transference eliminates the possibility of transference neurosis and resistance and guides the process to the genetic figure the therapist currently represents. So this technique not only reduces resistance but, in so doing, speeds access to the unconscious conflicts from the past that are being enacted in a disguised form through the transference. Therapists can become intensely uncomfortable about the patient's positive feelings toward them and must guard against discouraging their direct expression.

Herein lies another important distinction between ISTDP and traditional models of dynamic psychotherapy. Whereas the transference is avoided in the early stages of traditional analytic work and eventually becomes the focus for working through, the initial work in ISTDP is largely transference based. As the transference feelings are experienced and directly linked with genetic figures, transference distortions steadily decrease. The real relationship and the therapeutic alliance assume increasing precedence over time.

In this case, feelings and fantasies about the therapist were dealt with before shifting focus to the material regarding past figures. The patient imagined killing the therapist's husband, which would, he surmised, evoke despair and rage in her.

De-Repression of the Primal Scene

PATIENT: You wouldn't want anything to do with me. I would feel like I messed everything up. I'd end up alone again.

THERAPIST: So you end up alone again—the loser. That's happened before, huh?

PATIENT: With my mother. I had almost given up, but I wanted her.

THERAPIST: Because you remember a real closeness between them and that she would respond to your father.

PATIENT: Yeah, I remember watching them kiss passionately when I was 5 or 6 and wanting that. I also remember, in our last house, I was about 11 and I walked in on them. She was in his arms—they were naked and smiling. I said, "Oops," and walked out. My father was sitting on the edge of the bed and my mother was sitting on his lap, with her arms around his neck. They were smiling.

The longing to hold the therapist on his lap is now clearly related to this image of his mother and father. His desire to take his father's place will be visualized. This will also make his beginning remarks about guns and a fight to the death very meaningful.

THERAPIST: So your mother's body was very exposed then.

PATIENT: I saw she had beautiful breasts. She looked really sexy, smooth skin, and smiling.

THERAPIST: So she was clearly enjoying herself—smiling, and no tics or signs of anxiety.

PATIENT: My father was too, which I rarely saw.

THERAPIST: So there was something very special there and you wanted some. What is the impulse?

PATIENT: I wanted her, there's no doubt about that.

THERAPIST: How would you get her?

PATIENT: I would look at him and say, "OK, you've had enough." I'd grab my mother and say, "She's mine now." He'd say, "Hey, that's my wife. You don't know how to treat her, what she needs."

THERAPIST: So he would put you down. How do you feel toward him?

PATIENT: It's bullshit—he didn't help her, didn't treat her right.

THERAPIST: You feel you could do better.

PATIENT: I would beat him out the door. I'd punch and disable him. Knock him unconscious. Kick him, then drag him out, and leave *him* out in the hall and close the door. Then I'd grab her and make love to her. I want to touch her all over. I want to be the one who makes her feel great.

The patient goes on to detail a scene of mutually satisfying love-making. In his fantasy, his mother gives herself over to him. He has full access to her and she is enjoying his intense interest in her.

Further De-Repression

PATIENT: This is what I wanted—how I see it. The actual contact with my mother is great. The problem is that my father is lurking in the hallway.

THERAPIST: So you are still haunted, like the other night at home—listening for every sound, looking over your shoulder.

PATIENT: I can't let him keep lurking. I'd shoot him. There's a 22 caliber in his closet.

THERAPIST: You knew about this gun?

PATIENT: Yeah, I shot it.

THERAPIST: When?

PATIENT: Not until I was 11 or 12.

THERAPIST: So, the same age.

PATIENT: I had just killed something for the first time. My eyesight started going at that time (myopia). I wanted to shoot but didn't want to kill anything. I was out with a friend, who was trying to get a bird. I said, "Let me have a shot," but I never thought I'd hit it.

THERAPIST: So you knew about this gun, how to shoot and that you could kill.

PATIENT: I used to take it out and play with it—just take it out of the case and look at it. I was interested in it.

THERAPIST: And now we can see why. It's all coming together—the rage toward your father for keeping your mother all to himself, your wish to get rid of him so you can have her to yourself, and your fear of these powerful feelings and impulses.

PATIENT: The way I see it is that, after I'm done with my mother I realize he'll be back and then I go get him. He'd be lying on the carpet, naked. I'd shoot him in the chest a couple of times. His arms are splayed, his mouth open.

THERAPIST: How do you feel when you look at him?

PATIENT: A mix. Powerful but sad. I didn't want this. I felt I had to. He wouldn't let me near her. I wanted him to let her love me. I didn't want to kill him to get it. And I wanted her to give me some of the love and attention she gave him. It's the only time I ever saw her relaxed and happy.

This material, along with a wealth of developmental data gathered throughout the course of this man's treatment, suggests that his mother was very detached from him and that his father actively encouraged this distance. In fact, when as a young boy, he attempted contact with his mother, she would become anxious and symptomatic. The patient's father would literally pull him away from his mother and say, "See what you're doing? Go to your room, leave her alone."

So here is a case where detachment was actively encouraged and affectionate contact clearly punished. It is no wonder then, that reaching out and directly expressing his desires for affectionate contact would be experienced as dangerous and avoided at all costs. His initial detachment with the therapist was a replication of this pattern. Although ultimately self-defeating, this pattern of interaction ensured safety. For him, being unobtrusive—appearing to need little contact—was the only way of gaining any proximity to his mother. For the patient to achieve deep insight, an understanding of how that pattern of attachment was developed, what it was designed to preserve, and how it currently backfires all had to become conscious. In addition, having an experience with the therapist that directly contradicted this experience was deeply affecting. The therapist's active and persistent attempts to know him in an intimate way, while simultaneously pointing out the pain and self-defeat in detachment, constituted a very specific corrective emotional experience and was experienced as profoundly healing.

There was every indication that this young man had been deprived of the loving, affectionate care of his mother and was taught to be tough, manly, and independent very early in his life. In addition, his mother was very ill and frequently left the home for days and weeks at a time, deactivating the normal attachment behavior between mother and child. He maintained whatever proximity he could to his mother by requesting nothing of her.

When, at the age of 11, he found his parents in bed together, what seemed to surprise him most of all was that they were relaxed and smiling. He repeatedly talked about her smile as he recounted this memory. I believe this is what he craved most. In his fantasy, he talked about having uninterrupted access to her, which *she* found pleasurable. He wanted to touch her and "make her feel great." He wanted to be the one to bring a smile to her face. He had never found a way to do this. From this experience, he concluded that sexual contact was something, perhaps the only thing, that would evoke a warm response from her. It could be argued that the fantasy of satisfying her sexually was born of compliance—a way to give her what he felt she wanted.

Material revealed in the next session could be viewed as support for this hypothesis. He spontaneously reported the fantasy of himself as a baby and child, lying on a blanket in a field next to his mother. What he felt most strongly was a desire to be suckled at the breast—to be able to touch, smell, and taste his mother. This longing was experienced as far deeper and more primary than the genital sexual longing he initially became aware of and, in many ways, was more difficult and less socially acceptable for a grown man to acknowledge. These two levels of desire need not be mutually exclusive. Most marriage and sex therapists (Schnarch, 1991; Zilbergeld, 1992) agree that an integration of these longings and desires deepens adult attachments and is a sign of health. In sexual ecstasy, boundaries are blurred and blissful regression is experienced. Adults must be secure in themselves and their relationship to be able to achieve this.

A TABOO ON TENDERNESS?

In our society, power, toughness, and a lack of sentimentality are viewed as hallmarks of maturity. To be tender, gentle, and sentimental is considered "babyish." There seems to be an especially strong prohibition against these feelings in men. Since sexual prowess is equated with power and toughness, men frequently sexualize their longings for closeness.

Ian Suttie (1937, 1988) suggested that there is a taboo on tenderness far more stringent than that against sexual feelings and impulses. Suttie is considered by many to be one of the most pivotal figures in the movement away from mechanistic drive theory to an object-related attachment theory. He hypothesized an impulse toward tenderness and affection that was social rather than biological in nature and was derived from self-preservation instincts rather than genital appetite. The aim of this impulse was considered truly interpersonal and required, for its satisfaction, "the awakening of an adequate response of appreciation and tenderness in the other person" (White, 1937).

This was graphically depicted in the Detached Observer's fantasy. He imagined awakening a response in his mother that he had not been able to evoke during his life. Suttie hypothesized that being pushed away by mother at an early age (which he referred to as "psychic weaning") would be particularly distressing because it constitutes the deprivation of contact which had been enjoyed "from time immemorial" (p. 87). This was contrasted with the pain of being deprived of sexual gratification, something that might be desired but had never been experienced.

Suttie felt that, whenever this primary need for succor was frustrated or thwarted, anxiety and "neurotic maladjustment" would result. One of the distortions Suttie observed was that of sexualization of a desire for affectionate contact. The other, also evident in this case, was that of detachment. It is important for us, as clinicians, to help our patients sort out their longings and expand their repertoire of expressive behaviors, so that sexual activity becomes but one of many ways for expressing loving feelings.

The Man with Primary Impotence

Where there is a history of sexual dysfunction, working with sexual feelings and impulses, particularly as they emerge in the transference, is of critical importance. The man described here reported a history of primary impotence. His first experience in attempting intercourse, at age 16, resulted in the loss of his erection and inability to penetrate his girlfriend. This became a consistent problem that had plagued him for many years. The success achieved in this case is especially notable, since primary impotence has been a sexual dysfunction associated with severe psychopathology and carries with it a very poor prognosis, even with traditional sex therapy (Singer-Kaplan, 1974).

It became apparent from the beginning of treatment that the source of this man's difficulty had to do with a fusion of sexual and aggressive impulses. During the initial evaluation, his pervasive defenses against any meaningful closeness with the therapist were targeted. This resulted in an outpouring of grief over how superficial his relationships had been. Later in the session, following a 10-minute break, the resistance against meaningful contact with the therapist returned. This time, pressure on the defenses resulted in the experience of anger toward the therapist. The patient reported an impulse to "knock you over in the chair, flip you over and fuck you up the rear." The spontaneous expression of an impulse toward rape indicates a fusion between sexual and aggressive feelings. Before we can attempt to remediate such a problem, we need to understand how the fusion develops.

The material that emerged in this case provides a possible answer. Following the breakthrough of the sadistic impulse toward the therapist, the patient began to weep and recalled how his mother had insisted on wiping his bottom, even when he was 7 and 8 years old, by laying him across her lap. Although there was something stimulating and gratifying about this contact, he also became aware of a fury toward his mother for using him for her own gratification. The patient's father worked nights and, because his mother was afraid of being alone, she had the patient sleep with her. One night, when he was about 5 years old, he witnessed a marital rape. He woke up to hear his mother screaming and imploring him to go get a hammer and clobber his father.

The genesis of the fusion between sexual and aggressive feelings couldn't be clearer. He had learned, in an intense and direct manner, to associate sex with violent aggression. In his experience, both at home and in his tough city neighborhood, the notion that men take women aggressively was repeatedly reinforced. Being tender and loving was equated with being "soft"—"a sissy"—something to be avoided at all costs. These early experiences were highly traumatic and largely excluded from his conscious memory. The fantasy of raping the therapist served as a disguised memory of sorts. As the fantasy of raping the therapist faded and the memories of trauma from the past came into focus, the feelings associated with these early incidents could be approached directly.

If his sexual difficulties were the result of intense and terrifying feelings associated with past trauma, the reliving and reworking of these feelings in a direct manner should result in a relief of symptoms.

THERAPEUTIC STRATEGIES FOR DEALING WITH THE FUSION OF SEXUAL AND AGGRESSIVE IMPULSES

When there is a significant fusion of sexual and aggressive impulses, the first task is to disentangle the two by draining the reactive sadism. This frees up the sexual feelings and impulses, which then need to be integrated with loving feelings. This session, from the midphase of treatment, will illustrate the beginning integration of sexual and loving feelings. This work also served to enhance the patient's sense of separateness from his mother and helped him to consolidate a sense of self based on his own needs and desires rather than those internalized from his mother.

The Emergence of Sexual Longing in the Transference

THERAPIST: That's a big smile.

PATIENT: I'm a little nervous about seeing you, but it's nice to see you. It's both. I'm nervous but it's nice to see you—a friendly face.

THERAPIST: So you have some warm feelings toward me.

PATIENT: Yes (uttered in an exaggerated tone with laughter).

THERAPIST: You get nervous about the positive feelings.

PATIENT: (now in a genuine and thoughtful tone). Yes, yes I do. I'm very nervous. Maybe it has to do with you being a woman.

THERAPIST: What's anxiety provoking about having positive feelings toward a woman?

PATIENT: With a woman, well, a potential lover.

THERAPIST: When did you become aware of these feelings toward me?

PATIENT: When I came in and saw you. I looked at you and, in fact, I looked at your legs. I said to myself, "Nice legs."

Integrating Sexual and Loving Feelings

THERAPIST: So there's a sexual flavor to these warm feelings.

PATIENT: Yes, and it's very difficult to talk about. With women it's difficult to let them into what I'm feeling. Not to digress, but isn't this separate from feelings of friendship and warmth? Isn't the sexual a separate kind of thing? I've always separated them.

THERAPIST: So this is really important, isn't it, and maybe it explains some of the heightened anxiety. You try to keep sexual and loving feelings separate but you have both feelings here toward me.

PATIENT: Yes, in fact, I've been thinking about you and fantasizing about you in a sexual and romantic way.

THERAPIST: And how about today? You notice my legs. What's the impulse? Is there a fantasy?

PATIENT: It wasn't an image but a feeling. It's forbidden territory. From the neck up is OK, but below is forbidden.

THERAPIST: So, if you can't split the loving and sexual feelings, you'll split me in two. This is a very strong tendency in you.

PATIENT: They've never gone together. I could never masturbate to the thought of a girlfriend. It was something forbidden, taboo, violating. I would imagine a friend's mother or a teacher.

THERAPIST: But now they exist together. You have both warm, loving feelings toward me and sexual feelings.

PATIENT: I look at your body and your face but I almost separate them. Your face looks beautiful to me, you look beautiful to me. But when I go down past the neck I go, "WOW, that is sexual!"

THERAPIST: How do you experience these feelings?

PATIENT: It's a feeling of longing and desire, to take you, your arms, your shoulders, to hold you and fondle you. It's luscious—it's wonderful. I'm allowing myself to feel this.

THERAPIST: You say it feels luscious. So now it feels good—not so scary or forbidden.

The anxiety attendant to his sexual feelings is being stripped away, and he's allowing himself to enjoy these feelings and desires—all of which compose a new experience.

T-P Link

THERAPIST: And what is it like to let me know about them?

PATIENT: Usually I fear rejection—that you will resist me and say no. Very specifically, I picture rubbing you along your shoulders and your arms. It feels great to me but feels dissociated from you. As soon as I see your face, I think of rejection (suddenly sits up in his chair). It's like I'm fucking my mother! Oh shit, you know what I mean?

THERAPIST: How did that come to your mind?

PATIENT: That's the most taboo. Suddenly I got an image of my mother in a blue dress with white polka dots. I loved that dress, it had a sheen to it. I remember sexual feelings and it comes back to me, the feel of her belly—seeing her in her girdle.

The patient's initial comment, "It's like fucking my mother," certainly surprised me, and I was suspicious that he was being provocative or sarcastic, as he had a tendency to be. However, the immediate and specific association to his mother in a particular dress, followed by a spontaneous link with his current fetish-like preference for women to wear silky slips and nightdresses, indicated a genuine unlocking of unconscious feelings and memories.

THERAPIST: Just like now, you love the feel of silky fabric over a woman's body.

PATIENT: Yes, and how the feel of her belly gives me excitement.

THERAPIST: So it starts here with letting yourself feel the sexual arousal toward me and then your mother comes to mind, along with memories of those feelings from the past.

PATIENT: I can see her in the bedroom and remember holding her, the warmth and softness of her belly—the hips and buttocks too, which I go crazy over now.

THERAPIST: So what do you want to do?

PATIENT: Rub her behind with my hands. I get aroused. Feeling the soft, fleshy contour of her hips and I move into the vaginal area and I want to fondle and finger her. That feels like a building excitement and a hunger. It's funny, in the fantasy, I look up at her, so I'm small.

THERAPIST: And what do you see?

PATIENT: I see her face, like a Mona Lisa smile—a knowing, understanding smile. She's not angry. She says to me, "Now you know you're supposed to . . ." Oh, I mean . . .

THERAPIST: What's that like—if she's not angry and rejecting but wants you?

PATIENT: Very uncomfortable.

It is very important to follow the out-pouring of material and not to make assumptions about the direction it will take. Although the patient, and probably the therapist, expected the mother to be viewed as a sexually rejecting figure, the slip of the tongue in the previous vignette, along with other supporting material, indicated that the patient felt his mother had sexual desires for him. It was these desires that frightened him.

THERAPIST: Later you did feel she had sexual feelings toward you and you remember those lascivious looks. What about in the fantasy, is she lubricated?

PATIENT: She's lubricated, yeah, ready. Wow, that's wild. Right now I don't feel upset about it. I don't even feel bad about it. I can imagine it feeling wonderful and I don't feel so much the prohibition and horror. There was a lot of sexual feeling there. She used to wipe my ass and my cock was on her lap. I picture fondling her vagina. She's wet. I'm getting hotter and hotter exponentially. I'm erect and I enter her and we're having intercourse and it feels great. Then I look at her face. It's my mother's face and it's old and pale. I don't like it. It doesn't feel good. Her body and her face don't go together. I look at her face and it's, "Oh, yuck!"—a definite turnoff.

Again, the spontaneous flow of associations provided the context for understanding his earlier experience in the transference. The focus on the split between the therapist's face and her body "below the neck," reflected an existing split between feelings and perceptions associated with his young and older mother.

Erotic Attachment to Mother as a Defense against Grief

THERAPIST: What's the feeling now?

PATIENT: Real sadness. I feel real, real sad (starts to cry). I'm holding back, pushing it down, and I want to go back to when I'm fucking her.

THERAPIST: So you go back to her young body and the sexual feeling now to avoid looking at her. She's old and the feeling is sadness. To face her deterioration and death is painful, and you're tempted to go back to the warm, comforting body you remember when you were a boy.

PATIENT: The pain and anguish of watching her deteriorate—seeing her die a piece at a time. Watching someone you love deteriorate is a terrible, terrible thing. This goes deep (crying). I've been having this feeling about young bodies. There's a resentment. I like to look at these young bodies but there's something scary about it—something taboo.

THERAPIST: You've just allowed yourself to face the feelings and fantasies toward your mother, which you sensed she also had toward you. What was really taboo was you having those feelings toward a young, age-appropriate woman. Like in your masturbatory fantasies as a boy—you couldn't let yourself imagine wanting your girlfriend sexually and you would substitute a mother figure. You've been true to her, holding onto her, and it's been very hard to let go. As you see her as she is and say good-bye, it seems to feel like a betrayal.

The material suggests that what was taboo in this man's experience was the opposite of the traditional oedipal situation. His mother wanted him erotically attached to her and became angry and jealous when he became interested in age-appropriate girls. When he was as young as 5 years old, his mother chose him over his father to share her bed. In addition, she attempted to have her young son be her protector and get rid of her abusive husband.

PATIENT: Yeah, I wonder about that.

THERAPIST: Facing the loss is very hard—you want to find a substitute (patient had recently started an affair with a woman in her mid-40s who, like mother, had an old face).

PATIENT: It feels like my mother is inside of me. I've been worried about getting too old. I remind myself that I'm only in my 30s. It feels like my mother. She's dying and beyond help.

THERAPIST: So even if you have to die with her, you stay true. Both of you had difficulty saying good-bye. It seems you can't bear to leave her behind and go on with your life with a young woman. Would she want this?

PATIENT: She's always been so fucking selfish. She never had my best interest in mind. She only thought of herself and when I tried to do things for myself, like take music lessons, she'd curse me. I feel like I'm possessed.

THERAPIST: Do you want her inside or do you want her out?

PATIENT: OUT!

Ousting the Parental Introject

THERAPIST: How do you imagine that?

PATIENT: I picture allowing myself what I want. Being with a beautiful woman who is not neurotic. (In the past, he had displayed an uncanny ability to find women who were just as intrusive, controlling, and abusive as his mother had been.) I want to talk to her directly on the outside. "Get out of me. I'm not your baby boy! I'm not your baby boy! (He starts to cry.) There's nothing I can do for you. I don't want to die before I have lived. I won't let this happen."

This last vignette seems a powerful example of the role of pathogenic beliefs in the maintenance of psychopathology:

Pathogenic beliefs warn the person who holds them that the pursuit of desirable goals, for example, to be independent, happy, or relaxed, or to have a good marriage or satisfying career, will endanger the person or others. To avoid these dangers, the person may renounce valued goals, and may develop inhibitions and symptoms. (Weiss, 1993, p. v)

This patient adopted his mother's views. She quite literally told him she would die without him. In addition, she directly blamed him for her own deterioration and damned him to a life of misery and suffering as punishment. "You should live the life I lived," was a statement he heard repeatedly and a command he had lived out quite faithfully.

He was hostage to the fear of violating his mother's dictates and gave up his desires to ward off the feared consequences. Whereas in the case of the Detached Observer, the patient was able to reconcile his needs with what he imagined his mother would want for him, in the present case, the patient's mother actually wished him a life of misery and suffering. There was no way to undo this painful reality. It had to be faced and dealt with in some way other than the slavish compliance that had dominated his past.

Psychotherapy was necessary to expose and then disconfirm the pathological beliefs adopted through the relationship with his mother. The de-repression of his mixed feelings toward his mother would not have been sufficient to eradicate the pathological beliefs associated with them. His understanding of the rules governing interpersonal relations had to be examined and repudiated. By the end of the session just depicted, he was able to declare, with feeling and conviction, that he would no longer allow himself to be controlled by the fears and beliefs he had adopted at an early age. In facing that which he could not control (his mother's happiness), he was able to focus on that which he could affect—his own. A new sense of freedom ensued.

Those patients whose parents have consciously or unconsciously wished them ill must accomplish on their own the task of finding a will to live. This can only happen when they face and work through the painful reality of their parents' destructiveness. As Marie Cardinal (1983) put it, "Until you learn to name your ghosts and to baptize your hopes, you have not yet born; you are still the creation of others."

Bettelheim (1983) has suggested that achieving a separation from the internalized aggressor requires "an appropriate life-affirming counterforce," like psychotherapy. Up until the time this man entered treatment, his conscious and unconscious goals were in direct opposition to one another. Consciously, he wanted to be free, happy, and healthy. Specifically, he wanted to be able to love and be sexually expressive with the woman of his choice. Unconsciously, this was forbidden. He continued to comply with his mother's wish that he live a miserable life, as she had, and, in so doing, stay loyal to her. As the unconscious feelings and memories came into view, a new alliance could be formed between his conscious and unconscious wishes, such that fulfillment of his needs and desires would be possible. Following this work, the patient formed a stable, loving, and actively sexual relationship with a woman who was both available and responsive, for the first time in his life.

Increased Freedom of Choice

This vital work also highlights the crucial element of choice in the selection of attachment figures. The issue is not simply one of having the ability to establish closeness and intimacy versus isolation and detachment, but one of expanding the arena of conscious choice over these matters. Emotional closeness is not necessarily good and healthy in and of itself, any more than keeping an emotional distance from others is necessarily pathological. It is frequently just as important to solidify patients' ability (and right) to keep a distance from those who would be damaging to them, as it is to enhance their tolerance for genuine intimacy with those who are responsive.

Many patients suffer because they are not able to protect themselves from the intrusiveness of others. The patient described here had an exceptionally intrusive and controlling mother from whom he was helpless to protect himself. As an adult, he tended to re-create this interpersonal drama by choosing women who were intrusive, controlling, and frequently violated his privacy in grossly inappropriate ways. For example, one woman he was dating broke into his home after a quarrel. Since she cleaned his apartment, fed the cats, and left flowers, she denied the incident involved any hostility or violation of his rights. It became just as important for him to learn how to keep a distance from women like that as it was to be able to pursue and become intimate with the kind of warm, responsive women he actually desired.

The goal is for patients to learn to be his or her own gate-keeper—allowing close to them only those individuals who are loving, while keeping a conscious distance from those who are damaging. In the novel *Like Water for Chocolate* (Esquivel, 1989), the necessity for this deep understanding of oneself as a prerequisite for achieving healthy, mutually gratifying relationships is beautifully depicted:

> My grandmother had a very interesting theory; she said that each of us is born with a box of matches inside us but we can't strike them all by ourselves. . . . Each person has to discover what will set off those explosions in order to live, since the combustion that occurs when one of them is ignited is what nourishes the soul.

She went on to say that it was equally important:

> To keep your distance from people who have frigid breath. . . . If we
> stay a good distance away from those people, it's easier to protect
> ourselves from being extinguished. (Esquivel, 1989, pp. 115–116)

GENDER DIFFERENCES IN RESPONSE TO TRAUMA

It has been noted (Herman, 1992; van der Kolk, 1987) that men who
have been abused and traumatized as children tend to identify with the
aggressor and become victimizers as adults. Women, on the other hand,
tend to consolidate an identity around their victimization and repeat a
pattern of being victimized in their intimate relationships. In both cases,
there is a deep fusion of sexual and aggressive feelings. What differs is
the outward manifestation and behavioral sequelae of this fusion.

Most in the field have attributed these differences to socio-cultural
influences that shape gender-related behavior. For either gender, the behavior, whether it's called acting out or the repetition compulsion, is
often viewed as a way of defending against remembering and experiencing a whole range of painful and disruptive feelings associated with traumatic memories. As the defensive element of the behavior is stripped
away, the expressive element achieves dominance.

In the case just reported, the patient re-enacted early trauma in
which sex and violence were directly associated by victimizing women
he considered weaker than himself. He would use them and discard
them without regard for their feelings. In the following case, a woman
who learned to associate love with pain re-enacts early trauma by being
involved with men who use and exploit her.

The Masochistic Artist

This 40-year-old professional woman of considerable beauty, intelligence, and accomplishment came for treatment because of a marital
break-up that had precipitated an intrapsychic crisis. She was questioning both why she was having such a difficult time extricating herself
from a clearly unsatisfactory marriage and what had motivated her
choice in the first place. She entered treatment shortly after leaving her
husband of 12 years and resuming an affair with an old lover. She was
tormented by anxiety and guilt regarding this affair, which reinforced

the painful sense she had of herself as weak and immoral. That she was separated and had endured many years of deprivation and mistreatment by her husband did not seem to factor into her understanding of her own behavior. Each time she would begin to entertain the notion of choice regarding her marriage, she would be overcome with anxiety and guilt, insisting she must try ever harder to reconcile with her husband.

During her marriage, the patient had become very successful in her career while her husband floundered. As soon as she had become established, he quit his teaching post and never regained any semblance of financial or professional stability. He became increasingly demanding of her in every way—to stay slim and ever more successful in her career, yet remain beholdened to him. No matter how much she accomplished, he was never satisfied. In fact, all her accomplishments were diminished and devalued by him. This pattern of control through demands and criticism paralleled the relationship she had with her mother. From the outset of treatment it was this mother-daughter dynamic that was most clear, not only in her relationship with her husband, but also in relationship to the therapist. This particular T-C-P link was the focus of early interpretive work.

The patient's lover seemed to resemble her father. She described both as "Boy Scouts"—sweet, kind, responsible, and unassuming. The patient was initially reluctant to examine the relationship with her father and tended to regard it as unimportant. In the session to be recounted here, she reported having seen the movie *Cape Fear*. Her reactions and associations to the film were directly connected to her father, who she was beginning to realize was very possessive of her. I decided to use this opening to explore her sexual life and relationships with men by asking about her masturbatory fantasies.

Exploration of Masturbatory Fantasies

THERAPIST: We haven't looked at your sexual development. When did you start masturbating and what are your masturbatory fantasies?

PATIENT: Well my fantasies started around the age of 6. Really my sexual fantasies always have been pretty masochistic—rape fantasies—things that are self-degrading.

THERAPIST: Let's look at one of the rape fantasies.

PATIENT: Well they can go all sorts of ways, like let's say a motorcycle gang or a burglar, but the heaviest one is about a family. I've been having that one more frequently lately.

THERAPIST: How does it go?

PATIENT: I'm in the country, looking for a piece of furniture, for example. There's a person who looks a little strange and he owns an antique shop. He wants me to look at something in the barn but it actually turns out to be a torture chamber. He proceeds to rape and torture me. Then we go up to the house and the family is all there. His wife is into this too. There are older children and younger children. I keep thinking, what is this all about?

THERAPIST: What's your idea?

PATIENT: Well, it's obviously about a father figure and a family. It seems indicative of a lot of things. If I examine it, I won't be able to use it as a fantasy. You see, I'm not blind to the dynamic in which I am always the victim. But it goes back so far. My worst fear is that I've been so damaged from an early age that I won't be able to change it. I feel kind of fatalistic about it.

This sexual fantasy actually depicts her own family constellation. There was a mother and father and two sets of children—older children from her father's previous marriage and she and her sister from her parents' marriage. Sexual fantasies seem to be a kind of window into the world of internalized object relations, defined here as an organization of mental representation of self and others that has been established early in life through the interaction between the child and significant others. In a thinly disguised way, sexual fantasies often reveal how the patient views intimate relationships, as well as revealing the source of these assumptions in the early family dynamics (Schnarch, 1993). As the patient will say later on, the fantasies are "symbolically fraught" and should not be understood as actual memories.

The patient arrived for the next session in a state of acute distress. She felt compelled to return to her husband, as if she were trapped and had no choice but to reunite with this depriving and emotionally abusive man. She then reported a dream that she felt was highly significant. Dreams are often offered during the phase of treatment when de-repression is at its height. The dreams are typically quite revealing, with little distortion evident.

Dream Work

PATIENT: I had this dream about my father. There was a man who was my lover. We made love and it was nice. Afterward, I sat and watched him—like Picasso's "Sleep Watchers." Then it was like a sci-fi film where the guy turns into a werewolf, except he turned into my father as a young man. He woke up and raped me—sodomized me. It was a dream within a dream. In the dream within the dream, I was trying to wake up and I thought "Oh, that's it, that's it." What this is, I don't know.

THERAPIST: When the man was a contemporary, the lovemaking was nice. Then he turned into your father and he raped you. How did that go?

PATIENT: I remember it was sodomy—penetration of the rectum. The clearest memory is what he looked like. It was so vivid. You know you forget what your parents looked like when they were young.

THERAPIST: What was your feeling in the dream?

PATIENT: Victimized.

THERAPIST: Any arousal?

PATIENT: No. I was frightened and I wanted to wake up. But it was more than that. It was a clue or a hint. It made sense. I felt like "I got it" that was the main feeling.

Defenses against Cognitive Clarity

In a sense, this patient doesn't let herself know what she knows about her father and his sexualized attachment to her. Although the patient has no memories of being sexually abused by him, a wealth of memories surfaced that suggested he was overly concerned about her interest in boys and tended to project his own sexual feelings and desires onto her in a highly attacking and critical manner. As early as age 6 (the age when her fantasies began), her father made comments about her interest in boys and their bodies while at a basketball game. When she was 10, she and her sister ran into some strange men on an island in a lake on their property. They made a hasty return to shore and reported the incident to their father. The patient's sister became hysterical, while she remained the calm one who got them safely to shore. Her father failed to attend to his daughter in distress or to the men on the island. Instead, he focused on the patient and her lack of emotional response, suggesting she must have been interested in the men and liked being there. Numerous other memories of his anger and jealousy regarding boyfriends were reported. The dream, then, seemed like a clear depiction of the way she experienced the relationship with her father. He became angry when she was involved with age-appropriate boyfriends (satisfying love-making with a peer in the first part of the dream), and behaved in an attacking fashion toward her (graphically depicted as a rape).

It is essential that we, as therapists, not jump to conclusions and take too literal or concrete an approach to dreams and fantasies. Again, there is no evidence that this woman's father actually raped or in any way physically molested her. Nevertheless, his reactions to her were experienced as harsh and punitive. In fact, this more subtle means of undermining her confidence as a young woman, increased her confusion about its source. The patient internalized the message that she was perverse and viewed herself in accordance with parental expectation. In so doing, she remained blind to her father's role in projecting his own unacceptable feelings and impulses onto her.

Patient Makes Her Own Interpretation

PATIENT: I've been thinking about this—there's something in these fantasies. My father was a prince because my mother was such a witch. He would come home and rescue me and my sister. He knew that. If my attention was diverted to someone else, then he would notice and tease me about it or diminish it, because then he couldn't be the only one to rescue me.

THERAPIST: Perhaps the dream was an expression of how you felt—that he was jealous and possessive. His taking you is graphically depicted in this dream. Unlike the fantasies, in the dream you are terrified; this is against your will, and there is no arousal. Let's look at how you feel toward your father for treating you like this.

PATIENT: The feeling is blocked. I think the awareness—the "Oh, that's it" is beneath that.

Here the patient confirms that it is essential to get in touch with affect first, before moving to interpretations. She seems to be saying that her inability to feel is a way to remain unaware. It's all a part of a numbed and foggy state she had maintained about her relationship with her father. Access to her feelings was the key to understanding.

Alice Miller (1986) has suggested that there is a special prohibition against awareness of parental deficiencies, particularly in cases in which the parents are narcissistically vulnerable themselves. In this case, the patient's mother was very disturbed and was a frightening figure for the patient. She clung to the idea that her father was a prince and would save her from her mother. It would have been too overwhelming for her to recognize the deficiencies in both of them, so she denied her perceptions of her father's difficulties and readily accepted his projections.

Encouraging such patients to focus on their internal experience and to articulate these feelings, is an invaluable aid in clarifying perceptions of self and other. Miller (1986) has stated that change occurs much more rapidly than previously considered possible when patients can articulate the childhood traumas they've experienced. These patients, whom I've referred to as self-sacrificing (Della Selva, 1991), focus on the feelings of others at the expense of their own experience. They do this so automatically, they literally don't know what they are feeling. Helping them to access and attend to their own feelings proves a reliable guide to their internal truth. At the same time, it is this very thing that has been forbidden and feels dangerous. The danger involved becomes clear in the next vignette.

Assessing the Dangers Associated with Feeling

PATIENT: I feel I have to give in—if I don't submit, I'll lose him.

THERAPIST: Let's see how that would happen.

PATIENT: I feel I can't struggle against it—that I have to hold something down inside me that wants to struggle against him but, oh (cries out in pain and reports that she's been having back spasms).

THERAPIST: What do you make of these back spasms coming now?

PATIENT: I feel like my body is punishing me, but that's a very upsetting thought—to think I need to be punished, if that's what it is. Or, maybe, that I'm just so used to it.

THERAPIST: This is all coming together now—you submit to this pain and hold down the anger inside you—the part that wants to fight against him. What would happen if that came out?

PATIENT: I feel like I'd want to kill him, really. I'd strangle him.

The Roots of Masochism

The question this patient raises is vital and one that's been a real point of contention in the field. Is masochism the result of the patient's need to suffer, or a re-enactment of traumatic interactions that have become an ingrained pattern of attachment? The ways in which we understand the origins of masochism will directly and profoundly affect our attitude toward patients and the therapeutic endeavor.

Davanloo (1988) has articulated the belief that masochistic patients have a need to suffer as punishment for their own violent and sadistic impulses. According to his view, these patients suffer from superego pathology. Consequently, treatment is directed toward the patients' sadism, guilt, and need for punishment through masochistic suffering. The danger in this approach is that patients feel blamed for their own suffering and are re-traumatized by the treatment. Should this occur, their sense of themselves as bad and deserving of punishment could be reinforced instead of being dispelled.

Although the notion of pleasure in suffering has a long history in psychoanalytic theory, this assumption has recently come under intense scrutiny (Shainess, 1986). There is increasing evidence that those who behave in a masochistic fashion are treating themselves the way they were treated as children. Their behavior constitutes an enactment of early, unconscious attachment patterns of behavior. In this way, patients' symptoms serve as a disguised means of communication.

When patients' defenses against feeling and remembering are eroded, the situations they faced as children become increasingly clear. As they are encouraged to face the rage toward parents and experience the grief over all that has been lost, symptoms that had previously served as disguised communications are rendered obsolete.

Since this woman tended to take on others' feelings and perceptions as her own, and stayed blind to her own internal truth, a focus on the experience of her true feelings was an essential step in the consolidation of an authentic sense of self. The patient was encouraged to experience the growing rage against her father. She declared a wish to annihilate him and peel off his skin, layer by layer.

THERAPIST: So you're no longer the submissive little girl. You are angry and you want to fight back. What is his reaction?
PATIENT: He doesn't have a chance.
THERAPIST: What does his face look like?
PATIENT: I don't want to see his face.
THERAPIST: Why not?
PATIENT: I don't want to see fear. I don't want to care about that. I don't care. I don't care.

Although the patient can be viewed as holding onto her anger as a way to avoid grief over the loss of her father, the anger is important in its own right. This woman has not been able to access and utilize her anger to protect herself in the past. This has rendered her quite vulnerable to being used and abused, particularly by men. Her determination to hold onto the anger and not sympathize with her father so readily was a safeguard against losing herself in the experience of another. Although the ultimate goal is for her to be able to experience her own feelings while maintaining some empathic contact with others, focusing exclusively on her own experience at this point in treatment seemed necessary to tip the balance. I decided not to push her to experience the grief at that moment and, as the material in the following session reveals, it was not necessary.

Re-Playing versus Re-Living

PATIENT: Before I felt like I was re-playing a situation from the past—literally re-playing it out of compulsion because there was something wrong with me. I couldn't really make my marriage work because something was wrong with me and I really am an adulteress and I really can't be trusted. And also the sense that when I go to someone who is loving, it's the wrong person—it's all a mistake. More recently, though, I feel like I'm actually re-living a trauma. Not just reconstructing a situation but actually re-living a trauma.

THERAPIST: And allowing yourself to experience all the feelings in reaction to it.

This statement, along with the material that will be revealed in a subsequent session, lends considerable support to the hypothesis that the source of this woman's masochism was a compulsive re-living of the early relationship with her parents. What she had been unable to remember and directly experience in relation to the past was re-played in her current intimate relationships. Once that repetitive dynamic became clear, and she began to experience the feelings of rage and grief she had repressed, her whole demeanor changed. There were immediate and dramatic decreases in symptomatology, and even more impressive, dramatic changes in her sense of herself, others, and the world. These changes will be illustrated in Chapter 7.

SUMMARY

As feelings of reactive rage and grief over losses are experienced and integrated into conscious memory, positive feelings toward the therapist, frequently linked to genetic figures, become prominent. These positive feelings can, and often do, include a sexualized longing for physical contact. In my experience, the anxiety and defensiveness that often accompany these feelings should not be minimized, nor should they be considered a mere consequence of unresolved anger. Frequently, these feelings and impulses are quite anxiety provoking in and of themselves. The dangers associated with their experience and expression have roots in the past and need to be exposed and re-evaluated for therapeutic change to occur. As anxiety wanes, tolerance for positive feelings and longings for closeness increase. These changes enhance the quality of the patient's current relationships.

CHAPTER 7

Working Through toward Character Change

> Man's main task in life is to give
> birth to himself, to become what
> he potentially is. The most
> important product of his effort is his
> own personality.
>
> *Eric Fromm (1947)*
> *Man for Himself*

For the therapeutic process to achieve rapid and enduring change in a patient's character, the intrapsychic system must be in a state of disequilibrium. Frequently, an external crisis in the patient's life begins this process. When no such crisis has occurred, or the patient's ego is constricted by the rigid use of character defenses, Davanloo advocates creating an intrapsychic crisis using the techniques of pressure and challenge to the defensive armor. The continual pressure to remain highly emotionally and cognitively involved in the therapeutic process keeps the resistance from returning and the characteristic patterns of adaptation from settling back in once the immediate crisis is over. This, in turn, facilitates the working through of core conflicts and solidifies character change.

WHAT IS "WORKING THROUGH"?

Freud considered the process of working through to be the feature of psychoanalytic treatment that distinguished it from other, more suggestive forms of therapy. Despite the lip service that workers in the field often give to the crucial nature of working through for the ultimate success of therapy, they have written less about this process than any other aspect of psychodynamic treatment (Weinberger, 1995). In addition, the lengthy nature of most psychodynamic treatment has made any systematic research into the process untenable. So, we'll begin with what has been written about this vital process.

Early in his work, Freud discovered that catharsis was a necessary but insufficient ingredient for the achievement of stable and enduring change. The process that occurs after an insight is obtained and leads to stable changes in feelings, attitudes, and behavior has been called "working through." During this process, insights are translated into observable changes in the patient's ego functioning. These changes include improved modulation of anxiety and affect, alteration in the patient's defensive structure, and modification of internalized images of self and other. Because all defensive processes originate in the ego, the functioning of the ego is altered when defenses are dismantled through the process of working through. Greenson (1967) wrote that working through operates "only on the ego," and for treatment to be considered successful, "the ego has to give up its pathological defensive function."

Working through is the "meat" of dynamic psychotherapy and constitutes the midphase of treatment. It is the longest and least predictable phase of therapy and varies most widely from patient to patient and therapist to therapist. In part, such variability may be due to the lack of guidelines for conducting this crucial aspect of the work. This is especially troubling because this phase of psychotherapy seems to have the greatest impact on outcome. Wachtel (1977, 1993) has suggested that most failures in psychotherapy are attributed to a lack of working through and rarely, for example, to a lack of insight. He reminds us that, in psychotherapy, as in life, it is follow-through that makes the difference.

THE PROCESS OF WORKING THROUGH

Nearly all definitions of working through involve the notion of repetition. According to Greenson (1967), during the process of working through "a variety of circular processes are set into motion in which insight, memory, and behavior change influence each other." As this process occurs, it needs to be repeatedly reviewed to deepen insight and further the process of change. In Intensive Short-Term Dynamic Psychotherapy, this type of circular process is set into rapid motion and maintained within an affectively charged atmosphere, speeding the process of working through.

We can only gauge the success of working through in a post hoc fashion, by observing changes that occur subsequent to our interventions. The depth and stability of these changes are put to the test when the patient faces a conflictual situation and displays the following changes:

1. A reduction in anxiety.
2. Decreased reliance on defensive processes.
3. An increase in emotional activation and freedom of affective expression.
4. Cognitive understanding of the relationship between feelings, anxiety, and defenses.
5. A newfound sense of mastery that overrides feelings of helplessness.
6. Increased adaptive capacity suggesting psychological growth.

Each of these elements will be briefly reviewed.

Reduction Changes in Anxiety

Although all dynamic psychotherapists understand the importance of the triangle of conflict (the relationship between impulse/feeling, anxiety, and defense), different schools of thought seem to place particular emphasis on one factor over the others when intervening in neurotic styles of behavior. The drive theorists view the strength of the impulses as the determining factor in neurotic maladjustment, and tailor their interventions to tame the impulses by increasing the role of secondary processes. In other words, "Where id was, let ego be." The ego psychological approach suggests that it is not the feelings or impulses themselves that cause the trouble, but the habitual use of pathological defenses against their full and direct experience. Consequently, their therapeutic strategy involves efforts aimed at an alteration of defense and resistance.

Yet another set of theorists (Dewald, 1972; Wachtel, 1977, 1993) have suggested that the *excessive anxiety* associated with feelings and impulses is the driving force behind neurotic behavior. This factor has been "relatively neglected" by psychodynamic theorists (Weinberger, 1995). Davanloo is an exception. The therapy he has developed, like many learning-theory based approaches to therapy, emphasizes the importance of *exposure* to anxiety-provoking stimuli. In ISTDP, patients are encouraged to face the problems in their life very directly. As the anxiety originally associated with forbidden feelings and impulses is reduced or eliminated, the pathological defenses that were designed to avoid that anxiety will no longer be required. Then, the adult ego will be free to adduce new and more adaptive strategies for the expression and satisfaction of feelings and desires. Working through can be conceptualized as a series of extinction trials in which affects become detoxified (Wachtel, 1977). The result is increased freedom of expression.

A reduction in anxiety is undoubtedly a goal of psychotherapy, but how can therapists help their patients achieve this goal? Dewald (1972) suggested that the gradual elimination of anxiety, guilt, and shame, so essential in the remediation of psychopathology, is the result of the "repeated exposure to rational perception and conscious integration" provided during the phase of working through. Davanloo would agree. Anxiety increases as the forbidden feelings and impulses are approached. Once the feeling breaks through the repressive barrier and is directly experienced without the feared consequences occurring, anxiety is reduced. This is particularly powerful when it occurs within the therapeutic relationship (Teyber, 1992). Patients tend to become bolder following such an experience, expressing themselves more freely. This typically results in positive interactions with others, further reducing the anxiety that was previously associated with affect.

Take the Woman with Panic Attacks (Chapter 5) as an example. The experience of anger was highly anxiety arousing for this woman, and she avoided it at significant cost. As the root of her dread was deeply unconscious, mere exploration of why she felt anger was dangerous would have yielded little of therapeutic value. Davanloo suggests that we expose the conflict by approaching it directly. As the patient talked about her anger toward her husband, the therapist applied pressure on the defenses to facilitate the actual experience of her rage. It was the direct and current experience of anger toward her husband for leaving her that provoked the impulses to kill him. As she faced the impulse to stab him, the image of her dead mother appeared. Then, the memories of the trauma associated with her mother's death and of the patient's last visit with her came into consciousness, providing an opportunity for the patient to relive (emotional) and then re-evaluate (cognitive) the situation from the perspective of an adult. As a child, she experienced an overwhelming sense of guilt about her mother's death. She was so filled with anxiety, lest anyone find out about the wish toward her mother, that she sealed off the entire experience from her consciousness, only to feel all the anxiety again whenever her husband was away on business. As an adult, she knew her wishes did not cause her mother's death. Instead of judging herself so harshly for the anger she felt toward her mother, she was able to feel some compassion for herself. The key factor in her recovery was the reduction in the underlying anxiety, which came about as a result of the working-through process. As this brief example illustrates, repeating in the present that which was experienced as traumatic in the past can create an opportunity to re-evaluate the danger inherent in the situations that were so frightening in the past. In this case, being separated from her husband no longer seemed dangerous. In fact, the patient reported feeling calm when alone and enjoying the freedom her husband's schedule afforded her.

In other cases, the anxiety attendant to affect is so strong it must be reduced before the underlying feeling can be approached. Inquiry is sometimes sufficient to diffuse the intensity of the anxiety. Making the link between the affect and anxiety can be the starting point for the inquiry. A statement such as, "You seem terrified of your own anger. What's your idea about that?" can begin to bring a perspective to bear on associations that are old and have not undergone any revision since childhood.

Evidence of Decreased Reliance on Defenses

Malan and Osimo (1992) have suggested that symptom removal alone is insufficient to accomplish character change. Indeed, for the process of working through to be considered complete, every symptom and pathological defense must be replaced with something adaptive. Clinicians spend most of their time and effort detecting defects in the regulation of affect and cognitive processing of their patients, rarely considering in any depth what non-defensive ego functioning actually looks like.

Norma Haan (1977) has filled in this gap by detailing the differences between coping (healthy adaptation), defending (neurotic solutions), and fragmenting (psychotic decompensation). Coping is defined by flexibility and conscious choice. Coping behavior is purposeful. In contrast, defensive behavior is rigid, channeled, and propelled by unconscious forces. Whereas defensive behavior is driven by the past and distorts the present, coping behavior is aimed at the future, while oriented to present reality.

These definitions can help us to be specific about the kinds of changes we are looking for in our patients. The goal of working through is to help patients become more conscious and purposeful in their behavior, employing flexible and adaptive choices. The *process* of living often changes more noticeably for patients than their specific behaviors. For example, patients who feel anxiously driven to prove themselves, like the Masochistic Artist (Chapter 6), may spend many hours at work. Following a successful treatment, they may be just as busy and productive as before, but they report a sense of freedom and delight in their work, rather than feeling driven by a need to perform and produce.

When changes begin to occur and the patient deals directly with a feeling or conflict that had been avoided by defensive means in the past, the contrast between the two should be highlighted. This gives the patient another opportunity to critically assess the differing experiences and outcomes, which further solidifies the new changes.

Increased Freedom of Emotional Expression Along with Cognitive Understanding: The Role of Integration in the Process of Working Through

Affective activation has been shown to be an effective means for gaining rapid access to core conflicts. As these conflicts come to life within the therapy session, they can be dealt with directly. This process provides a pathway for achieving a thorough intellectual understanding of emotionally felt experience—a vital ingredient for working through aimed at rapid therapeutic change.

According to Strupp and Binder (1984), who have conducted years of research on the process of change in short-term dynamic psychotherapy, the key to therapeutic success is "conceived of as the affective experiencing and cognitive understanding of current maladaptive patterns of behavior that repeat childhood patterns of interpersonal conflict" (pp. 24–25).

Initially, as defenses are abandoned, patients experience considerable depth of feeling. Davanloo insists that interpretive work, conceptualized as a cognitive re-analysis of the process, must *follow* these emotionally charged experiences within the therapeutic setting. At this juncture, the therapist can meaningfully focus on the repetitive patterns apparent in the patient's life and can begin to understand what one patient called "the elegant economy" of symptomatic behavior. What had seemed senseless now has meaning. With fresh insight into the meaning and function of patterns that have affected both past and current functioning, new options can be considered.

There seems to be a fairly wide consensus in both the clinical and research literature that the most effective and efficient method for speeding the process of working through is a two-pronged approach: (a) mobilize intense affect, and (b) examine the thoughts, memories, and beliefs associated with these feelings as they emerge in the affect-laden communications from patient to therapist. By including both affect and cognition in the process of analysis, the experiencing and observing functions of the ego are interwoven, facilitating integration of these two spheres.

Mastery and Competence

Achieving mastery involves overcoming helplessness. All the elements involved in working through discussed so far result in feelings of competence and mastery. Greenson (1967) wrote that patients deal with feelings of helplessness engendered by early trauma by "actively repeating the situation that once induced the original sense of panic." In so doing, "The ego which was passive in the original traumatic situation actively reproduces the event at the time it chooses, in circumstances favorable to it, and thus slowly learns to cope with it" (p. 178). This frequently happens within the therapeutic relationship. Patients test us out by doing their typical dance and waiting for a response. We need to respond differently from significant figures in the past so that the same old story has a new ending. According to Malan (1979), "What went wrong must go right, again and again."

Regardless of the particular goals achieved, character change has not been achieved until and unless a fundamental shift from passive to active involvement in one's own life has occurred. Research confirms the notion that enhancing a patient's sense of mastery is crucial to positive outcome (Weinberger, 1995). How is this achieved? In ISTDP, patients are encouraged to assume an active role in their own treatment. The therapist expresses an inherent confidence in patients' ability to face difficulties and cope at their highest level of ability. In addition to this somewhat general factor, more specific elements are also required to facilitate patients' growing sense of mastery. As patients become conscious of the particular thoughts and feelings they had previously defended against, they are free to deal with them in a rational and intentional manner, typically leading to more effective behavior. This effectiveness leads to a sense of mastery.

Research (Bandura, 1986, 1989; Hollan, Evans, & DeRubeis, 1990; Whisman, 1993) strongly suggests that a patient's attribution regarding the cause of change significantly affects long-term outcome. Those patients who attribute their therapeutic success at termination to their own efforts were able to sustain their gains, whereas those who attributed success to external factors, such as their therapist, tended to regress following termination (Bandura, 1986, 1989). These attributions relate to whether patients experienced a sense of mastery in dealing with their own problems or whether they felt "cured" by the therapist. Davanloo's techniques place a great deal of emphasis on patient responsibility. Patients often report that, while treatment was difficult, they feel proud of themselves for working hard and facing their problems. This seems to bode well for future success.

As patients gain experience with an active mode of dealing with situations and feelings they had passively avoided in the past, a new or renewed sense of enthusiasm for life emerges. New tasks are approached with vigor and old conflicts tend to be re-visited from this active, competent position. One patient, who had always felt completely helpless and overwhelmed in the presence of her mother, began to feel her own strength as she allowed herself to experience anger over the harsh treatment she had received at her mother's hand. She spontaneously said, "I'm 36 now, not a little 2-year-old. I could literally kill my mother with my own two hands." She then smiled and said she had started working out at a gym and was enjoying her newfound upper body strength. This feeling of mastery expanded her view of herself to include a power to affect her surroundings and interactions. She was taking stands at work and getting noticed by her boss. Such pervasive alteration in her functioning denote genuine character change.

Authors from James Mann (1973) to Alice Miller (1986) contend that it is essential to acknowledge the very real helplessness our patients experienced as children. However, this must be contrasted with their current ability to effect the world. It is this crucial distinction in our patients' view of themselves—from a helpless child to an active adult—that must change for psychotherapy to be successful. It was just this sort of change that occurred, during the therapeutic process, in the case of the Man with Primary Impotence (Chapter 6). When treatment began, he defined his problem as a pervasive sense of helplessness. He reported feeling small and weak and as if he had no solid center of being. He contrasted this to his colleagues, who seemed like competent adults. After the session detailed in Chapter 6, he was able to declare that he was no longer his mother's baby, but a man willing and able to make his own choices in life. This kind of change will endure over time and affect all future behavior.

From Regression to Growth

Change occurs as the *result* of a process of integration and application of the knowledge obtained in therapy. When concrete and stable change in behavior occurs, we conclude that the conflict that had previously prevented adaptive functioning has been "worked through." In more operational terms, we can say that conflicts are worked through when there is evidence in each corner of the triangle:

1. A reduction in anxiety.
2. An increased tolerance for the experience of affect.
3. Decreased reliance on defenses. In addition, we look for an expanded capacity for intellectual and creative functioning, and an increased ability to form and maintain intimate relationships.

As this definition suggests, working through has been accomplished when growth resumes. Menninger (1958) suggested that it is the process of working through which facilitates the transformation from regression to growth. When this occurs, "The infantile aims and goals lose much of their compulsive force; the patient is then free to choose or to develop new techniques, aims and goals that are more adaptive and gratifying" (p. 75). He goes on to say that such a transformation takes "strenuous effort" and involves that rarely mentioned dimension of change called the will. Davanloo frequently speaks to the patient's conscious will to change and exhorts patients to assume control of their own behavior in alignment with their will. He has emphasized that our patients feel helpless, not only in dealing with the external world, but in the face of their own internal feelings and reactions. Both must be mastered for success to be considered complete.

IMPLICATIONS FOR TREATMENT

Before we can begin to understand and treat neurotic maladjustment, we must be explicit about our assumptions regarding what constitutes healthy functioning. How do we understand human nature? Are our most basic feelings and impulses anti-social and in need of strict restraint? So say the drive theorists. An alternative view is that our feelings and desires are basically healthy and sound, but when associated with anxiety, guilt, and shame, their means of satisfaction become distorted and ineffective. The solution depends on the definition of the problem. In the first case, renunciation of wish fulfillment is the answer. In the second, finding appropriate avenues for the direct gratification of basic needs would be the goal.

Davanloo's treatment model is based on the latter set of assumptions. His therapy was designed to boost the development of ego functions such that patients are able to operate at their highest level of ego-adaptive capacity. This includes the ability to relate to others in a clear and direct way, to work productively, and to fulfill their dreams and potential.

When symptomatic, patients defend against painful and anxiety-provoking thoughts, feelings, and memories in a way that prevents adaptive functioning in current life. The goal of treatment, achieved by the process of working through, is for the ego to attain or regain its ascendance. Then, those feelings or situations that used to arouse anxiety and generate the deployment of pathological defenses, are dealt with in a deliberate and adaptive manner. For this type of change in ego functioning to be maintained, each pathological defense must be replaced with an adaptive strategy for coping.

The power and strength of ISTDP is achieved by combining and integrating all the preceding strategies. Rather than focusing on one aspect of conflict, whether it be feelings, anxiety, or defense, to the relative neglect of the others, all of these vital ingredients are addressed as a totality. This involves linking the three corners of the triangle of conflict (feelings, anxiety, and defense). While in certain cases, one aspect of the triangle of conflict may be particularly troublesome and will require focused attention, it is the deep understanding of the inter-connectedness of feelings, anxiety, and defense that is considered necessary to resolve a conflict. To facilitate the process of working through, the triangle of conflict is then linked with the triangle of person (therapist, current figures, and past significant others). The goal is for patients to become cognitively and affectively aware of the repetitive patterns of interaction that have predominantly influenced their functioning. As patients actually experience the power of these dynamics in their life, particularly in the transference, they become consciously aware of the central issue or conflict that has been perpetuating these repetitions. This awareness creates the possibility of conscious choice regarding the satisfaction of their goals in a way that will facilitate growth and satisfaction with life, rather than fuel regression and perpetuate misery.

To achieve this end, some patients need more work in one realm than the other. So, even though ISTDP focuses a great deal on the experience of affect, the emphasis on insight and understanding is equally strong. In fact, greater time and effort may be devoted to the cognitive re-analysis of the triangle of conflict than in achieving affect-laden breakthroughs, especially with more fragile patients. It has been Davanloo's ability to deal equally well with each of these elements and to rapidly determine which patients require what kind of emphasis, that has contributed to the rapid and dramatic changes in those he treats.

This process has been operationally defined by Malan for purposes of training and research. His studies (Malan, 1976, 1979; Malan & Osimo, 1992), along with others investigating the effectiveness of STDP (Trujillo & McCullough, 1985), have provided data consistent with the view that successful outcome in psychotherapy is highly correlated with the frequency of affectively meaningful T-C-P links. This particular interpretation has been designed to facilitate an integration of cognitive and affective levels of experience.

TECHNICAL CONSIDERATIONS IN WORKING THROUGH

Once again, the differences between traditional analytic treatment and ISTDP are in technique, not theory or goals. Greenson (1967) espouses the traditional view that working through must be, by definition, a long and arduous process. In his classic text, he described how one particular insight was worked through over a period of 6 months of almost daily sessions. He went so far as to state that any rapidity in the process of working through would, by definition, be superficial and transient. We have since learned this is not the case. In fact, this condensed form of treatment can lead not only to rapid, but to deep and long-lasting change (Malan & Osimo, 1992).

The issue of a highly focused approach is critical. Rather than maintain "evenly hovering attention," Davanloo has suggested we return to Freud's initial therapeutic stance of "seizing the resistance by the throat." Paying special attention to the repetitive patterns in the patient's thoughts, feelings, defenses, and behavior in a selective fashion will accelerate the process of working through. Rather than finding patient's conflicts to be highly complex and "overdetermined," Davanloo has found they tend to be quite elementary in nature (Bauer & Kobos, 1987). What may appear to be a complicated picture of symptoms and defenses can often be viewed as derivatives of basic conflicts around love and loss, anger and betrayal. The process of working them through is accelerated by such clarity.

ISTDP employs the following active intervention strategies to facilitate the process of working through:

1. A high level of therapist activity.
2. A focus on the patient's current life (the C corner of the triangle of person, so often ignored in treatment).
3. Attention to change within and between sessions.
4. Encouraging the patient to assume an active, rather than passive, role in his or her own treatment and own life.

In ISTDP, the therapist makes quite clear that real change in behavior is the goal. We are not involved in an intellectual exercise or mere expansion of self-understanding. Patients come to our offices because they are suffering and want to change. The therapist positions him- or herself on the side of change, creating an alliance with the healthy part of the patient's ego. As soon as an insight is achieved or a declaration is made, the therapist applies some pressure on the patient to behave in accordance with these intentions. Questions such as "Then what are you going to do about the smiling, the diversion, and the avoidance of this feeling?" or "Let's see if you can take this opportunity to do it differently and let me know, directly, how you feel this growing anger toward me?" make it clear that change is expected to follow insight. This active encouragement to put insights into action within the therapy session provides a new experience—one of mastery—within a safe environment.

Although some may consider these interventions new and radical, they have a long history. Freud encouraged his patients to approach what they fear, not just in the analytic sessions, but in their daily lives. Freida Fromm-Reichman (1950) believed it was essential to "train" patients to test out any insight gained in therapy sessions by "investigating it in its relatedness to their practical living and to the conduct of their relationship with others" (p. 144).

The therapist not only encourages change but models persistence and follow-through by drawing the patient's attention to each change as it occurs and then processing how it feels to do things differently. This step is often neglected and may be partially responsible for the added repetitions often required to foster change. Focusing on a single instance of change in some detail and comparing it with past experiences enhances the contrast between the two. This provides another opportunity to assess the relationship between behavior and outcome—both how past defensive maneuvers have contributed to the perpetuation of suffering and how the present experience of direct affective expression leads to feelings of strength and competence. Such an analysis yields further impetus to change.

THE CENTRAL IMPORTANCE OF T-C LINKS

In traditional psychoanalysis, getting to the past seemed to be the goal. The transference pattern of behavior was used to achieve the end of reconstructing the past. All too often, the patient's current life outside the analysis was neglected. Ferenzi and Rank were the first to caution against this relative neglect and suggested a focus on T-C links, only going to the past as necessary to facilitate an understanding of the present conflicts. All three corners of the triangle of the person must be attended to for working through to be complete, but the transference and the past recede in importance over time, while changes in the present become the most significant aspect of the work.

PRACTICAL APPLICATION OF NEW LEARNING

During graduate school, I had an opportunity to train in the martial arts. Most of the training sessions were spent honing skills and techniques through repetition and drill. Within the group setting, sparring was structured and safe. The real question was, would the techniques learned in this environment be generalized to life on the street, where one might actually have to employ them? The teacher did not leave this to chance. At the end of each session, he would say, "Now it's practical application time." He would portrait scenarios in which students might need to use the techniques learned in class to protect themselves. This was of enormous value when I was jumped from behind one morning while walking to class. I could hear my teacher's voice in my head and quickly ran through my options. I was able to scare away the attacker. Without the bridge from technique to application provided by my teacher at the end of each class, I might not have been able to apply what I had learned. This is what we need to do in a systematic way during the working-through phase of therapy.

Therefore, in the practice of ISTDP, the therapist encourages active attempts at change within the hour and communicates quite directly to patients that changes in their current life are expected as well. When a change occurs in relation to the therapist, the implications for the patient's current life and relationships are addressed directly. This link is neither left to chance nor assumed to occur spontaneously.

For example, a woman came into a therapy session reporting fury with her husband, which she dealt with by withdrawing from him. During the session, she was helped to look at how this pattern of avoidance was being repeated with the therapist. The patient was encouraged to do things differently in the session, expressing her anger and frustration with the therapist in a direct manner. Following this experience within the therapeutic relationship, it was essential to return to the precipitating incident in the patient's current life and ask how she would like to deal with the anger toward her husband, having had this new experience as a viable alternative to her characteristic withdrawal. The new options were imagined and played out in fantasy.

Portraiting

The portraiting technique, discussed earlier as a useful tool in facilitating affective expression in the transference and to past figures, can function like a role play for current conflicts, providing a bridge between insight and action. This technique allows the patient to practice new behavior in the therapeutic setting and anticipate the outcome, before instituting it in the outside world. This kind of work expands the experiencing and observing functions of the ego, and enhances the patient's ability to integrate the two. It should be noted that both positive and negative reactions to the patient's changes should be anticipated. Although therapists tend to encourage openness and honesty, many of those the patient will encounter in "real life" will not. To avoid unnecessary disappointment, it is helpful to ask patients how they would feel if their new changes are not welcome.

Follow-Up Inquiries

The therapist needs to keep track of the process and to follow-up on changes from one session to the next. It is essential to check on possible delayed reactions to changes observed in the therapeutic setting, as well as to inquire about additional changes in their current life. It's not unusual for a depressive to feel buoyed by the direct expression of anger in a session, only to feel anxious and guilt ridden later on, reverting to defensive self-flagellation before the next meeting. The therapist must be alert to these possibilities and catch any regression as quickly as possible.

It is not necessary to wait for spontaneous offerings of change. If the patient does not mention what had been discussed previously, the therapist might ask, "I'm wondering what happened after our last session. You were wanting to be able to talk with your husband in a direct and forthright manner. How did that go?"

So, in a sense, working through is the process through which intention becomes reality. Freud (1937) also emphasized the importance of follow-up, suggesting that working through was only successful if the work enabled the patient to cope with future difficulties. This information can only be obtained by follow-up inquiries. Clinicians like Davanloo and Malan do this continuously, both while treatment is in progress and following termination.

CLINICAL EXAMPLES

The Masochistic Artist: Part 2

In the case of the Masochistic Artist (see Chapter 6), a marital crisis created significant psychic disequilibrium within the patient. The therapeutic work created further unconscious upheaval, as previously repressed feelings and memories began to surface. The patient began to face what she had always avoided knowing and feeling. Instead of dreading the reliving of the trauma, she reported a feeling of freedom and relief.

The Dawning of Hope

PATIENT: Things are coming to a crisis and I'm relieved. I was very upset after seeing you the last time. Then I drove around and went shopping for a couch, because I think a couch is going to make my life better (laughs with delight). I can invite people over. Slowly I began to feel better, then really better, then I actually started to feel happy. It's like a miracle. You know, the worst part of my feeling is that I'm completely alone and that I always will be and there's nothing I can do about it—and I always have been. The only thing I could do was find ways to avoid it. Only now I can admit I've always felt this way. In the past, I've denied it saying, "No, I'm really upbeat and a happy person." But it's really not true. I've always had this deep-rooted fear of being alone. I don't mean actually being alone but feeling alone. And, for the first time, I feel optimistic about not feeling that way— for the first time in my life.

There is a dramatic change in this woman's sense of time—from existential time in which pain seemed ever present, to real time, in which feelings come and go in response to current events. This is something James Mann (1973) has discussed in his writings. His time-limited psychotherapy focuses almost exclusively on the meaning of time and how this is affected by the inevitable losses that occur in our lives. The goal of his brief and focused treatment is to replace the patient's pervasive sense of helplessness and diffuse pessimism with realistic optimism.

In this case, the patient reported feeling realistic hope for the first time in her life, signifying major revisions in her view of herself and the world. This was not achieved through an intellectual or philosophical discussion but by facing, experiencing, and living through all the painful feelings she had previously avoided. Paradoxically, it was only when she was able to acknowledge that she had always felt alone, depressed, and powerless to do anything about it, that the possibility of change became a reality for her. She found freedom in speaking the truth about her own inner experience.

PATIENT: Now when I feel sad I don't deny it. Like the other day, I just gave into it and I put on candles and classical music, had a glass of wine, and took a bath.

The Development of Self-Care

For lasting change to occur in a patient's character, it is not sufficient for her to remember traumas from the past. In this case, the resulting sense of herself as damaged and, therefore, deserving of the poor treatment she received, needed to be dramatically altered to achieve lasting change.

In addition to the direct assaults many of our patients were subjected to as children, they were rarely protected from the abuse, and they suffer from a deficit in self-care and self-protection, which only develops with the receipt of nurturance. The development of this vital function must be facilitated therapeutically.

In this case, the emergence of self-care appeared after the patient expressed deep appreciation for her suffering as a child. In the following vignette, she eloquently describes the real benefit of facing the truth, however painful—she can take care of herself and soothe the pain rather than trying to avoid it, which only leads to a festering of the wound.

What is being referred to as "self-care" can be conceptualized as a new and adaptive way to reduce anxiety that also involves a change in the patient's view of herself. She can now master her internal upheaval, as well as deal with external events that may threaten her well-being.

PATIENT: I woke up this morning and thought, you know, this is a miracle, really, this whole process. It gives me this freedom for the first time in my life—that I don't have to repress this. I could actually move beyond it or accept pain because on the other side is something else. It's a feeling of self. I was going to say self-sufficiency but that's not it. It's like I'm inside with myself now. I'm not alone anymore. I'm in here with me. It's a funny thing.

Changes in Symptoms and Sexual Fantasies

The profound changes apparent in the patient's sense of herself and the world are translated into concrete and observable changes in behavior.

PATIENT: I see changes immediately. For example, I can't use the old fantasies anymore. This is really interesting because these are fantasies that go back 35 years. I couldn't construct this whole scenario—it was too obvious, too painful to me. Actually, then I focused on making love with my lover and imagined coming to orgasm as he came to orgasm.

THERAPIST: So it was a fantasy of mutual pleasure. No one was getting hurt, being forced, or humiliated.

PATIENT: It was sweet. I thought the whole switch was really dramatic.

Now the patient can imagine giving and receiving physical pleasure without pain needing to be involved. There is no longer anxiety, guilt, or fear of punishment following pleasure with a man of her choice. Freud (1930) wrote, "We are so made, that we can only derive intense enjoyment from a contrast, and only very little from a state of things." This woman can now allow herself to contrast the current possibilities with the painful limitations of the past. In so doing, her feelings, particularly pleasurable feelings, are intensified.

De-Repression of Feelings and Memories of "Rape" by Mother

PATIENT: My mother was always poking and prodding at me. She and my father would hold me down and pick the lint out of my navel. And my mother had this thing about enemas.

THERAPIST: What do you remember about the enemas?

PATIENT: It was in my mother's bathroom. What I remember is she'd put a towel over her lap and lay me over her and insert this and then there's this sensation of water coming in and the feeling that something bad might happen, like getting too filled up. It was scary—is it going to get too full? And, this is kind of interesting because it's sexual, in a way. I'd be lying there and she'd be patting me and soothing me, waiting for a number of minutes.

THERAPIST: What kinds of feelings do you notice when you go back to that now?

PATIENT: It's a feeling I still have, of being forced to submit.

THERAPIST: And the feeling inside?

PATIENT: A feeling of being trapped by love—trapped by this thing that's supposed to be good for you (crying). And no one to go to who would protect me.

THERAPIST: So inside there's a terrible feeling of helplessness. But, what about the feeling toward her?

PATIENT: I can see how my feeling is blocked because I feel I'm not allowed to be angry because she's doing it for my own good. I know I felt that way then. I felt outraged really and violated, but I couldn't feel that way then.

THERAPIST: Well you couldn't express it—you kept it down inside. But if you let that rise within you now, how would it want to come out?

PATIENT: We'd be in the bathroom and I wouldn't let her do it. I would kick her in the stomach, push her away and scream as loud as I could and punch her and run away. Because that is, like, a fight for something—it's self-defense. This is where it hits now—in defending myself that way—you see, I would get candy for being good, so sometimes I must have been bad, whatever that means, and so maybe I even did this. I was accused of being mentally ill by both my parents for having tantrums as a child. So to be really good and to submit was to be healthy.

THERAPIST: So your feelings were considered wild, dangerous, and crazy. Is that the way you see it now?

PATIENT: No.

THERAPIST: What is your feeling toward her now?

PATIENT: Rage.

THERAPIST: How do you experience it?

PATIENT: I go blank.

During an earlier segment of this woman's treatment, when we began to approach the rage she felt toward her father, the patient claimed she went blank. Her anger was so anxiety provoking that she wouldn't let it register. Now, as we begin to face rage toward her mother, she says she is blank again. Often patients say they don't feel anything. I have found that questions which guide the patient toward a focus on the feelings and sensations in their body will reveal they are, in fact, feeling a great deal. This certainly proved to be the case here.

THERAPIST: What happens in your body?

PATIENT: I feel I have a hole around my heart. I feel this sense of diminishment and a kind of cavernous feeling (crying). It almost feels like a boomerang shape, almost pulling down from my heart. I don't feel empty now—I feel I want to hold onto that feeling because it does turn into anger.

THERAPIST: So now you won't let it be flushed out or pushed down?

PATIENT: Yeah, it's my body. It's my body! It means it's me. It can't be violated, can't be washed away.

THERAPIST: But it's going to be a fight. You couldn't just say "Mommy, I don't want you to do that." She didn't listen.

PATIENT: I feel that I'd have to kill her. I have to protect myself.

THERAPIST: How?

PATIENT: I'm bigger than her now. I see myself strangling her and hitting her head against the tile and hitting her again and again and again until she's limp and then dropping her there by the toilet. I feel really pissed off. I feel like she's a piece of shit. I don't understand how someone could do that to a child and not hear them being in pain and just to think it doesn't matter (sobbing). I think it's unforgivable, it's unforgivable. To do that out of cruelty or I don't know what—it was killing me and I don't feel blank about it anymore. I feel I want to kill her in self-defense.

THERAPIST: It felt like she was trying to gut you—clean you out from the inside. There was no one to go to. Your father always sided with her. Your sister was glad it wasn't her on the hot seat, so it must have seemed like killing her would be the only way to spare yourself.

PATIENT: Exactly. Running away doesn't work. I want to get rid of her.

THERAPIST: Otherwise you stay in the struggle, like you have been.

PATIENT: It feels like I can have pleasure—physical pleasure. That my body doesn't feel pushed down, it feels opened up. It's empowering. It's like being inside your body in this way that's filling—occupying your body, your height, your mass—feeling your presence. That's the other side of it. It's odd. I see myself emerge from the bathroom, see myself in the mirror and see I'm a woman. I get dressed up, put on perfume and leave the house. I want to go out into the world now, as a woman. I don't feel like I'm going to get arrested. I'm free.

This fantasy illustrates the process of growth as it occurs. It begins with the deeply felt experience of rage. She moves from a helpless, victimized stance to that of a strong and capable woman. She not only expresses the anger toward her mother, but in so doing, separates from her and becomes a woman. She imagines leaving her mother's house and going out into the world. Love no longer needs to be torturous. She can seek pleasure for its own sake.

This case meets Malan's criteria for character change, as each pathological defense has been replaced with something adaptive. Both internal changes, such as her view of self and her capacity for self-soothing, and externally observable behavioral changes, such as the nature of her relationships, have undergone significant alteration. Follow-up confirmed the stability of these changes. In addition to changes in the areas of conflict, this patient reported growth and development in other areas. Her artwork had taken on new form and direction. She felt it was her best and most revealing work by far.

The Man with an Explosive Temper

This middle-aged father of three came to treatment for help in controlling his temper. During his opening statement, he reported a history of severe abuse by his own father and his resolution never to hit his own wife or children. He was, however, having verbal temper tantrums that frightened his family and were causing an increasing strain on everyone. He was especially troubled because he did not know what triggered these outbursts. He described them as coming out of the blue and being beyond his control.

Evaluation of Impulse Control

Careful evaluation of impulse control is absolutely essential in cases such as these, where an explosive temper is a presenting complaint. Detailed inquiry during the trial therapy revealed that these occasional temper outbursts were the result of the patient's more pervasive tendency to squelch his feelings. He was so terrified of anger that he habitually suppressed any experience of irritation. Over time, his anger and frustration would grow and exceed his capacity to contain it. Then, at some unpredictable moment, a small annoyance would send him over the edge and he would have a verbal temper tantrum. This experience would upset him greatly and only further reinforce his sense that anger is big, bad, and dangerous and should be avoided. This set the stage for the next round of suppression and eventual discharge. As this pattern was elucidated, the problem was reframed. Initially he identified anger as the problem. As the result of our beginning work together, he began to see that it was his *avoidance* of anger (as well as other painful feelings) on an ongoing basis that created the environment for this symptomatic disturbance.

The interpersonal consequences of his intrapsychic solution for dealing with affect were then enumerated. This man had a way of talking around any issue at hand and kept an emotional distance while appearing superficially engaged. He tended to get so derailed by the minutia of a story that he would loose the listener in the process. This became our focus, for if he continued to keep an emotional distance from the therapist, no progress would be possible.

Defenses against Emotional Closeness

THERAPIST: You've mentioned that several counselors you've been to see have fallen asleep during sessions. Not just one, but several. Are you aware that you have ways of losing people? You not only have various ways to distance yourself from others but you discourage others from coming close and getting interested in you.

PATIENT: I know. I put them to sleep with my rambling.

THERAPIST: Do you want to do that here with me?

PATIENT: No. I want to open up. I don't want to spend my life this way, but I get very nervous.

THERAPIST: Your anxiety is our indication that a lot of feeling is stirred up.

PATIENT: Yes.

THERAPIST: There must be a certain feeling toward me.

PATIENT: I'm not sure. I'm anxious and a little testy.

THERAPIST: Testy means what?

PATIENT: A little frustrated. I want you to have the answers, but I know it's up to me. I've got a wall around me, and you can do anything you like but it won't make a difference.

THERAPIST: Yes, you could defeat me. Is that what you want to do?

PATIENT: No.

THERAPIST: So could we look at the anger?

PATIENT: Well, it's only irritation.

THERAPIST: Now you want to water it down.

PATIENT: But it's only on the fringes—it's not a big anger.

THERAPIST: Isn't this a big part of the problem? You store up resentments and wait until you're in a rage and then there's the last straw and you explode.

PATIENT: You're right but it's difficult. The wall is high. It scares me, facing the emotion. I don't know what's down there.

THERAPIST: You're very anxious about the anger.

PATIENT: Yeah.

THERAPIST: How do you feel the anger inside?

PATIENT: (big sigh). I don't know. I don't feel it.

THERAPIST: What do you feel?

PATIENT: Frustrated. Like a mouse in a corner with a cat waiting.

THERAPIST: So you're playing a cat-and-mouse game here with me around the anger. Is that what you want to do?

PATIENT: No.

THERAPIST: Will you let yourself feel it?

PATIENT: Physically I do. It's tight inside and there's tingling then numbness. I get cold.

THERAPIST: The feeling of anger gets covered over—you go cold. There's something terrifying about letting yourself feel this anger toward me.

PATIENT: Whenever I've shown emotions, people have shunned me. There's always been a negative reaction. I get hurt. When I've turned to someone for comfort, I get chastised and berated.

THERAPIST: Any indication that will happen here?

PATIENT: I don't know. I know you're here to help, but it's happened so many times.

THERAPIST: So you've decided to give up? No one has a chance with you, huh? Then how are we going to find out?

PATIENT: We're not.

THERAPIST: So there's no potential here. You've decided it's a lost cause.

PATIENT: No, not a lost cause, just a difficult cause.

THERAPIST: What are you waiting for? Do you imagine it will be any easier 2 years from now? All you do is hold onto your suffering. In fact, you've been saying it's getting worse and your wife is ready to walk out.

PATIENT: I know. But I'm embarrassed by the emotion. I go out of my way to avoid it.

THERAPIST: The cover-up spares you some feared hurt and humiliation.

PATIENT: Yeah, but it's short.

This last comment is of great significance, revealing an internal shift from an alliance with the defense of detachment to a turning against the defense, as its cost is keenly experienced. This evoked grief and provided the first unlocking of his unconscious.

Breakthrough of Affect

THERAPIST: It looks like there's a lot of feeling right now.

PATIENT: Yeah, but it's not anger. (Patient puts his head in his hands and sobs. There are waves of sobs for three or four minutes during which time the therapist waits quietly.)

THERAPIST: It sounds like this pain comes from a very deep place. Could we look at this together?

PATIENT: I wish I knew where that came from.

Here is where the process of working through, in which affect and understanding are integrated, begins. The patient has an emotional experience but says he does not understand it. This is a large part of his difficulty. He suddenly experiences intense feelings, as if they come out of the blue. The therapist needs to guide the patient through the experience with the goal of deepening his cognitive understanding of what the emotion is all about.

Cognitive Re-Analysis

THERAPIST: It's vital that we understand it. What is the painful feeling like?

PATIENT: In my chest. I feel very sad as I listen to you and think about how I'm pushing my family away.

THERAPIST: You've been keeping all these feelings inside and no one really knows you.

PATIENT: I have such a hard time telling someone how I feel. I'm always afraid of their reaction.

THERAPIST: How about here with me? How did you see my reaction?

PATIENT: With you, I don't know.

THERAPIST: What's it been like to open up to me? You've been brutally treated in the past and it's understandable that you're afraid, but you've kept everyone out, not just the bad guys. So what's it like to open up?

PATIENT: I feel a little better. The sadness comes because I see myself doing it over and over again. In the past week, I think of how often I've kept feelings in and backed off from others.

This spontaneous link between the experience in the transference, and his current relationships signals a deepening awareness of the meaning and impact of his defensive withdrawal. Now an exploration of the underlying feeling, leading to its origins in the past, can occur.

THERAPIST: What came to you when the feelings surfaced?

PATIENT: How I've been berated. My father used to . . . (starts to cry again). My father made me feel like a baby if I cried (crying and voice is small and squeaky, like that of a small, frightened child). If you got hurt, even physically, he'd yell at you. We weren't allowed to cry. And my mother never consoled us. It didn't matter how bad it was.

THERAPIST: So, to cry would be to invite more assaults.

Linking the Triangles

Now the two triangles can be meaningfully linked. The patient is aware that he gets anxious about strong mixed feelings and backs off in a number of ways, remaining alone. As the previously avoided feelings are approached in the transference, the patient makes a link to his interactions with others in his present life. Finally, critical memories from the past are exposed, rendering the link between the triangle of conflict and the triangle of person complete. This is the essence of working through in ISTDP. As these patterns are worked and re-worked in an emotionally charged atmosphere, that which had been avoided is now directly experienced. This provides both a corrective emotional experience and a living alternative to previous modes of interaction. Now the patient is in the position to realistically assess how he wants to live. Conscious choice becomes possible.

De-Repression

The patient entered the next session without hesitation. He revealed that the opening in the previous session had provided him with access to long-buried memories and feelings.

PATIENT: I wanted to talk to you about two things that happened during the week. I had two flashbacks. I was driving home one night after our last session and, out of nowhere, I had a flashback to the time my father killed our dog and beat me. I know I was very young because I was still in the crib. The first thing I saw was my father beating my mother with a belt. I could literally hear her scream. I had visions of him killing the dog, even though I didn't see it. He beat him to death behind the woodpile because he had bitten me. I know I got beaten too, but I don't remember it. My mother tried to intervene and she got beaten—that's what I remember. I recall looking through the spokes of the crib.

Facilitating Recall of Pivotal Life-Events

The nature of memory, particularly with reference to memories that surface during the course of psychotherapy, has become a source of heated debate (Loftus, 1993; Trierweiler & Donovan, 1994). There have been serious concerns about how to ascertain the truth regarding memories that surface after many years. Strong opinions have been formed on both sides. One camp suggests that memory narratives are "at best, fallible representations of life episodes" (Dickman & Sechrest, 1985; Trierweiler & Donovan, 1994). Others (Herman, 1992; van der Kolk, 1987) have emphasized the harmful effects of our failure to accept the validity of memories presented in psychotherapy. There is a need to develop guidelines for practicing clinicians that are based on empirical evidence as well as theoretical grounds.

Evidence is accumulating that the fallibility of memory may have more to do with poor investigative technique than with distortions in memory per se (Bower, 1981; Geiselman et al., 1985; Loewald, 1976; McCloskey & Zaragoza, 1985). To correct this, it has been suggested that therapists approach the work of memory retrieval with a tight focus, asking patients for elaboration, with an emphasis on concrete physical details, sensory experiences, and emotional activation (Trierweiler & Donovan, 1994). In other words, patients should be encouraged to talk about what they remember in great detail, including what they saw, smelled, heard, and felt at the time. Davanloo has intuitively done just this by asking patients to immerse themselves in recalled experience and extracting detail about such things as date and time of the memory being evoked, clothing worn, facial expressions recalled, and the like. This type of work serves multiple functions, including aiding uncovering and working through, by encouraging patients to paint the scene in great detail and re-live the emotional experiences associated with the memory.

In the case being presented here, working on the triangle of conflict in the transference created an opening into the unconscious. The patient reported having a flood of strong memories of pivotal and traumatic experiences his character defenses had been designed to avoid recalling and re-experiencing. As these memories were explored in the therapeutic setting, the feelings that accompanied them became our focus.

THERAPIST: What's the feeling that accompanies this memory?

PATIENT: Very sad and upset. Emotionally, I plunged. There was immense sadness seeing my mother getting beaten. I wanted to talk to my wife about it. I feel I can talk to her lately and realize that, as I start to share with her, I'm not getting the negative response I anticipate. She's warm and comforting. She hugged me.

Cyclical Psychodynamics

This passage suggests that the patient has been able to use the insight gained by his experience in the previous session to make real changes in his current life—the ultimate goal of treatment. Instead of repeating the past by withdrawing and depriving himself and others of the opportunity for emotional closeness, he opened up to his wife. Instead of rejection or humiliation, he found comfort, further reinforcing the new changes in him. Defensive withdrawal has been replaced by active engagement, signifying substantial character change.

This type of reciprocal interaction between insight and behavior change is at the heart of a theory called cyclical psychodynamics, developed by Wachtel (1993). This theory places particular emphasis on the dynamic interplay between intrapsychic conflicts and internalized object relations on the one hand, and current interpersonal dynamics on the other. To facilitate working through and character change, it has been suggested that changes need to occur in both the internal representations of self and other and in concrete, observable behavior. Further, it is suggested that changes in one area can effect the other in mutually reinforcing ways. Although traditional psychoanalytic theory seems to suggest that internal changes must occur first, with behavior change to follow, there is also evidence that this process can happen in the reverse.

Interpersonal experience can have a profound effect on internal images, fostering revisions of existing internalized models of self and other. In this case, the patient allowed the therapist into his inner emotional world. He was not berated, as he had been in the past. Rather, he found that the sharing of himself was profoundly healing. Something changed in his assumptions about himself and others that was rapidly translated into his interactions with his wife. He opened up to her and found she was warm and receptive. This further solidified the changes that began in the previous session. Many clinicians feel that this type of experience facilitates the replacement of outdated, negative parental introjects with compassionate alternatives.

In addition to the impact of this corrective emotional experience on this man's internal representations of self and other, the experience of complex transference feelings created an opening into the unconscious, as vital memories of early abuse surfaced in a dramatic way. Now the intense and conflictual feelings associated with the abuse could be worked on directly, at the source.

THERAPIST: What's the feeling now, when you go back to that incident?

PATIENT: Anger. Anger at my father for his brutality. It's also the only time I can remember my mother stepping in and she got a terrible beating.

Memory of Homosexual Rape

Now the patient recalls a highly traumatic incident from his adolescence. He is able to view his response in light of this new and deeper understanding of how his early experiences affected him.

PATIENT: The second flashback was the rape. I was so naive and unprotected. Should I have seen signs that he was capable of this? Why did I get into the truck with someone I'd only met once? The thing that bothers me most is the passive submission. I thought of fighting back but didn't. When it was over and we walked out, I had the gun. He said to me, "I'm not nervous because I know it's not loaded" but I know I had a bullet in my pocket. I can remember rubbing the bullet in my hand but being numb and feeling sick. When I got home, I burst into the house crying, "This asshole raped me! He fucked me up the ass!" I remember my father saying, "Watch your mouth—your mother is here. What's the matter with you?" Later, in the police car, he said to the officer, "All this started when the Beatles came out." I thought, "What in the world is he talking about?" I was terrified.

THERAPIST: Even there, your father is totally oblivious and insensitive. What else came to you about this flash?

PATIENT: Remembering his grabbing me from behind and pushing me on the bed. He threatened me—take your clothes off or I'll beat you up. He sucked on me but I didn't get hard because I was so scared. When I look now I get angry at myself for submitting.

THERAPIST: You had learned to submit to violence and wanted to come out with your life. Now you feel angry. Even then, you thought of the bullet in your pocket. What did you want to do?

PATIENT: I would have killed him—no doubt in my mind. Rage so bad I wouldn't shoot him, I'd beat him to death with the gun. The bullet wouldn't be enough.

THERAPIST: How do you see it?

PATIENT: I had a golden opportunity to hurt him but didn't. I was on the bed. He was bent over with his back to me. With a good swift kick I could have rammed his head into the door jam and either run out of there or beat the shit out of him. He was a big, muscular man. I remember seeing him in court and being afraid of his size. It was totally isolated and secluded there and no one knew where I was.

THERAPIST: What's the impulse now?

PATIENT: That I would turn quickly and hit him in the head with the gun. Beat his head into the ground. No doubt about it because it's an image I've had in dreams before.

THERAPIST: What happens?

PATIENT: He dies. I beat him to death with the gun butt.

THERAPIST: What do you see?

PATIENT: Head smashed to a bloody pulp. A mess.

THERAPIST: What do you feel?

PATIENT: Relief. He violated me, hurt me, and I've retaliated.

Link with His Father

THERAPIST: Your father violated you too. You must be angry with him.

PATIENT: I'm angry for all the times he beat us. I could kill him. I turned on him once when he kicked my brother and he put my head through the coffee table. And I got yelled at by my mother! I'd beat his face in. No doubt. I'd beat his face in and be crying in a rage at getting back at him.

THERAPIST: What happens in this image of unleashing the rage toward him?

PATIENT: I'd be crying—tears of rage. I'd want to yell and scream. Father always yelled and screamed. His mouth would go. Verbally berating us. I did this when I'd get into fights.

THERAPIST: What do you want to say to him?

PATIENT: "You rotten son of a bitch. Don't ever touch me again. Don't touch my mother or any of us." It's a relief. The weight of the world off my shoulders. I would love to say to him, right now, "You mope and cry over what's happened to your kids (with the exception of the patient, they are unemployed, alcoholic, or in jail), and you're too stupid to know it's all your fault."

THERAPIST: You want him to suffer with that.

PATIENT: Payback is a bitch, but it serves him right. I just had a flash. There's so much anger over the fact that we loved him and wanted him to treat us as a father, not another bully. "Damn it, I wanted you to love me like a father should. You cheated us out of something we needed desperately." If he had been loving and compassionate, we would have learned that instead of learning to turn on those we love.

It is of critical importance that all the mixed feelings toward significant others be experienced as fully as possible. This patient felt murderous rage and agonizing grief in relation to his father, but also a deep longing for closeness—a yearning to love and be loved by his father—that he has also defended against and was adversely affecting his relationship with his own son. The next session will clearly reveal the impact the previous work has had on his current ability to form an intimate bond with his son.

P-C Link Regarding the Father-Son Relationship

There was a 2-week break between the last session and the one reported here. The patient continued to work at a high level of ego-adaptive capacity. The roles assumed by patient and therapist have changed profoundly. The patient is doing most of the active work now, with the therapist observing and responding.

PATIENT: I want to tell you about Valentine's Day. I thought it was ridiculous that there were no cards for sons. I finally found the perfect card. I made a conscious effort to add something personal and I spent a lot of time on this. I acknowledged that I've been hard on him but love him. I gave him the card and he started to cry. I asked, "What's the matter?" He was bawling—tears rolling down his face (patient begins to cry). He said, "Thank you so much," and sat on my lap (more crying). I just held him while he cried. We sat for 10 or 15 minutes. My emotions were so mixed. I felt so bad that I had caused him pain and uncertainty—that a card could unleash that. At the same time, I was elated—it was a door that I opened. From that point on, I noticed that, even if I feel angry, I stop and talk to him about it.

This man's harshness with his son has been replaced with compassion. The entire family has benefited from his treatment.

THE REPETITION COMPULSION

The notion of repetition is included in nearly every definition of working through available, with more traditional analysts assuming this will be a time-consuming endeavor. In large part, this is attributed to the strength and tenacity of the resistance. Although various types of resistance have been cataloged, the "repetition compulsion" is considered the most difficult to deal with therapeutically.

The tendency for patients to repeat and re-enact their internal conflicts externally in one situation after another has been referred to as the repetition compulsion. The repetition compulsion is "a theoretical construct consisting of two elements: (a) the unconscious instincts (sexual and aggressive) seeking expression, and (b) the ego's attempt to master old traumatic conditions or events associated with an infantile neurosis" (Strupp & Binder, 1984, p. 22).

According to drive theory, it is the first of these two elements, the strength of the impulses, that is the culprit in creating and maintaining psychopathology. Kernberg (1975, 1976) is a contemporary advocate of this theory, suggesting that patients with borderline personality organization have exceptionally strong innate aggressive drives. Yet, it is the second element mentioned by Freud, regarding the ego's repeated attempts at mastery, that has received the most clinical and empirical support over the years. Initially, Freud considered the tendency for patients to repeat in the present what has occurred in the past as a resistance to remembering. Eventually, as his focus shifted from the primacy of impulses and the operation of the pleasure principle to a theory based on the ego's adaptation through the reality principle, the notion of repeating in an effort to achieve mastery gained prominence.

How can repeated exposure to traumatic events in dreams, fantasies, and behavior be explained? The nearly universal nature of this phenomenon suggests that it contains an adaptive function. Traumatic events are, by their nature, outside ordinary experience. Accordingly, repeating in the present traumatic events and reactions from the past may be driven by the individual's need to assimilate and integrate powerful yet discrepant information into one's ongoing theory of how the world works (Epstein, 1994; Janoff-Bulman, 1992). If, as hypothesized (Epstein, 1994; Stern, 1985), there is a fundamental motive to assimilate emotionally significant experiences into a coherent conceptual system of how the world works, material that can neither be ignored nor readily assimilated will keep re-appearing in an attempt at integration. Conceived of in this way, the repetition compulsion is adaptive because it creates opportunities for assimilation and adaptation to current reality, taking unusual and traumatic events into account.

A good deal of research data supports the view that we humans are hypothesis testers who need to assimilate new incoming information into our ongoing view of the world (Stern, 1985). It seems we will not rest until a problem is solved. As early as the 1920s, Zeigarnic found that there was consistently greater recall of unfinished than finished tasks.

Lewin (1951) suggested that tension arises within the system when a task has not been completed. This tension creates energy that drives the organism toward completion. When the goal is accomplished, the tension is released and the material is forgotten. He also found that the more emotionally involved the individual was in the problem and/or the more emotionally significant the outcome, the greater the tension created when the problem was unsolved or the task unfinished. Again, this tension creates the energy that drives the system toward mastery and completion of the task at hand.

Although resistance to change poses a problem in psychotherapy, Janoff-Bulman (1992) has suggested that resistance to change in our operating assumptions about self, others, and the world is adaptive most of the time and is, therefore, revised or abandoned with great reluctance. She refers to this "cognitive conservatism" as a trait characteristic of the species, designed to provide the kind of stability, coherence, and predictability that foster the feelings of security so necessary for daily survival. We seem to develop theories of unity and consistency to make sense of a complex and frequently chaotic world. We are then highly motivated to maintain consistency and to support our own hypotheses (Aronson, 1968). This need contradicts the desire to change that brings many to psychotherapy. Janoff-Bulman's point is that this resistance cannot simply be chalked up to psychopathology. In fact, she's saying that, in most instances, it is healthy and adaptive to cling to our familiar guiding principles because they work most of the time. The question then becomes how to help patients overcome this resistance to change when necessary.

WHEN INSIGHT DOES NOT LEAD TO CHANGE

In the two cases presented in this chapter, the work in the transference was effective in unleashing previously repressed memories and feelings regarding significant figures and events from the past. The implications of these revelations for the present rapidly became clear and the patients made dramatic changes in their current lives, which further reinforced the internal changes that began in psychotherapy. Things do not always progress so smoothly. Sometimes insights, even emotionally experienced insights in the transference with links to the past, do not lead to changes in the patient's current functioning. How can this be explained?

Most dynamic psychotherapies subscribe to the notion that increasing patients' understanding (insight) of their repetitive patterns of interaction with others will help them more clearly define their difficulties and, in so doing, will facilitate problem solving. When this does not occur, even after a period of working through in which the pattern and its negative consequences are elucidated in many different situations, resistance is usually considered the factor responsible for the impasse. In particular, a transference resistance is suspected. Perhaps the gratification of the relationship with the therapist outweighs the patient's motivation to get well. Alternatively, getting well would mean facing separation and loss. If this is avoided, treatment could go on indefinitely.

In ISTDP, the transference relationship is monitored throughout treatment. Particularly at the inception of treatment, analysis of the transference pattern of behavior, with a strong emphasis on the negative consequences of defense and resistance, occupies a good deal of time and energy. As treatment progresses, the transference distortions are reduced and largely eliminated. A working alliance based on a collaborative relationship becomes ascendant and work on current and past relationships takes center stage.

For example, if a tendency toward dependency is noted early on in treatment, it could be anticipated as a potential barrier to rapid movement. This kind of anticipation can be pivotal in preventing an impasse or an aborted treatment. Davanloo has paid particular attention to self-defeating patients who seem motivated to destroy their chances for success and sabotage treatment in the process. This is most likely in cases where there is a history of failed relationships. I treated a young man who complained of being unable to sustain a relationship with a woman. During the initial evaluation, it was revealed that three previous psychotherapies had been aborted after several months of treatment. As soon as things started to get emotionally stirred, he would bolt. I asked him why this treatment would be any different. During that first session, when motivation was high, he declared his intention not to act on the impulse to flee when it would inevitably arise, but to talk about the feelings underlying the impulse. He did not break off treatment but completed it successfully. In cases like this, no substantive work on the patient's current life can occur until the potential for self-sabotage in the treatment has been directly addressed.

Others (Crits-Christoph & Barber, 1991) have suggested that these explanations are insufficient to explain the numerous instances in which insight fails to lead to behavior change. It has been hypothesized that symptoms can assume "functional autonomy," becoming habitual and gradually independent of their original source (Wachtel, 1977). For example, a young boy may become passive and subservient with authority as a compromise between his anger at being controlled by authoritarian parents and his need to defend against it. Yet, over time, his passive-aggressive procrastination becomes habitual and part of his character. These responses no longer occur just when the fellow is angry, but have become a habitual mode of functioning that is independent of circumstances. These authors suggest that insight into the original source of this dynamic will be of little value in facilitating change. They suggest behavioral treatment in these cases because interpretation alone seems to be of little value.

By focusing intensively on the negative, self-defeating consequences of a reliance on character defenses, Davanloo has offered us a powerful alternative strategy. In particular, the ways in which these character traits will sabotage treatment if not abandoned are enumerated. Again, the focus is directed toward the vicious cycles infecting the individual's current functioning rather than toward the vicissitudes of the basic drives. Since patients often retreat to the past to justify their present behavior, such an approach would reenforce, rather than dismantle, defenses. Instead, the ISTDP therapist focuses on the ways that patients avoid responsibility for perpetuating their own suffering. The focus should remain on patients' behavior in the here and now, with some pressure to change, lest the therapeutic relationship end in another failure.

SUMMARY

In ISTDP, the process of working through—in which both affective and intellectual modes of experience are integrated and lead to stable changes in behavior—begins with the initial evaluation and continues throughout treatment. According to Davanloo, affect must come first, but should be followed by a cognitive re-analysis of the process, in which both the triangle of conflict and the triangle of person are meaningfully linked. Research confirms the hypothesis that such interventions are significantly associated with the achievement of enduring character change.

CHAPTER 8

Termination and Follow-Up

> May the spirit never die
> Though a troubled heart feels pain
> When this long winter is over
> It will blossom once again
> *Loreena McKennitt**

It seems fitting to approach the subject of termination by coming full circle, ending with the last verse of the song "Breaking the Silence," quoted at the start of Chapter 1. When psychotherapy comes to a successful end, the painful process undertaken by someone with a troubled heart leaves the person feeling renewed.

The issue of termination involves two basic questions: when and how? The longer and more protracted dynamic psychotherapy has become, the more often innovations tailored to reducing its length have appeared. In fact, in his paper entitled "Analysis Terminable and Interminable," Freud (1937) lamented that analysis was frequently a protracted affair and advised that we should attempt to shorten its duration. In this spirit, Freud, Ferenzi, Rank, and Alexander all experimented with setting a termination date to accelerate stalled treatments.

In Intensive Short-Term Dynamic Psychotherapy, the length of treatment, while relatively brief (1–40 sessions), is open-ended. Termination is tied directly to the achievement of therapeutic goals. Therefore, in contemplating the end of treatment, we must return to its beginning. We can only decide whether the patient is well by understanding the

---

*From "Breaking the Silence." Music and lyrics by Loreena McKennitt.

nature of the presenting illness. It all gets back to the goals of treatment. According to Freud:

> First, the patient must no longer be suffering from his former symptoms and have overcome his various anxieties and inhibitions and, secondly, the analyst must have formed the opinion that so much repressed material has been brought into consciousness . . . that no repetition of the patient's specific pathological processes is to be feared. (1937, p. 320)

Once these goals have been achieved to the satisfaction of patient and therapist, the issue of termination needs to be addressed.

Davanloo, following Freud's lead, considers termination when therapeutic goals have been met. Ultimately, however, those goals can only be considered stable if the patient proves capable of weathering *future* storms without regression. Routine follow-up interviews with patients who have terminated treatment would be required to make this assessment. Freud discussed a few incidental follow-up reports on patients previously treated, but did not make follow-up a standard practice. Malan, Davanloo, and those they have trained, routinely conduct follow-up visits at 1-, 5-, and 10-year intervals. This practice allows the therapist to identify failures, learn from mistakes, and determine who is helped by this method of psychotherapy.

Malan (1976) has reported encouraging findings which suggest that those patients who responded well to treatment not only maintained their gains over time but were better yet at 5-year follow-up. Such findings indicate that the brief, accelerated form of dynamic psychotherapy being described here does, in fact, remove obstacles to development and that the process of change continues well after treatment formally ends.

So, most short-term dynamic psychotherapists, like their colleagues engaged in traditional long-term psychotherapy, aim to terminate treatment when the stated goals have been reached. How the actual process should proceed is a matter of debate, however. Whereas Firestein (1978) found no consensus of opinion about how to handle termination in the analytic community, there is greater agreement among the short-term dynamic psychotherapists. In general, practitioners of ISTDP continue the same technical approach of working the triangles right up until the last session. As termination approaches, interpretations are geared toward an understanding of how the experience of separation and loss is tied to the central conflicts affecting the patient. With a few exceptions, there also seems to be agreement that patients must face all their mixed feelings about ending, but that the magnitude and importance of this phase of treatment for the outcome of treatment is quite variable.

Both the when and the how of termination will be discussed in this chapter. Special problems associated with termination and techniques to facilitate a healthy process of separation will be outlined. Clinical vignettes will illustrate the process.

HOW IMPORTANT IS THE TERMINATION TO OUTCOME?

Malan's Research

Malan (1978) has suggested that termination, per se, is of variable importance for outcome, depending on the patient and the presenting complaints. He warns that "termination should not be over-valued into a fundamental principle." He found that a "radical" approach, in which the transference pattern of behavior was interpreted early and repeatedly, resulted in uncomplicated terminations, as the psychic conflicts responsible for neurotic interactions had been worked through during the midphase of treatment. Once these conflicts were resolved and noticeable changes had occurred in the patient's life, the topic of termination tended to arise naturally and be dealt with easily.

The following factors seem to be responsible for this:

1. The focus on defense and resistance early in treatment.
2. Intensive working through in which the triangles of conflict and the person are repeatedly linked to consolidate insights.
3. Examination of the transference pattern of behavior from the beginning of treatment.
4. The highly collaborative effort between patient and therapist.

Consequently, patients frequently reported feelings of satisfaction about a job well done. While they reported some sadness about saying good-bye to the therapist, who had been a valued ally in their journey, it was typically mild and associated with good feelings.

In contrast to the uncomplicated termination just described, Malan found that, with those patients for whom loss was a focal issue, the handling of termination was absolutely crucial to outcome. The final phase of treatment in these cases tended to be longer, requiring three to five highly focused sessions.

The concept of a corrective emotional experience is most relevant during termination. Malan (1979) makes it clear that we must help patients come to a new ending. This new ending is not an attempt to provide for patients what they were deprived of in the past, but rather to help them face past and current failures directly. The therapist helps patients to bear all the rage and disappointment following these failures (including the limits of psychotherapy). This is what is new and corrective—having someone who will bear all the feelings with them. According to Malan, this type of experience helps patients give up impossible longings for endless nurturance or restitution and facilitates their ability to enjoy the satisfactions available in their current life.

Sifneos's Findings

Sifneos (1979) is in general agreement with Malan regarding the process of termination. He has emphasized that the therapist must be alert to signs of progress and make a point of recognizing evidence of change. This is an important and often neglected issue. We, as therapists, can become so focused on defenses and symptoms, that we fail to recognize and respond to the changes evident in the patient. The therapist's lingering doubts about the possibility of rapid and enduring change can slow down the pace of growth as well.

His research suggests that symptom removal is not the factor most likely to change following short-term anxiety-provoking therapy. Rather, the patients' *concern* about their symptoms or attitude toward them is what undergoes significant change. Most successfully treated patients leave therapy with increased self-esteem and a sense of understanding themselves better (Sifneos, 1979).

The therapist expects patients to feel ambivalent about termination and communicates this, normalizing such a response. Feelings of accomplishment are acknowledged, as well as the inevitable sadness that will accompany the end of therapy. Additionally, Sifneos helps patients anticipate the future, and how they will apply what they have learned to conflicts and difficulties they will inevitably confront in life.

According to Sifneos, 50% of the patients treated with brief dynamic psychotherapy raised the issue of termination spontaneously once progress on their presenting difficulties had been made. In the other 50% of the cases, it was the therapist who brought up the subject of termination when progress had clearly been made. In these cases, there was some initial reluctance, followed by agreement.

Mann's Findings

Termination is a major focus in Mann's (1973) time-limited psychotherapy and is an issue from the start of treatment. Therapy is strictly limited to 12 sessions, and the date for termination is set at the end of the first session. "Mann believes that throughout treatment, patients are aware of the inevitability of termination and organize their defense mechanisms to guard against the pain of the loss" (Bauer & Kobos, 1987, p. 276). At the same time, the awareness of the end, from the beginning of treatment, tends to evoke feelings and memories about past losses, which can be reworked during the therapy. The theory underlying this treatment model suggests that all the rage, guilt, and grief attendant to separations and losses from the past were not able to be experienced and expressed at the time of their occurrence. Any such avoidance must be eliminated if therapy is to be considered successful. The therapist actively encourages the full experience of all these mixed feelings about the impending loss. It is believed that this new ending will be a maturational experience for the patient (Mann, 1973).

Davanloo's Findings

When considering preparedness for termination, Davanloo (1979) looks for "total resolution of the central neurotic structure of the patient's problems manifested by the total replacement of the maladaptive neurotic pattern with an adaptive pattern associated with cognitive and emotional insight into the dynamic structure of his difficulties" (p. 21). He has suggested that such radical goals, amounting to cure, can be achieved in 10 to 15 sessions for a highly functioning neurotic and in 25 to 40 sessions for those patients with a character disorder. Termination is less of a distinct phase in ISTDP, as it has been in motion from the beginning. The aim is to work consistently at the patients' highest level of ego-adaptive capacity. Each insight is worked and re-worked in a focused manner before moving on to another area of conflict. As each area of difficulty is worked through, the core neurotic structure is disassembled. By the end of treatment, patients are functioning very well, with a great deal of insight into their own internal workings. Consequently, the chance of regression at termination is very limited.

Because termination is tied to the goals of therapy, it is impossible to set a date at the start of treatment. Still, the idea that treatment will be brief and accelerated is communicated, in both word and deed, from the inception of treatment. When patients call to schedule their initial appointment, they are told they will undergo an extensive evaluation requiring several hours. This evaluation will determine the nature of their difficulties and whether this form of treatment is indicated. They are also told that, should they be selected for therapy, they will be seen on a weekly basis until their problems are resolved. This clearly communicates that the aim is to *resolve* their problems and to do so in an efficient manner. In this way, the end is present from the beginning.

In uncomplicated cases, where there is an absence of ego fragility or traumatic early losses, termination tends to be a brief and straightforward process lasting one or two sessions. Where there has been early or traumatic loss, the termination phase is particularly important and typically requires three to five sessions.

According to Davanloo's (1978) clinical research, termination is broached by 70% of the patients with an oedipal focus and only by 20% of the patients with character disorders. In the latter case, patients tend to cling to the therapist despite clear progress. It is up to the therapist to call this to patients' attention, and to deal directly with the pain and anger being avoided by holding onto the relationship. Davanloo's focus on patient activity and responsibility throughout the process discourages pathological dependence on the therapist, and greatly reduces the possibility of protracted terminations.

Davanloo's approach to psychotherapy is radical in many ways, including his decidedly optimistic view of the power and strength of dynamic psychotherapy (Bauer & Kobos, 1987). He communicates an inherent belief (based on a careful assessment of ego functioning) in his patients' capacities and urges them to work at their highest level of ability. This optimistic stance extends to the process of termination, which he views as no more difficult than any other stage of therapy. In fact, because defense and resistance are persistently and thoroughly dealt with early in therapy, a strong therapeutic alliance takes over as therapy continues. In most cases, the therapist's role becomes easier as the process progresses and patients do more and more of the work on their own. Rather than assuming that termination will be experienced as a traumatic loss, Davanloo uses the patient's reactions as another opportunity to "explore and deal with unresolved feelings concerning past and current relationships." Often there is a celebratory air to the ending of treatment as both patient and therapist revel in the gains that have been made.

FACTORS AFFECTING TERMINATION

The Effect of Therapist Expectations

Most of the material written on termination focuses on patient variables. In particular, previous experiences with loss are considered a primary factor in determining how a patient will respond to termination. It is also essential to consider therapist variables. The therapist's theoretical orientation and expectations about how termination (not to mention our own feelings about and defenses against loss) will be experienced are very likely to influence the process (as well as outcome). If we expect the termination to be traumatic, we may search for confirming evidence of such a reaction. Conversely, our confidence in the patient's ability to deal with this loss in an adaptive way will also have an impact.

I have found that doing routine follow-up relieves some of the pressure on both patient and therapist to have everything tied up neatly by the termination date. One cannot always predict a patient's reaction to termination ahead of time. Follow-up sessions provide the opportunity to explore any reactions that might occur *after* termination and to rework difficult areas still troubling the patient.

Need for Specificity and Flexibility

When planning termination, it is essential to be case-specific. The therapist must be flexible when determining when and how to go about termination, rather than relying on a rigid set of fixed criteria. Occasionally, a patient will have an unexpected reaction to the termination once a date is set. Allowing for an extra session or two to work this through tends to solidify change in the patient.

The real question is how to determine what would be best for a given patient. Malan (1979) has suggested that the therapist be aware of how separations were handled by the patient's parents and to use this as a guideline, by making sure the ending goes differently. This prevents the possibility of re-traumatizing the patient and provides for a corrective emotional experience.

I have had a couple of cases in which patients quite consciously decided to continue in treatment despite clear and profound changes in all areas of their functioning. In one case, a young woman decided to allow herself the "luxury" of some extra sessions once the work had been completed because, as the first of eight children, she had always been forced to grow up and be independent prematurely. In response to my comment that we be "as efficient and effective as possible," she said, "Efficient and effective? Forget it. I've done that all my life. I'm paying for this, and I'm going to allow myself to have a little longer than is absolutely necessary. I've had it with always making do with the absolute minimum."

This statement, in and of itself, was evidence of profound change, as she had always been subservient and self-sacrificing in the past and would never directly declared her needs to another in such a forthright manner. That she could stand up to me and declare her intent to allow herself some leeway was extremely important. She was able to have a new experience during the termination phase of treatment rather than repeating the old, in which she would move along at another's insistence.

It was essential that I recognize this and accommodate to it, rather than push for termination and, in so doing, re-traumatize the patient. This is an example of how crucial the handling of the termination can be. Failure to allow the patient to take some extra time could well have resulted in a therapeutic failure.

This brief example highlights the importance of understanding the patient's experience of separation and loss within the context of all that has materialized during the treatment. Specificity is never more important than when determining a means for terminating treatment that serves to solidify the changes made throughout the course of therapy. More detailed cases in which a deep understanding of the patient's central conflicts influences the work of termination will follow.

CLINICAL EXAMPLES

Uncomplicated Termination

Patients who enter treatment with a clearly demarcated focus and erect few barriers to meaningful communication with the therapist work rapidly, effectively, and consistently right up until the end of treatment. They meet their goals and tend to raise the issue of termination themselves. The end of treatment tends to be viewed as an achievement and the primary feeling toward the therapist is that of gratitude.

The Gentleman Scorned (Chapter 2) finished treatment in only 10 sessions. The work was focused on helping him gain access to his anger, particularly toward women, and expressing it in direct and appropriate ways. In the past, he had alternately internalized his rage and become depressed or acted out in a defiant manner. Even in the second case, he would end up feeling guilty and like a failure, with depression the final result. So, in addition to being able to freely and appropriately express his anger, the patient wanted to be able to do so and maintain a good feeling about himself. He felt significantly improved and as if he had achieved his stated goal in coming for therapy. By taking the initiative in broaching the topic of termination, he was displaying evidence of significant change from a position of passivity and smoldering resentment toward women, to one of assertiveness. Even though I had some reservations about the depth and stability of his changes at first, his interaction with me suggested the changes were robust. Termination was a fairly straightforward review of the process and only required one session. At follow-up a year later, the patient reported continued progress.

Mother's Little Angel

This middle-aged mother of three came to see me at the urging of her primary physician who was unable to convince her that, despite all medical evidence to the contrary, she was not dying of cancer. Inquiry revealed that the onset of her symptoms—which included anxiety, panic, depression, and a host of somatic complaints—began 6 months prior to consultation, following the wedding of her eldest son. She also reported that her daughter had recently become engaged and her youngest son would be graduating from college in 3 months. As we explored her reactions to the loss of her role as mother, she told me that her mother had died of cancer just as she was preparing to leave home and become independent at the age of 18.

The patient displayed some intellectual insight into the meaning of her current difficulties by saying, "I feel I'm somehow re-living the traumatic experiences of loss from the past." The following material was then revealed. She was conceived in an attempt to assuage her parents' guilt and grief over the death of their youngest son, who died at the age of 4 when he wandered off and fell into a gully that was ablaze with leaves and debris. Her mother called her "my little angel," a role she also played for her father and two brothers, 9 and 11 years her senior. She recalled a happy childhood in which she was doted on and was frequently the center of attention.

Until the age of 9 or 10, her home was a safe and happy place. All this came to an abrupt halt when her oldest brother returned home from the armed services in a state of paranoid psychosis. The brother she had adored was now a terrifying figure who would fly into uncontrollable rages without provocation. Her father refused to have him hospitalized, leaving the rest of his family in an unprotected state. Her father would escape to work, leaving his grown son alone with his wife and younger daughter. The patient's mother became anxious and physically ill. In anger, she banned her husband from their bedroom. Again, the patient was recruited to compensate and replace the lost object—in this case, her mother's husband. She became her mother's mate and protector, even sleeping in her bed every night. During the patient's adolescence, her mother's health deteriorated markedly. Despite this, she refused to seek medical help. The patient watched helplessly as her mother was eaten away by breast cancer.

This patient had a solid early childhood and showed no signs of ego fragility. She had developed a compliant and subservient facade in response to parental demands, caring for others while repressing all feelings of anger toward them. In psychotherapy, she was able, for the first time, to directly experience her rage toward her mother for using her as a substitute husband, withdrawing from life, and committing a slow and excruciating suicide. The direct experience of anger toward her mother, while anxiety provoking at first, was extremely liberating. Her fears of dying of cancer disappeared and she was able to deal with her feelings regarding the separation from her own children in a new and healthy manner. This was achieved by developing an adult relationship with them, rather than repeating the past in which she would hold onto them by being sick and needy, as her mother had done. In addition, having access to her anger enabled her to be assertive with her husband and co-workers. She was no longer everyone's caretaker. Her newfound energy was focused on her own life, revitalizing her marriage, solidifying friendships, and taking on more responsibility at work. Her family, friends, and physicians all noticed and applauded the substantial changes in her, which further reinforced them.

After 12 psychotherapy sessions, she felt ready to end treatment. The termination was uncomplicated and marked by feelings of gratitude and pride. Can substantial change occur this rapidly or was this a mere flight into health? Let's evaluate her progress vis-à-vis her presenting complaints. All symptomatic disturbances had disappeared and were replaced by adaptive strivings. She was no longer depressed, and reported that her sense of humor had returned, that she felt spontaneous and flexible in her dealings with others, and had a deeper sense of closeness with family and friends.

The Emergence of a "New Self"

In the last session, she said, "I don't just feel like my old self, I feel I'm better than ever. I'm proud of myself for facing all the pain from the past and I feel it's strengthened me so that I'm better prepared for difficulties in the future." All these results seemed to indicate real progress and did not constitute an avoidance of deeper work through a flight into health. The termination was uncomplicated. She expressed her gratitude toward the therapist but also felt proud of herself for taking advantage of what the therapist had to offer.

At the time of termination, there was every indication of a full recovery. This case exemplifies the type of change in ego functioning that Menninger (1958) described when referring to criteria for termination. He stressed that, rather than the patient becoming his "old self," he'll become "an enlarged, an improved, indeed a new self." By the end of treatment, Mother's Little Angel had accomplished the task of becoming whom she could potentially be and was a woman in her own right.

The Manic-Depressive's Daughter: Part 2

It has been said that the central goal of psychoanalytic treatment is to release the patient from reliance on pathogenic defenses so that she can "confront the realistic problems of his life as a mature human being" (Munroe, 1955, p. 323). Just this sort of transformation, from reliance on avoidant defenses, to dealing adaptively with the daily problems in life, is illustrated in the following case. Treatment consisted of 25 psychotherapy sessions.

Review of Current Changes

PATIENT: My life seems to be getting in order. There's an improved quality of life. Even this week. My husband was gone on business, and it was last minute but my son coped.

THERAPIST: And so did you.

PATIENT: Yeah. I felt like I did a great job. I was tired but it was a physical tired, not emotional, like being drained or frazzled or depleted. It was different. It felt different.

THERAPIST: You even feel good about the way you handled it and are more confident as a mother.

PATIENT: Yes, much more confident. It's really amazing how . . . maybe I've been preparing, and last week was like a final exam with him gone all week. It was ok so I feel pretty good about that.

As was noted in Chapter 7, symptomatic and characterological difficulties must be replaced with adaptive alternatives for a patient to be considered truly improved. This woman, who had been highly self-critical all her life, could now feel genuinely good about dealing well with a stressful situation. In particular, she had been desperately insecure about her capabilities as a mother and arranged it so that she was never alone with her children. Now, she reported feeling more confident in her abilities and was able to function independently in the role of mother. Not only was she able to perform the necessary maternal functions, she felt good about herself and took pleasure in motherhood.

Emotional Changes

THERAPIST: It really seems to me that the internal blocks—those unresolved feelings and conflicts from the past—have largely been resolved and now you're freed up. You are involved and effective—no longer anxious and withdrawn.

PATIENT: I think that's right. I feel liberated from the past. It is really incredible. I'm tearing up.

THERAPIST: Tell me about that—you obviously have a lot of feeling.

PATIENT: As I drove here, I thought I don't feel haunted by it anymore. The past is there—it's my history and it has shaped me but it doesn't haunt me. Now when things happen currently, I don't hark back to those feelings of helplessness and hopelessness. It's very different. It's amazing.

THERAPIST: So you feel at peace. I remember this being a primary goal. In the first session, you said, "I just want to be free." As we talk about this, you get tearful. Could we look at that?

PATIENT: It's an emotional thing to feel something I've carried around for so long, even when it wasn't acute, to have it not there is amazing.

THERAPIST: I wonder if you were so used to it, you habituated to it and didn't realize what a heavy weight it was. Only now that it's lifted, do you realize how heavy it was. It's sad. I also sense some feeling toward me. It is wonderful that you're doing so well, but then it means saying good-bye.

PATIENT: Yeah. It's sad, but I like to think you're still there if I should need you.

The termination presents another opportunity for facing feelings around loss. Is it a problem that the patient wants to hold onto the idea that the therapist is still alive and available? In this case, I think not. This woman lost both her parents at an early age and adapted by becoming highly self-sufficient. Her ability to trust and rely on the therapist seems a sign of health and one to be supported not undermined.

This woman now fits all the criteria for termination of an analysis as outlined by Nacht (1965):

1. An absence of suffering.
2. Modification of the structural and dynamic whole of the personality (changes in ego functioning).
3. The removal or minimizing of internal obstacles to health, happiness, and achievement.
4. The ability to live in harmony with oneself and with others.
5. Increased capacity to adjust to externally provoked frustrations.

That these results were obtained after only 25 sessions in this case and 10–12 respectively in the previous two described, is powerful support for the unique efficacy of this method of treatment. Short term does not mean compromising when it comes to goals. One can have far-reaching goals and achieve them within a brief time, given the right combination of patient, therapist, and technique. Even though the cases described in this chapter thus far were complex and involved a good deal of traumatic loss, the terminations were smooth. With the Gentleman Scorned, the negative transference feelings, while strong, were identified immediately and worked through in speedy fashion. The two women just described had primarily positive feelings toward the therapist throughout treatment, which were maintained even in the face of separation.

COMPLEX REACTIONS TO TERMINATION

Mann (1973) places a great deal of emphasis on the work of termination. The goal of the time-limited psychotherapy he has developed is to aid the patient in developing and maintaining a positive view of self and others, even in the face of the inevitable losses of life. Because reactions to loss are the focus of treatment, working through patients' reactions to termination, particularly in regard to the central issue that brought them into therapy, was deemed essential for successful resolution of the patients' difficulties. Mann stressed that this work could be as difficult for the therapist as for the patient. He contends: "The therapist must not hesitate to examine with the patient all the feelings and fantasies" that arise during this phase of therapy. In fact, he considers the therapist's resistance to dealing actively with the feelings around separation the primary cause of "analysis interminable." He also contends that the work of termination is the most difficult to teach trainees. We, as teachers and supervisors, must consider whether we contribute to this difficulty by our failure to focus on this phase of treatment and all that it demands from both patient and therapist.

In the following clinical vignettes, you'll notice how the therapist directly addresses the mixed feelings about termination and encourages the kind of "affect-laden" interaction Mann feels is optimal for the resolution of feelings around separation and loss.

CLINICAL EXAMPLES

The Masochistic Artist: Part 3

PATIENT: I'm feeling really good these days. It's wonderful. I feel calm and happy and productive. I feel this tremendous sense of relief—I'm on a better track.

The patient opened this session with a statement about her subjective sense of happiness and went on to detail all the changes in her life. These included the improved sense of well-being described in her opening statement, mutually gratifying personal relationships, an ability to assert herself in professional arenas, and a new productivity in her work.

Patient Raises Possibility of Termination

PATIENT: I saw a friend yesterday who's ending therapy and I thought, "Maybe I could do that."
THERAPIST: So you've been thinking about ending.
PATIENT: Only recently—in the past 2 weeks or so.
THERAPIST: Look at what you've told me today. The obvious question is "Why would you need to come here anymore?" You're better.
PATIENT: Yeah! One thing that's always impressed me about you is that you've been so encouraging. You just don't slowly sort of begin to

deal with your life—you get better. You actually get better and you are able to leave some of this shit behind and be a person—a better person—someone capable of getting pleasure from life. That has always been a big draw for me to you—this hopefulness—that I won't be stuck in this mire forever and that there's a possibility for real growth.

Feelings of Hope and Confidence

Although critics of Davanloo's methods (Strupp & Binder, 1984) voice concern over how harsh and demanding the treatment seems, patients frequently report the kinds of feelings this woman expressed. Positive and hopeful feelings are engendered by the therapist's active involvement and expectation for change and improvement. Particularly at termination, patients report feeling proud of themselves for working so hard and accomplishing what they set out to do (Flegenheimer, 1982). Sometimes this kind of positive response is evident earlier in the treatment process. I recall one patient who said, in response to my challenging her defenses against closeness, "I know you probably expect me to be angry but I feel moved and deeply grateful that you care enough to dig a little. No one has ever made this kind of effort to get to know me beyond the surface."

This is what Davanloo means when he refers to the complex nature of the transference feelings evoked by this intensive method of treatment. Patients feel hopeful and even excited about facing what they have avoided, while feeling increasingly confident in their own abilities to deal effectively with life.

Our expectations are powerfully felt by our patients, so we must examine them carefully (Frank, 1961; Stotland, 1969). If we expect patients to be fragile and to need a great deal of time to be able to deal more effectively with life, in all likelihood that is what will occur. In contrast, if we expect patients to work at their highest level of ability, challenge them to stretch, and are equally willing to work hard and deal with difficult material as it arises, they will often be heartened and rise to the occasion, as the Masochistic Artist demonstrated.

Accepting the Good

In the case of the Masochistic Artist, love had become equated with pain and suffering. The patient had a history of difficulty in accepting good things. During the phase of working through, there was accumulating evidence that she was beginning to take good care of herself (eating well, allowing herself to rest, buying a couch and making a comfortable home, etc.), but her ability to allow others to care for her in affectionate and loving ways was untested. This juncture in the treatment process proved an ideal time to test this out in the transference. I was very impressed with, as well as moved by, the changes this woman was reporting. In addition to all the changes she was discussing, there were very noticeable changes that are not reflected in the transcripts. These included a change in her appearance, speech, and manner of relating to the therapist. She behaved in a relaxed and confident, yet direct and engaging manner. I felt it was important to reflect and confirm these changes and to assess her ability to accept positive feedback. It should go without saying that any such comment on the therapist's part must be genuinely felt, as it was in this case.

The Sharing of Feelings at Termination

THERAPIST: So what's it like to hear me reflect on all the changes and to tell you how different it feels to be with you?
PATIENT: I feel kind of teary. It's emotional. It's important to me because I believe in you and what we've done together. I feel this is something we've done together. It's very moving and touching to me.

This response, both in word and in the manner she received it, suggested that the patient was quite receptive to positive interactions. She was able to feel touched and to express that directly. At the same time that she was able to receive positive feedback, she gave in return by emphasizing the joint nature of our venture. This kind of spontaneous interaction was a clear reflection of her newly developed capacity to form mutual and reciprocal relationships. Further material revealed these kinds of changes in her current relationships outside therapy.

Improvement in Intimate Relationships

It is my feeling that a focus on the relationship as it develops is of central importance. Malan and Osimo (1992) have reported that the quality of intimate relationships has proven the most difficult change to effect in patients. Could this be an artifact of the treatment regimen in which the focus is too exclusively intrapsychic in focus? Davanloo's focus has shifted over time. Originally, he too focused almost exclusively on intrapsychic phenomena. Gradually, he began focusing on patients' defenses against emotional closeness and illustrating to patients the effect their intrapsychic functioning had on interpersonal relationships. In most cases, it is the difficulty in establishing and maintaining satisfying relationships that brings people into treatment. Sharpening our focus on the quality of relating, including work on the development of the therapeutic relationship, may facilitate substantial and enduring change in this critical area of functioning. In addition, careful monitoring of changes as they occur in the patient's current relationships should reinforce changes within sessions.

Internalization of the Therapist and the Therapeutic Process

PATIENT: I was just thinking I wanted to tell you how important it's been for me to be able to come here. I've been moving and getting things in order and it's all going so well. I'm enjoying my life and my friends. It has to do with what has happened here in therapy. It's been very important to me.

THERAPIST: It sounds like it's not just therapy that has been important but that you have a lot of feeling toward me.

PATIENT: I do. It's more like a friendship than I thought it would be. Initially, it was like I was talking out loud to myself in the room, but I've become increasingly aware of and empathic with you. I really feel we've done this together. I will miss you. Even though I know we're not friends, there's an importance to the feelings I have for you.

THERAPIST: There's a depth of feeling. There are tender feelings and a sense of closeness. So, for us to say good-bye is painful too.

PATIENT: I miss you but I carry your words around with me. A lot of this has been internalized. It's missing being here with you but it doesn't feel like the process will end—it will continue inside me.

Once again, readiness for termination can only be assessed in terms of our goals. In ISTDP, as in psychoanalysis, the goals go beyond symptom removal to include alterations in ego functioning. According to Alexander and French (1946), this is accomplished by "inducing emotional discharge in order to facilitate insight, and exposing the ego to those unresolved emotional constellations which it has to learn to master" (p. vii). This therapeutic work has as its aim an increase in "the patient's ability to find gratification for his subjective needs in ways acceptable to both himself and the world he lives in" (Alexander & French, 1946, p. 26). In the case being presented, this has been accomplished. The patient has dealt with her traumatic past and all the intense and previously terrifying feelings she experienced in reaction to recalled events. Now she felt free from the compulsion to repeat her past and could find new and gratifying means for working productively and for loving.

In addition to alterations in ego functioning, particularly the observing, anticipatory, and integrative capabilities, the nature and quality of parental introjects have also changed during the therapeutic process. In the case just described, the patient's ability to care for herself and to allow others to care for her in a nurturing way indicated a change in the nature and quality of her parental introjects. The patient stated that she had internalized both the therapist's voice and the analytic process. She was now able to do for herself what the therapist once did with her.

In addition to facilitating change in self-care and her ability to form mutually gratifying relationships with others, the internalization of the therapist makes separation possible without a feeling of traumatic loss. Patients frequently say things like "I don't feel like I'm losing you because I have you inside of me." This process of internalization seems to parallel that which occurs in normal development and allows a child to separate without undue anxiety. One evening, following a brief separation in which my 7-year-old son spent a weekend alone with his father, I asked, "Did you miss me?" "No," he said, "You see, I have this picture of you in my mind—standing in front of the house." This internalized image of me and our home offered my son a sense of security that enabled him to separate without distress. This is the kind of process we seek to facilitate therapeutically in our patients.

How this occurs remains a matter of debate (Wachtel, 1993). Luborsky and Mark (1991) have suggested that "internalization is a gradual process by which external interactions between the person and others are taken in and replaced by internal representations of these interactions (Crits-Christoph & Barber, 1991, p. 116). More specifically, Ellman (1991) has suggested that it's the "analyst's equanimity in the face of conflict" that needs to be internalized so that the patient can face post-treatment conflicts with a similar attitude.

The Man with an Explosive Temper: Part 2

Several authors (Horner, 1984; Novick, 1982; Sterba, 1934) emphasize the importance of the patient's ability to perform self-analysis as an indicator of preparedness for termination and a safeguard against future deterioration. In the case of the Man with the Explosive Temper (see

Chapter 7), there was evidence of both symptom removal and the replacement of pathological defenses with adaptive alternatives. The patient's relationships were becoming closer, richer, and truly reciprocal. In the following vignette, he tells the therapist of a recent incident in which strong feelings were evoked. Following the experience, he was able to understand the personal meaning it had for him. This was particularly important in this case because he came for treatment stating that strong feelings seemed to come out of the blue and he'd have no idea what triggered them. Evidence of self-understanding in which emotional and cognitive insights were integrated, suggested a readiness to end treatment and carry on the work by himself.

Evidence of Capacity for Self-Understanding

PATIENT: My wife and I went to the theater to celebrate our anniversary. We have a new and deeper closeness now. We saw a dramatic production of *Phantom of the Opera*. I had read the book and knew that the manager of the opera house was the Phantom's father. The Phantom had been hiding because he was deformed by something his mother drank in an attempt to abort him. His father doesn't tell him who he is until he's been shot by the police, but the Phantom said he'd always known. I thought of you because I saw a connection between the play and my own father and me. I was really crying. I was so sad because this was me and my story. I identified with the Phantom— being wounded by rejection. He took so long to realize he was my father. His death won't be as painful as the loss of that bond.

Much of the therapeutic work in this case involved freeing the patient to experience directly all the intense and conflicted feelings toward his brutal and sadistic father. Prior to treatment, his characteristic methods for defending against these feelings had left him in a state of detached confusion punctuated with sudden and unintelligible emotional outbursts. This pattern was adversely affecting all his interactions, at work as well as at home. Now that he was able to feel and understand his emotions, he could use all his capacities to decide on an appropriate way to deal with them, increasing his personal confidence as well as improving his relationships with others. He was especially grateful that the deep understanding he had developed of himself had expanded his capacity for genuine compassion for others resulting in newfound closeness with family members. In addition, his ability to understand his emotional reactions provided a reliable safeguard against repetitions of the past.

Defensive Withdrawal Replaced with Relatedness

PATIENT: This is it, huh?

THERAPIST: How are you feeling about that?

PATIENT: I had an interesting experience on Sunday. I am a convert and was asked to speak about the program for adults interested in joining the church. I did it on Sunday and I broke down. I got through the talk but I cried. I felt embarrassed, but after the Mass I received an outpouring of warmth from others.

THERAPIST: What about it was so moving?

PATIENT: Memories of my grandfather, whom I talked about. I wasn't able to get to his funeral and I feel awful about that. He was more of a father to me than my own father. We would pitch horseshoes, fish together, ride in his pickup. I was the first grandchild and I spent a lot of time with him. These new relationships with priests and other men in the class reminded me of him. That's when I cried. When I left the podium, I got a standing ovation. My family came over and surrounded me with love and support. Others came over with tears in their eyes, all choked up. Even strangers came up to me and said how moving it was. It felt good to have these people respond.

This last vignette, along with the previous sessions in which the patient revealed a newfound ability to love his wife and children, demonstrate the kind of change in the quality of relating that Menninger (1958) has described. He wrote that "above everything else in life he wants to love and be loved, and realizes that he can give love and get love and also that he can hate effectively when necessary" (p. 158). Relations with others assume a real specificity. He can love and open up to those he has chosen to be close to and stay away from or confront those who are a threat. Both were essential in this case, as the patient had previously been unable to protect himself from violence. In fact, during the course of treatment, his home was vandalized. He was able to take firm and appropriate steps to apprehend the offenders and to protect himself, his family, and his home from violence.

The Man with Primary Impotence: Part 2

Return of Symptoms at Termination

In the analytic literature, one frequently finds reference to the phenomenon in which old symptoms return as termination is approached. This is certainly not a universal phenomenon and only occurs in a small percentage of patients treated with ISTDP. Should this kind of regression occur, it is an indication that specific feelings and defenses regarding separation and loss need to be worked through (Trujillo & Winston, 1985). This was the case with the Man with Primary Impotence (see Chapter 6). This highly dependent man had experienced a great deal of gratification from the intense and sexualized relationship with his mother. In treatment, he became more and more aware of the underlying rage toward his mother for holding onto him and using him in ways that interfered with his optimal development. Still, as termination approached, old fears about being alone, along with the anger and pain associated with loss emerged. The re-appearance of passive-dependent defenses accompanied this upheaval. In addition to current feelings regarding the impending loss of the therapist, termination revived feelings about losses from the past that had not yet been mourned.

Evidence of Regression as Termination Approaches

The patient came into the session described in the following vignette saying he could feel himself reverting to procrastination as a way to avoid ending the therapy and facing all the feelings associated with the loss. This insight was crucial and directed the session toward the emotions that were being avoided.

PATIENT: I felt anxious coming here today because I haven't been working. I feel like a kid who doesn't have his homework done. I'm reacting to the pressure to get moving—I procrastinate.

THERAPIST: You cling to this old pattern of interaction in which you play the naughty boy and then I am either the harsh mother who scolds or the indulgent one.

PATIENT: And on and on. I like the times when I feel motivated and I move. The only way to do it is to do it.

THERAPIST: Let's look at what gets in your way.

PATIENT: I'm getting stuck in my head but there's pain inside. I'm sad and frustrated about the thought of ending. I told my friend about what I've been doing here. He said he felt sad about the things I had told him, but I couldn't really open up to him emotionally. I tried. I made the decision to tell him about these things but emotionally I didn't open up. I'm scared of overwhelming sadness.

THERAPIST: You have to pass through the pain to be free to open to others. It can be frightening and the temptation is to pull back but . . .

PATIENT: It's like swimming. It's cold at first, but if you plunge in it's great.

The patient proved highly motivated and had a good deal of intellectual insight into the meaning of his current difficulties with procrastination. In fact, he had enough insight to know that awareness alone wasn't sufficient to produce lasting change. The problem was an emotional one. The mechanisms this patient had developed during childhood to avoid painful and frightening feelings have interfered with the development and maintenance of close relationships in adulthood. He spelled this out quite clearly when discussing a current friendship. Toward the end of this sequence, he seemed to be encouraging himself to approach rather than avoid these painful feelings by using the swimming metaphor. The same struggle he had elaborated on in his current relationship with a friend needed to be outlined in the transference.

Feelings and Defenses in the Transference

THERAPIST: Here too, do you notice that each time the sadness starts to well up, you avoid my eyes and look at the floor? You keep a distance from me to avoid these feelings.

PATIENT: I look at you and it starts to hurt. I want to look you in the eye and tell you, but I'm avoiding it. There's a lot of tension but some excitement too. There's a part of me that isn't helpless with you anymore. I feel a strength from my center. It's charged—there's something strong inside.

Comparing New and Old Ways of Dealing with Loss

As we approached the grief-laden feelings he feared, the patient reported feeling strong and capable. At this point in treatment, he became aware of the positive consequences of using new, adaptive means of dealing with feelings, as well as the negative consequences of reverting to outmoded defenses. Processing how it feels to interact in this new way is essential in consolidating the changes. Often patients regress to avoid new feelings and experiences, not just to flee those from the past. In this case, to be a strong, capable man means facing the loss of the therapist.

Processing the Effect of New Changes

THERAPIST: What is it like to feel like a strong man with me?

PATIENT: I've been thinking about saying good-bye to you. Then I heard about someone who saw you for 2 years, and I thought "That gives me an out." I think I'm afraid to say good-bye. Then I also think she got more time than me.

THERAPIST: Feeling scared to leave and avoiding and procrastinating came after you found out about this other patient?

PATIENT: Yeah, and I thought she's pushing me out and now I'm clinging.

THERAPIST: What is your feeling toward me then?

PATIENT: I don't know why I'm afraid every time I think of leaving. I want to leave with a good feeling but it's painful. I don't know what a good parting is—I've never had it.

THERAPIST: Parting while retaining the good feeling. This certainly never happened with your mother.

Two things seem to be going on here. On the one hand, the patient is trying to do things differently, while resisting a regressive pull in the face of an impending loss. An additional factor has emerged regarding competitive feelings reminiscent of rivalries with siblings. Defending against these feelings, which had not been previously worked through, added fuel to his defensive clinging. Both issues needed to be addressed. The patient's ensuing associations indicated that the rivalrous feelings were most prominent. To avoid this material could seriously interfere with his goal of ending treatment in a positive manner.

Competition and Sibling Rivalry

PATIENT: I used to have this dream where I would smash my sister's head and she'd be tied to a cross. Dead—with stuff leaking out of her head and some other member of the family would come and say "Let's go," but I couldn't let go. I couldn't believe what I had done. There was terrible pain and a longing to change what had happened. How could I live with this? I feel it's bad. I'm wrong to leave (crying). I feel so responsible. It's my fault. My mother and sister were in such a bad way. How can I leave them behind and have a good life?

Talking about ending the therapy and finding out that another patient had been involved in longer term therapy revived competitive feelings toward siblings that had not come up in the therapy previously. This concurrence of events provided the opportunity to rework these feelings and to understand his tendency to cling to his mother in the past and to the therapist in the present as manifestations of maladaptive defenses against feelings of competitiveness with rivals. By having a special closeness with his mother, he felt he could "beat" his siblings. When he became conscious of this, the cost attendant to this strategy began to outweigh the gains. He now felt he had won by losing. Not only did he end up saddled with a demanding, histrionic mother, but his relationships with his siblings suffered. Following this session, he began to reach out to his siblings in an attempt to develop a new sense of closeness with them as adults. In addition, he recognized how this pattern of competitiveness was repeated with peers with detrimental effects.

Finding a New and Adaptive Way to Say Good-Bye

Another important aspect of the work required at termination involves finding new ways to say good-bye. In the present case, simply putting an end to his tendency to procrastinate by working dutifully to the end of treatment would constitute progress but not substantive change.

Procrastination and regression need to be replaced by something adaptive. He made it very clear to the therapist that he had a specific goal in ending treatment—to say good-bye while maintaining the positive feelings he genuinely felt toward the therapist. This was something he had never been able to accomplish in the past. His goal could not be achieved by passing over the negative, competitive feelings and the guilt they engendered, but only by facing them directly. This material provided another opportunity to do so.

Special Consideration with Victims of Trauma

Nearly all the patients being described in this chapter experienced significant trauma in their childhood, whether the result of a mother's manic depressive illness, a brother's psychotic decompensation, or brutal beatings by a sadistic father. According to Judith Herman (1992), who has devoted herself to the treatment of psychological trauma, termination should begin when "the survivor no longer feels possessed by her traumatic past," but, having dealt with it directly, feels free. This was expressed by the Manic-Depressive's Daughter when she said she no longer felt haunted by the past. As the patient is able to face the trauma and mourn for the "old self," a new self begins to develop. The damaged, victimized self begins to be transformed by a process of integration with the survivor self who has courageously faced the horrors of the past (Herman, 1992).

Mother's Little Angel reported feeling proud of herself for having faced all the trauma in her past and said she felt stronger and like a new and improved version of her old self.

In accordance with Malan's dictum that each pathological defense be replaced by something adaptive, Herman (1992) suggests that the replacement of a sense of helplessness and isolation with a feeling of empowerment and reconnection is a crucial factor in the recovery of patients who have been traumatized. "Having come to terms with the traumatic past, the survivor faces the task of creating a future" (p. 196). For health to be restored, it is necessary but insufficient to deal with the past. The patient must develop a revised sense of self which should include:

1. A reduction in physiological reactivity.
2. The ability to bear emotions associated with trauma.
3. Authority over memories such that they are neither repressed nor intrusive.
4. Memories of trauma that form a coherent narrative integrated with feeling.
5. A sense of self that is no longer damaged.
6. Close and trusting relationships with those who warrant it.
7. A system of belief and meaning that includes the experience of the trauma.

The Man with an Explosive Temper seemed to exemplify these changes. In addition to dealing with the past, this man found a new and enriched means for relating to his family and the community at large. Toward the end of treatment, his internal changes produced far-reaching changes in his functioning. He was able to use his own experience to understand, on a deep emotional and personal level, the struggles of others. By sharing his experiences with others, he was able to transform hurting into healing—perhaps the ultimate sign of recovery.

The treatment process did not simply stop the past from repeating itself by removing the negative, damaging cycle of explosive anger and fear but facilitated a transformation in which real growth and reparative connections replaced hostile interactions.

THE CRUCIAL SIGNIFICANCE OF FOLLOW-UP

We are all indebted to Dr. Malan, who was the first clinician to systematically study the process of brief dynamic psychotherapy. This work included detailed follow-up interviews years after psychotherapy had been terminated. Such data are essential to determine whether our interventions are truly curative. The Tavistock group developed a rating scale to categorize patient response to treatment both at termination and follow-up (Malan, 1963). The criteria for success were as follows: 0 indicated no change; a score of 1 represented some symptomatic improvement but no evidence of greater coping skills in the area of the core conflict; a score of 2 reflected meaningful symptomatic improvement plus evidence of new coping strategies for dealing adaptively in previously conflictual situations; and a score of 3 indicated broad change beyond the specific conflictual area to reflect greater coping in relationships with both men and women and better performance at work. Malan's (1976) data suggest that those who were scored "improved" (a score of 2 or more) at termination maintained or exceeded this level of functioning at 3- to 5-year follow-up. In fact, 50% of those who scored a 2 at termination, moved up to 3 at follow-up.

It is also important to note that Malan (1978), in disagreement with Mann (1973), has found that awareness of follow-up interviews in no way dilutes feelings about termination, which is still felt to be absolute. My experience is consistent with Malan's view. It seems that, like the phenomenon of transference, the feelings at termination are so robust, it is unnecessary to try to preserve them by adhering to a rigid structure in which there is no contact after termination.

Davanloo (1978) reported that of 130 patients deemed suitable for ISTDP, 115 were successfully treated in an average of 20 sessions. These positive results were maintained in follow-up interviews conducted between 2 and 7 years posttreatment. Davanloo engaged patients in an active reassessment of the process at follow-up. Both patient and therapist watched videotaped segments of treatment. Davanloo asked for feedback from patients and elicited their comments about what they had found helpful. Of significance was a frequently reported perception that the patients had done most of the work themselves. They tended to report feeling "free" or "like a new person," attesting to the dramatic changes that had occurred as a result of their hard work.

Clinical Evidence of Further Improvement at Follow-Up

The Masochistic Artist: Part 4

THERAPIST: Well, how are you?
PATIENT: I'm great. It's been a particularly good time for me since about last September. We ended in July and I spent the summer with my

husband. I realized I was playing something out that I just couldn't do anymore, but I needed to try it and to do it without you. I had to try being with him from this new position of self-awareness and re-sourcefulness that I have attained. The marriage seemed immutable. There was no openness. He continued to see me in a very fixed way and saw himself as the injured party. He wouldn't move. The message was that I would have to make amends. I could feel myself being eroded, and I just couldn't do it. So, by the end of the summer, it was clear the marriage was over.

When he left, I felt such relief. There were feelings of loss—anger and sadness—but I felt like myself. Life has become rich. Things really took off after that and it's been steady ever since. I'm optimistic about myself and the world.

THERAPIST: This is very interesting because you seemed to know all of this at the end of treatment. Still, you're saying it was important to test it out in reality. I remember you saying that you wanted to be with your husband now that you no longer had a need to be used and abused. You wondered if you had pulled this from him and if you no longer needed him to be an oppressor he might be free to change. It does take two to tango. You seemed to know that your changes would cre-ate change in the relationship. Either you could grow together or it would be over.

Post-Termination Transference Reactions

THERAPIST: Now the part you didn't seem aware of, and you didn't men-tion until today, was something going on between you and me—be-cause you say you had to do it without me.

PATIENT: I didn't realize it until the fall, after my husband left. I had this dynamic in my life where people would offer suggestions and I was very susceptible to that. I had to make sure I wasn't just reacting to others' expectations but was exerting my own feelings.

THERAPIST: You wanted to be certain you weren't submitting to what you thought I wanted you to do. There was such intrusiveness in the past it was difficult to tell where the other left off and you began.

PATIENT: This is interesting in my friendships too. I notice how I tended to mirror their expectations and suppress my own. Now that I'm sep-arated and getting divorced, I see how others play out their fantasies and fears on me. I'm much clearer when someone is projecting their concerns onto me and I can address it directly. Like with my friend . . . (gives concrete example).

The changes noted at termination in this woman's ability to form and maintain relationships that were positive and not sado-masochistic have been solidified over time. She is aware of her own dynamics and more sensitive to unconscious forces affecting others. In addition, she reports discussing these things freely with friends, all indicating significant growth. That enormous changes have occurred cannot be disputed. What was responsible for these changes needs to be clarified. Following Davanloo's lead, I invite the patient to explore this with me.

Feedback from Patients on Factors Responsible for Change

PATIENT: So there's a whole new level of intimacy in my friendships.

THERAPIST: It really sounds like you feel released from this bondage. Obviously, this was a successful treatment. What do you think was responsible for the change?

PATIENT: Something very basic. Feeling someone being so sympathetic and empathic with a pain I was suffering. It sounds so simple and, in a way it is, but when you spend all your time and emotional energy denying that or feeling you're not entitled to it—because I really internalized my mother's voice. So I think that feeling I'm entitled to the pain, it's there, and I can bear it, made me understand how the avoidance of that pain set up this whole pattern of defensiveness. The other thing was your being very challenging and tough about bringing it back to the original source of pain and asking me how I actually feel it, cutting through the layers so I could really experience it. I don't know what else to say. It just makes it more difficult to return to denial. The layers get discarded.

The patient made clear that her therapy provided two essential ingredients that enabled her to change. The first was a feeling of *empathic connection with the therapist,* and the second was *the rigorous examination of feelings,* both present and past. This feedback confirms the hypotheses formulated by Malan and Davanloo regarding both the specific (focus on the triangles) and nonspecific (empathy) factors responsible for the powerful results obtained with ISTDP.

PATIENT: Now if I start in on self-loathing, I just stop it because I see it as very destructive and it's really not me.

This statement reveals how the patient's ego has assumed control. The harsh and punitive superego, which had been dominating her functioning in all areas previously, now has a back seat. If it tries to assert itself, she recognizes it as destructive and puts a stop to it.

PATIENT: There are immediate rewards too, so it's not just an abstraction. There's more pleasure in life, more intimacy—so it's very reinforcing.

Here the patient confirms one of the central hypotheses proposed by Wachtel (1993) regarding the cyclical nature of changes in the intrapsychic and interpersonal spheres of functioning. The internal changes beget external changes that are noticed and, in this case, reinforced by others. With her husband, these changes were not welcomed. Rather than revert to previous pathological accommodations to him, she left the marriage and selected those who enhanced her health.

PATIENT: I've been dating some, and I think I see things much more clearly. I speak up for myself and don't just go along with the man. I'm also done with guilt. I say, "This is what I want and you'll have to decide if that's ok with you."

As Malan and Osimo (1992) have reported in their follow-up studies, the change from passivity to active self-assertion is one of the most consistent findings in patients who respond to this form of treatment.

THERAPIST: So you take care of yourself but don't assume responsibility for others. You are clear about your needs and expectations and expect others to do the same.

In a subsequent follow-up interview a year later, the patient reported that her sexual relationships with men have taken on a quality of mutual pleasure and satisfaction. Previously, she had not been able to have an orgasm in the presence of a man. Now she was able to come to orgasm regularly.

Response to Subsequent Difficulties

As Freud suggested back in 1937, we can only tell if our interventions are curative if patients can face new difficulties without regressing. Both the Man with an Explosive Temper and the Manic-Depressive's Daughter began their follow-up interview by saying that things in their lives were still stressful, but they were handling the problems in their lives in new and more adaptive ways.

The Manic-Depressive's Daughter: Part 3

THERAPIST: So how are you?

PATIENT: Well, I'm actually ok, which is surprising since we've had a very difficult time of it. My younger son was found to have some serious medical problems. I feel certain that if I had not done the work with you previously, I would have gone under with this one. But, now I deal with it, and my husband and I deal with it together.

THERAPIST: How do you account for this—that the previous work prepared you to deal with this crisis with some sense of equilibrium?

PATIENT: Because it's just about now, it's not about the past and because I have a closer relationship to my husband and some basic confidence in my ability to be a good mother. If I didn't have all that, this crisis would have sent me over the edge.

We cannot guarantee our patients will have lives free of pain and trauma. In fact, Wolberg (1965) has suggested that we prepare patients for the inevitability of struggles in life. Can our treatment have a prophylactic effect, insulating our patients from future symptoms when such upheavals occur? These cases suggest that it can. By enhancing the ego functioning of our patients, we help prepare them to weather these storms in adaptive fashion.

SUMMARY

Termination is dealt with in a straightforward fashion in ISTDP and requires little in the way of special care. Rather, the same tenacity in breaking through defensive avoidance and the same encouragement to face all the mixed feelings evoked by the loss of the therapist—which have characterized the treatment from the start—continue until the end. Termination is not considered traumatic. Losses are a part of life, and it is the way they are dealt with that is the focus of intervention. Allowing patients freedom to end in new ways that will consolidate positive feelings about the self and others is the ultimate goal. Whereas loss cannot be prevented, regret about feelings unexpressed or actions not taken can be addressed and prevented. In addition to finding new ways to say good-bye to the therapist, termination provides another opportunity to mourn past losses.

Follow-up interviews provide patient and therapist with the opportunity to review the process of therapy, to access the extent of change, and to note new or recurring problems. My experience has paralleled that reported by Malan and Davanloo, suggesting that the changes occurring during ISTDP are generally maintained and strengthened over time.

References

Alexander, F., & French, T. M. (1946). *Psychoanalytic therapy principles and application.* Lincoln: University of Nebraska Press.

Aronson, E. (1968). The theory of cognitive dissonance: A current perspective. In L. Berkowitz (Ed.), *Advances in experimental social psychology* (Vol. 4). New York: Academic Press.

Balint, M. (1957). *The doctor, his patient and the illness.* New York: International University Press.

Bandura, A. (1986). *Social foundations of thought and action.* Englewood Cliffs, NJ: Prentice-Hall.

Bandura, A. (1989). Human agency in social cognitive theory. *American Psychologist, 44,* 1175–1181.

Bauer, G. P., & Kobos, J. C. (1987). *Brief therapy: Short-term dynamic interventions.* Northvale, NJ: Aronson.

Beck, A. T. (1976). *Cognitive therapy and the emotional disorders.* New York: International University Press.

Been, H., & Sklar, I. (1985). Transference in short-term dynamic psychotherapy. In A. Winston (Ed.), *Short-term dynamic psychotherapy.* Washington, DC: American Psychiatric Press.

Bettelheim, B. (1983). Preface and afterword. In M. Cardinal, *The words to say it,* pp. x–xii, 297–308. Cambridge, MA: VanVactor & Goodheart.

Bower, G. (1981). Mood and memory. *American Psychologist, 36,* 129–148.

Bowlby, J. (1970). *Attachment and loss* (Vol. 1). New York: Basic Books.

Bowlby, J. (1973). *Separation: Anxiety and anger.* London: Tavistock.

Bowlby, J. (1980). *Loss: Sadness and depression.* London: Tavistock.

Brenner, C. (1976). *Psychoanalytic technique and psychic conflict.* New York: International University Press.

Breuer, J., & Freud, S. (1895). Studies in hysteria. In J. Strachey (Ed.), *The standard edition of the complete psychological works of Sigmund Freud* (Vol. 2). London: Hogarth Press.

Bucci, W. (1985). Dual coding: A cognitive model for psychoanalytic research. *Journal of the American Psychoanalytic Association, 33,* 571–607.

Cardinal, M. (1983). *The words to say it.* P. Goodheart, (Trans.). Cambridge, MA: VanVactor & Goodheart.

Crits-Christoph, P., & Barber, J. P. (Eds.). (1991). *Handbook of short-term dynamic psychotherapy.* New York: Basic Books.

Davanloo, H. (1978). *Principles and techniques of short-term dynamic psychotherapy.* New York: Spectrum.

Davanloo, H. (1979). Techniques of short-term dynamic psychotherapy. *Psychiatric Clinics of North America, 2,* 11–21.

Davanloo, H. (1980). *Short-term dynamic psychotherapy.* New York: Aronson.

Davanloo, H. (1990). *Unlocking the unconscious.* New York: Wiley.

(1986a). Intensive short-term *dynamic* psychotherapy with highly resistant patients: I. Handling resistance (pp. 1–28).

(1986b). Intensive short-term dynamic psychotherapy with highly resistant patients: II. The course of an interview after the initial breakthrough (pp. 29–46).

(1987a). Intensive short-term dynamic psychotherapy with highly resistant depressed patients: I. Restructuring ego's regressive defenses (pp. 47–80).

(1987b). Intensive short-term dynamic psychotherapy with highly resistant depressed patients: II. The royal road to the dynamic unconscious (pp. 81–100).

(1988). The technique of unlocking the unconscious: I. (pp. 101–124).

Davanloo, H. (1990–1991). Core Training in Montreal, Canada.

Davis, D. (1988). Transformation of pathological mourning into acute grief with intensive short-term dynamic psychotherapy. *International Journal of Short-Term Psychotherapy, 3,* 79–97.

Della Selva, P. C. (1991). The emergence and working through of preverbal trauma in short-term dynamic psychotherapy. *International Journal of Short-Term Psychotherapy, 6,* 195–216.

Della Selva, P. C. (1992). Achieving character change in IS-TDP: How the experience of affect leads to the consolidation of the self. *International Journal of Short-Term Psychotherapy, 7,* 73–87.

Della Selva, P. C. (1993). The significance of attachment theory for the practice of intensive short-term dynamic psychotherapy. *International Journal of Short-Term Psychotherapy, 8,* 189–206.

Dewald, P. A. (1972). *The psychoanalytic process.* New York: McGraw-Hill.

Dickman, S., & Sechrest, L. (1985). Research on memory and clinical practice. In G. Stricker & R. H. Keisner (Eds.), *From research to clinical practice* (pp. 15–44). New York: Plenum.

Duncan, I. (1927, 1955). *My life.* New York: Liveright.

Ellman, S. J. (1991). *Freud's technique papers: A contemporary perspective.* Northvale, NJ: Aronson.

Emde, R. N. (1989). The infant's relationship experience. In A. J. Sameroff & R. N. Emde (Eds.), *Relationship disturbances in early childhood: A developmental approach* (pp. 33–51). New York: Basic Books.

Engel, G. (1961). Is grief a disease? *Psychosomatic Medicine, 23,* 18–22.

Epstein, S. (1994). Integration of the cognitive and the psychodynamic unconscious. *American Psychologist, 49,* 709–724.

Esquivel, L. (1989). *Like water for chocolate.* New York: Doubleday.

Fairbairn, W. R. D. (1954). *An object-relations theory of the personality.* New York: Basic Books.

Ferenzi, S. (1924). *Further contributions to the theory and technique of psychoanalysis.* New York: Brunner/Mazel.

Ferenzi, S., & Rank, O. (1925). *The development of psychoanalysis.* New York: Nervous and Mental Disease Publishing Company.

Firestein, S. (1978). *Termination in psychoanalysis.* New York: International University Press.

Fisher, S., & Greenberg, R. (1977). *The scientific credibility of Freud's theories and therapy.* New York: Basic Books.

Flegenheimer, W. V. (1982). *Techniques of brief psychotherapy.* Northvale, NJ: Aronson.

Fosha, D. (1988). Restructuring in the treatment of depressive disorders with Davanloo's intensive short-term dynamic psychotherapy. *International Journal of Short-Term Psychotherapy, 3,* 189–212.

Frank, G. (1961). *Persuasion and healing.* Baltimore: Johns Hopkins Press.

Freud, A. (1937/1966). *The ego and the mechanisms of defense* (rev. ed.). Madison, CT: International University Press.

Freud, S. All references are to *The standard edition of the complete psychological works of Sigmund Freud* (Volumes 1–24.). London: Hogarth Press, 1953–1974 (SE).

(1894). The neuro-psychoses of defense. *SE 3:* 45–61.

(1895). Studies of hysteria. *SE 2:* 255–305.

(1900). The interpretation of dreams. *SE 4/5.*

(1914). On the history of the psychoanalytic movement. *Standard Edition,* Vol. 14 (1957). London: Hogarth.

(1914). Remembering, repeating and working-through. *SE 12:* 147–156.

(1917). Mourning and melancholia. *SE 14:* 243–258.

(1920). Beyond the pleasure principle. *SE 18:* 3–64.

(1923). The ego and the id. *SE 19:* 1–66.

(1924). The economic problem of masochism. *SE 19:* 155–170.

(1926). Inhibitions, symptoms and anxiety. *SE 20:* 75–175.

(1930). Civilization and its discontents. *SE 21:* 59–145.

(1937). Analysis terminable and interminable. *SE 23:* 209–253.

(1949). An outline of psycho-analysis. *SE 23:* 139–207.

(1950). Extracts from the Fleiss Papers. *SE 1:* 173–280.

Friedman, S. B., Chodoff, P., Mason, J. W., & Hamberg, D. A. (1963). Behavioral observations on parents anticipating the death of a child. *Pediatrics, 32,* 610–625.

Friedman, S. B., Mason, J. W., & Hamburg, D. A. (1963). Urinary 17-hydroxycorticosteroid levels of parents of children with neoplastic disease. *Psychosomatic Medicine, 25,* 364–376.

Fromm, E. (1947). *Man for himself.* Greenwich, CT: Fawcett.

Fromm-Reichman, F. (1950). *Principles of intensive psychotherapy.* Chicago: University of Chicago Press.

Geiselman, R. E., Fisher, R. P., MacKinnon, D. P., & Holland, H. L. (1985). Eyewitness memory enhancement in the police interview: Cognitive retrieval mnemonics versus hypnosis. *Journal of Applied Psychology, 70,* 401–412.

Gill, M. (1982). *The analysis of transference.* Volume I. New York: International University Press.

Glover, E. (1958). *The technique of psychoanalysis.* New York: International University Press.

Goin, M. K., Burgoyne, R. W., & Goin, J. M. (1979). Timeless attachment to a dead relative. *American Journal of Psychiatry, 7,* 988–989.

Greenberg, J. R., & Mitchell, S. A. (1983). *Object relations in psychoanalytic theory.* Cambridge: Harvard University Press.

Greenson, R. (1967). *The technique and practice of psychoanalysis.* New York: International University Press.

Haan, N. (1977). *Coping and defending.* New York: Academic Press.

Herman, J. L. (1992). *Trauma and recovery.* New York: Basic Books.

Henry, W., Sims, J. H., & Spicey, S. L. (1968). Mental health professionals in Chicago: Some preliminary observations on origins and practice. In J. M. Shlien (Ed.), *Research in psychotherapy.* Washington, DC: American Psychiatry Association.

Hollan, S. D., Evans, M. D., & DeRubeis, R. J. (1990). Cognitive mediation of relapse prevention following treatment for depression: Implications of differential risk. In R. E. Ingram (Ed.), *Psychological aspects of depression* (pp. 117–136). New York: Plenum.

Horner, A. (1984). *Object relations and the developing ego in therapy.* New York: Aronson.

Horowitz, M. J. (1979). *States of mind.* New York: Plenum.

Jacobs, S., & Ostfeld, A. (1977). An epidemiological review of the mortality of bereavement. *Psychosomatic Medicine, 39,* 344–357.

Janoff-Bulman, R. (1992). *Shattered assumptions.* New York: Free Press.

Janov, A. (1970). *Primal scream: Primal therapy, the cure for neurosis.* New York: Putnam.

Kernberg, O. (1975). *Borderline conditions and pathological narcissism.* New York: Aronson.

Kernberg, O. (1976). *Object relations theory and clinical psychoanalysis.* New York: Aronson.

Kübler-Ross, E. (1969). *Death and dying.* London: Tavistock.

Laikin, M., Winston, A., & McCullough, L. (1991). Intensive short-term dynamic psychotherapy. In P. Crits-Christoph & J. B. Barber (Eds.), *Handbook of short-term dynamic psychotherapy* (pp. 80–109). New York: Basic Books.

Lewin, K. (1951). *Field theory in social science.* New York: Harper & Row.

Lewis, C. S. (1961). *A grief observed.* New York: Bantam.

Lindemann, E. (1944). Symptomatology and management of acute grief. *American Journal of Psychiatry, 101,* 141–148.

Lindemann, E. (1945). Psychiatric aspects of the conservative treatment of ulcerative colitis. *Archives of Neurology and Psychiatry, 53,* 322–325.

Lindemann, E. (1979). *Beyond grief.* Northvale, NJ: Aronson.

Loftus, E. F. (1993). The reality of repressed memories. *American Psychologist, 48,* 518–537.

Loewald, H. W. (1976). Perspectives on memory. In M. M. Gill & P. S. Holtzman (Eds.), *Psychology vs. metapsychology: Psychoanalytic essays in memory of George S. Klein* (pp. 298–325). New York: International University Press.

Luborsky, L., & Mark, D. (1991). Short-term supportive-expressive psychoanalytic psychotherapy. In P. Crits-Christoph & J. P. Barber (Eds.), *Handbook of short-term dynamic psychotherapy* (pp. 110–136). New York: Basic Books.

Malan, D. H. (1963). *A study of brief psychotherapy.* New York: Plenum Press.

Malan, D. H. (1976a). *The frontier of brief psychotherapy.* New York: Plenum Press.

Malan, D. H. (1976b). *Toward the validation of dynamic psychotherapy.* New York: Plenum Press.

Malan, D. H. (1978a). Exploring the limits of brief psychotherapy. In H. Davanloo (Ed.), *Basic principles and techniques in short-term dynamic psychotherapy* (pp. 43–67). New York: Spectrum Publications.

Malan, D. H. (1978b). Evaluation criteria for selection of patients. In H. Davanloo (Ed.), *Basic principles and techniques in short-term dynamic psychotherapy* (pp. 85–97). New York: Spectrum Publications.

Malan, D. H. (1979). *Individual psychotherapy and the science of psychodynamics.* London: Butterworth.

Malan, D. H. (1980). The most important development in psychotherapy since the discovery of the unconscious. In H. Davanloo (Ed.), *Short-term dynamic psychotherapy,* (pp. 13–23). Northvale, NJ: Aronson.

Malan, D. H. (1986). Beyond interpretation: Part I and II. *International Journal of Short-Term Psychotherapy, 1*(2), 59–82, 83–106.

Malan, D., & Osimo, F. (1992). *Psychodynamics, training, and outcome in brief psychotherapy.* London: Butterworth.

Mann, J. (1973). *Time-limited psychotherapy.* Cambridge: Harvard University Press.

Mann, J. (1991). Time-limited psychotherapy. In P. Crits-Christoph & J. P. Barber (Eds.), *Handbook of short-term dynamic psychotherapy* (pp. 17–43). New York: Basic Books.

McCloskey, M., & Zaragoza, M. (1985). Misleading postevent information and memory for events: Arguments and evidence against memory impairment hypotheses. *Journal of Experimental Psychology: General, 114,* 1–16.

Menninger, K. (1958). *Theory of psychoanalytic technique.* New York: Basic Books.

Miller, A. (1986). *Thou shalt not be aware: Society's betrayal of the child.* New York: Meridian.

Moffat, J. (Ed.). (1986). *In the midst of winter: Selections from the literature on mourning.* New York: Random House.

Munroe, R. (1955). *Schools of psychoanalytic thought.* New York: Dryden Press.

Nacht, R. (1965). Criteria and technique for the termination of analysis. *International Journal of Psychoanalysis, 46,* 107–116.

Novick, J. (1982). Termination: Themes and issues. *Psychoanalytic inquiry, 2,* 329–366.

Parkes, C. M. (1970). The psychosomatic effects of bereavement. In O. W. Hill (Ed.), *Modern trends in psychosomatic medicine.* London: Butterworth.

Parkes, C. M. (1975). Unexpected and untimely bereavement. *In Bereavement: Its psychosocial aspects.* New York: Columbia University Press.

Parkes, C. M., Benjamin, B., & Fitzgerald, R. G. (1969). Broken heart: A statistical study of increased mortality among widowers. *British Medical Journal, 1,* 740–743.

Peppers, L. G., & Knoff, R. J. (1980). *Motherhood and mourning.* New York: Praeger.

Pine, F. (1985). *Developmental theory and clinical process.* New Haven, CT: Yale University Press.

Ranko, S., & Mazer, H. (1980, 1983). *Semrad: The heart of a therapist.* Northvale, NJ: Aronson.

Raphael, L. (1983). *Bereavement.* Northvale, NJ: Aronson.

Reich, W. (1933). *Character analysis, 3rd ed.* New York: Touchstone.

Reich, W. (1987). Character resistances. In D. S. Milman & G. D. Goldman (Eds.), *Techniques of working with resistance* (pp. 41–116). Northvale, NJ: Aronson.

Reitav, J. (1991). The treatment of character pathology with Davanloo's intensive short-term dynamic psychotherapy, Part I: Management of resistance. *International Journal of Short-Term Psychotherapy, 6,* 3–25.

Schnarch, D. M. (1991). *Constructing the sexual crucible: An integration of sexual and marital therapy.* New York: Norton.

Schoenewolf, G. (1990). *Turning points in analytic therapy.* New York: Aronson.

Seward, G. H. (1962–1963). The relation between psychoanalytic school and value problems in therapy. *American Journal of Psychoanalysis, 22–23,* 138–152.

Shainess, N. (1986). *Sweet suffering: Woman as victim.* New York: Bobbs-Merrill.

Shand, A. F. (1920). *The foundations of character.* 2nd ed. London: Macmillan.

Sifneos, P. (1972). *Short-term psychotherapy and emotional crisis.* Cambridge, MA: Harvard University Press.

Sifneos, P. (1979). *Short-term dynamic psychotherapy.* New York: Plenum.

Singer-Kaplan, H. (1974). *The new sex therapy.* New York: Brunner/Mazel.

Sklansky, M. A., Isaacs, R. S., Levitor, E. S., & Haggard, E. A. (1966). Verbal interactional levels of meaning in psychotherapy. *Archives of General Psychiatry, 14,* 158–170.

Stark, M. (1994). *Working with resistance.* New York: Aronson.

Sterba, R. F. (1934). The fate of the ego in analytic therapy. *International Journal of Psychoanalysis, 15,* 117–126.

Stern, D. (1985). *The interpersonal world of the infant: A view from psychoanalysis and developmental psychology.* New York: Basic Books.

Stotland, E. (1969). *The psychology of hope.* San Francisco: Jossey-Bass.

Strupp, H. H., & Binder, J. L. (1984). *Psychotherapy in a new key.* New York: Basic Books.

Suttie, I. (1937, 1988). *The origins of love and hate.* London: Free Association Books.

Teyber, E. (1992). *Interpersonal process in psychotherapy: A guide for clinical training.* Pacific Grove, CA: Brooks/Cole.

Trevor, W. (1991). Reading Turgenev. In *Two lives* (pp. 1–222). New York: Penguin.

Trierweiler, S. J., & Donovan, C. M. (1994). Exploring the ecological foundations of memory in psychotherapy: Interpersonal affordance, perception, and recollection in real time. *Clinical Psychology Review, 14,* 301–326.

Trujillo, M., & McCullough, L. (1985). Research issues in short-term dynamic psychotherapies: An overview. In A. Winston (Ed.), *Clinical and research issues in intensive short-term dynamic psychotherapy.* Washington, DC: American Psychiatric Press.

Trujillo, M., & Winston, A. (1985). Termination. In A. Horner (Ed.), *Treating the neurotic patient in brief psychotherapy.* Northvale, NJ: Aronson.

Vaillant, G. (1993). *The wisdom of the ego.* Cambridge, MA: Harvard University Press.

van der Kolk, B. A. (1987). *Psychological trauma.* Washington, DC: American Psychiatric Press.

Wachtel, P. (1977). *Psychoanalysis and behavior therapy.* New York: Basic Books.

Wachtel, P. (1993). *Therapeutic communication.* New York: Guilford.

Weinberger, J. (1995). Common factors aren't so common: The common factors dilemma. *Clinical Psychology, V2N1,* 45–69.

Weiss, J. (1993). *How psychotherapy works.* New York: Guilford.

Whisman, M. A. (1993). Mediators and moderators of change in cognitive therapy of depression. *Psychological Bulletin, 114,* 248–264.

White, W. A. (1937). The origins of love and hate by I. D. Suttie. *Psychoanalytic Review, 24,* 458–460.

Winnicott, D. W. (1965). *The maturational process and the facilitating environment.* New York: International University Press.

Wolberg, L. R. (1965). The technique of short-term psychotherapy. In L. R. Wolberg (Ed.), *Short-term psychotherapy.* New York: Gruner Stratton.

Zilbergeld, B. (1992). *The new male sexuality.* NY: Bantam.

Author Index

Subject Index